The Teen Advantage Collection

Level-Up Your Life With Practical Skills, Money Smarts, and A Growth Mindset

Ben Clardy

Contents

Practical Life Skills for Teens

PERSONAL FINANCE FOR TEENAGERS

Growth Mindset for Teens

Practical Life Skills for Teens

Your Guide To Becoming A Capable, Confident and Independent Teenager With Real-World Skills Not Taught In School - Manage Money, Cook, Self-Care & Many More!

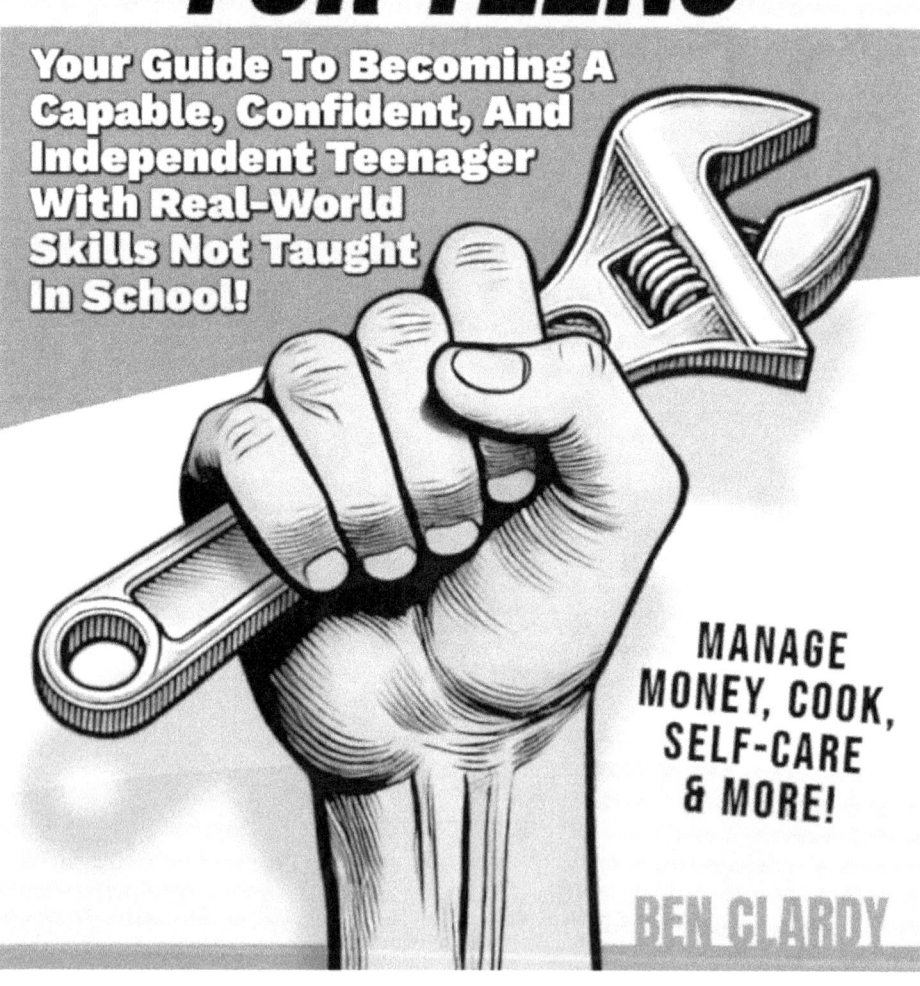

PRACTICAL
LIFE SKILLS
FOR TEENS

Your Guide To Becoming A Capable, Confident, And Independent Teenager With Real-World Skills Not Taught In School!

MANAGE
MONEY, COOK,
SELF-CARE
& MORE!

BEN CLARDY

Chapter 1
Thinking Skills

You are today where your thoughts have brought you; you will be tomorrow where your thoughts take you.
—James Allen

To kick things off, let's focus on the most critical area of all—the 6" or so between your ears. That'd be your brain or, more specifically, *your mind*.

Ever feel like your thoughts are running wild and in all directions like a pack of energetic puppies? Don't worry; we've all been there. In this chapter, we'll explore the power of your thoughts, how they shape your reality, and most importantly, how to harness them to bend reality to your will.

Critical Thinking

Anyone with a skull full of grey matter can think, but those who are able to think in a manner that is independent, clear, and rational are *critical thinkers*. Anybody can do it, but it takes practice. The trouble is that people are generally told what to think throughout their lives and, therefore, never develop the skill of thinking *critically* for themselves. Not you, though... you're different!

Picture critical thinking as connecting the dots in your mind—forming your opinions, diving into analysis, and ultimately reaching an intelligent conclusion. To get there, you ask questions beyond the usual "yes or no" variety. Instead, you must dive into the "whys" and "hows."

Example:

Imagine scrolling through your feed and stumbling upon a viral post about a new study claiming that drinking seven cups of coffee daily will make you a genius. It sounds incredible, right? You feel a little jittery just thinking about it. But hold up —let's engage the brain and think about this *critically*...

First, question the source. Is this post from a credible health news outlet or a random meme page? Look for the study itself. Find the original source of information rather than relying on second-hand news, which almost inevitably tends to twist and obscure the facts.

Next, dive into the context. Does the article explain who conducted the study and who funded it? Knowing who's behind the info can reveal a lot about why it was presented in a certain way. *Was it a coffee company* that made the claim? Hmm, the plot thickens!

Now, analyze the claims. Seven cups of coffee a day sounds a bit much, doesn't it? (twitch, twitch) Check out what other experts are saying. A quick search might show you that most health experts recommend moderation. See, those claims are already looking a bit shaky.

Finally, think about the implications. Sharing misleading health advice can be harmful. It's not just about not spreading fake news; it's about being a responsible online community member.

By questioning the source, understanding the context, analyzing the claims, and considering the consequences, you've just navigated the maze of misinformation like a true critical thinker.

So, next time you come across a sensational claim, remember to put your cerebral supercomputer to work. Who knows? You might save your friends from believing they can drink their way to Einstein status, one cup of coffee after another and another and another and...

Creative Thinking

Let's dive into the exciting world of creative thinking, where the sky's the limit and your imagination knows no bounds. Being a creative thinker isn't just about coming up with cool ideas; it's about exploring new horizons, solving problems innovatively, and embracing the unique quirks that make you—well, you!

So, how do you unleash your inner creative genius? The good news is that there are endless possibilities waiting for you to explore.

Let's break it down:

Think Outside The Box: Choose a random word or object—it could be anything from "banana" to "umbrella" to "spaceship." Now, brainstorm ways that this word could be related to your problem or task at hand. At first, this might seem like a stretch—after all, what does a banana have to do with solving a problem or planning a birthday party? But that's precisely the point. By forcing yourself to make connections between seemingly unrelated concepts, you're training your brain to think outside the box. Maybe the shape of a banana inspires a new approach to solving a complex problem, or perhaps the vibrant colors of an umbrella spark ideas for a creative art project.

Try Reverse Thinking: Instead of approaching a problem in the usual way, try flipping it on its head. Begin by envisioning the end goal and then trace back the necessary steps to reach it. This approach can uncover unconventional solutions that may not have been considered otherwise.

Set A Timer: By artificially limiting how much time you have to think, you might force a brilliant idea to the surface as your mind races to find a solution. 60 seconds or so should do it. Extra points if you use a ticking timer for added artificial stress. It kinda feels like a bomb scene from an action movie. *tick *tick *tick *tick... Sounds a bit out there, I know, but it works! Just don't flip your lid when the buzzer goes off.

Daydream: Our most creative ideas often emerge when relaxed and not actively focused on a task. Take breaks from screens and distractions to allow your mind to wander freely. Sometimes, the best solutions come when you're not trying so hard to find them.

As you can see, there are countless ways to embrace creative thinking. So, explore, experiment, and let your imagination run wild.

Making Good Choices

Life is a series of choices—big, small, and those that make you pause and wonder. Making good decisions is like being the captain of your own ship; you steer, navigate, and sometimes brave stormy seas. But what if I told you that you have the power to *make firm and good decisions* that set the course for your life's journey?

Life is like a choose-your-own-adventure book and each decision you make shapes the plot. Each little choice you make, whether big or small, ultimately contributes to your life's path in one way or another. The clothes you wear, whether you keep a clean or messy room, and the friends you choose—all impact your life's outcome. *The choices you make are the building blocks of your future*. This is why developing the habit of making good choices is essential.

The trickiest part about making good choices is that they can often be the most difficult. For instance, doesn't it sound nice to play video games, eat junk food, and skip cleaning your room? Sure, it does, but doing those things regularly will impact your life in negative ways. If you did those things long term, you'd be out of shape, unorganized, develop poor eyesight, and may not have much of a social life. Build the habit of making tough but good decisions, and you're doing your future self a HUGE favor.

Now, let's talk about how emotions affect our decision-making. Have you ever made a choice based on how you felt in the moment, only to regret it later? I know I sure have. We've all been there. Emotions can steer your decisions in odd directions—sometimes helpful, sometimes way off course. But fear not; understanding your emotions is like having a GPS for your feelings. It's about knowing why you feel the way you do and how to navigate those emotions to steer your ship in the right direction, even in the midst of life's emotional storms.

Here's something else that can help your decision-making skills...

Let me introduce you to BRAIN & GUT—the dynamic decision-making duo. Some choices are as clear as a sunny day, like knowing that 2 + 2 equals 4. That's your brain talking. But then there are those moments when your gut nudges you in a direction that logic can't quite explain. It's like having two guides—one armed with facts and figures (brain), the other with instinct and intuition (gut).

So, when should you listen to your brain, and when should you trust your gut? In those situations, you must balance rational thinking and intuitive nudges. When you weigh the feedback you get from your brain and gut, you're navigating the thin line between certainty and uncertainty. The right answer, more often than not, is found somewhere between the two.

Problem-Solving Strategies

Whether choosing between two birthday parties or figuring out how to share the Xbox without a family feud, problem-solving is a skill you need. You don't have to know all the answers; you need a strategy, a game plan for when life throws a curveball your way.

Have you ever faced a problem that seemed so complex that you felt there was no solution? Your first instinct might be to run for the hills. But wait—don't hit the panic button just yet. Breaking down big problems into bite-sized pieces is an excellent way of simplifying the complex.

Here's a simple example:

Bedroom Disaster Remediation

Your bedroom *was* a disaster waiting to happen, but then it *actually happened*. Not all at once, but gradually over days and weeks—almost so slowly that you didn't even see the mess until it was too late. Currently, where there used to be open floor space, there is now a vast assortment of clothes, belongings, magazines, and—*is that a half-eaten sandwich??* There are narrow foot-trails of bare floor connecting the door to the bed to the dresser to the closet to the... *seriously, who leaves a half-eaten sandwich lying around?* At this point, your bedroom seems too overwhelming even to start cleaning, but it must be done. Here's how to get it done by simplifying the problem.

Breaking Down The BIG Problem

Divide the room into distinct areas: closet, desk, bed, and shelves.

Tackle One Section at a Time

- **Closet**: Start by sorting clothes. Make piles to keep, donate, and throw away. Organize the kept clothes by type and color.
- **Desk**: Clear off all papers and supplies. Sort papers into keep, recycle, or shred. Organize school supplies into drawers or organizers.
- **Bed**: Make the bed and arrange pillows. This instantly improves the overall look and makes it feel more manageable.
- **Shelves**: Remove everything from the shelves, dust them, and then return only the items you need or love.
- **Set Time Limits**: Dedicate a specific amount of time to each section, say 30 minutes. This prevents fatigue and keeps the task manageable.
- **Take Breaks**: Take a 5-10 minute break after each section. This helps to refresh and maintain motivation.
- **Outcome**: By addressing each section individually, what seemed like an insurmountable task became completely achievable. Within a couple of hours, the bedroom was organized, and the initial overwhelming feeling was replaced with a sense of accomplishment.

A Simple Problem-Solving Sequence

Let me share a neat little playbook for effective problem-solving. These six steps are your roadmap when you are stuck with a problem that seems insurmountable:

- First things first—what's the problem? It's like creating a treasure map; you must know where "X" marks the spot.
- Let's dive deeper. Why does this matter to you? What's at the heart of the issue? Understanding the *why* will give you direction.
- Get those creative juices flowing. List all the ways you could tackle the problem. Consider them all without judgment. Everything from sensible to a bit out there.
- It's time to play judge and jury. Look at the pros and cons of each solution. Cross off the ones that don't cut it, and rate the rest. We're getting closer to the winning solution.
- You've picked your champion solution. Now, how will it work in the real world? Plan it out.
- Once you've implemented the plan, check how it went. What worked well? What didn't?

Now go out there, face those challenges, and remember, not all problems are roadblocks; some are just detours to a better solution.

Developing a Growth Mindset

Having what's known as a *growth mindset* can make all the difference in facing many of life's challenges. Think of a growth mindset as your secret weapon against self-doubt and fear. Your success hinges on the belief that dedication and hard work can cultivate your abilities rather than viewing them as innate, unchangeable traits from birth. *That's a sentence worth reading again.* In other words, it's the belief that you can conquer any mountain, slay any dragon, and achieve your wildest dreams with belief, effort, and perseverance.

Having a growth mindset means believing—truly believing—that you can achieve anything you put your mind to and commit to the process of making it happen.

Let me tell you something that may be hard to believe but is one of the most genuine things I can say to you:

You're capable of far, FAR more than you think you are.

When you believe this too, the sky is the limit for your accomplishments. Do yourself a big favor. Believe in yourself.

Embracing a growth mindset can level up your thinking skills. Imagine your brain as a muscle. The more you exercise it, the stronger it becomes. Adopting a growth mindset allows you to flex your mental muscles and expand your capacity for creativity, problem-solving, decision-making, and dream-achieving.

Instead of seeing challenges as roadblocks, you view them as opportunities for growth and learning. Did you fail a math test? No problem—it's not a reflection of your intelligence but a chance to learn from your mistakes and improve. Adopting a growth mindset when facing challenges unleashes your complete potential. It enables you to confront even the most challenging endeavors with assurance.

But the journey doesn't end there. Developing a growth mindset isn't just about facing challenges head-on. It's also about embracing the power of reflection and continuous learning. Picture this: after slaying a particularly challenging dragon, you take a moment to reflect on your battle strategies. What worked well? What could you have done differently?

By analyzing your experiences and learning from successes and failures, you're sharpening your thinking skills and laying the groundwork for future victories. Remember, the quest for knowledge is never-ending, and each new lesson learned is a stepping stone toward becoming the ultimate hero of your own story.

Wrap-Up

Remember that sentence that I said was worth reading again?

Well, here it is again:

Your success hinges on the belief that dedication and hard work can cultivate your abilities rather than viewing them as innate, unchangeable traits from birth.

It's important because not only is it true, but it also flies in the face of one of society's most damaging lies—the lie that your fate is predetermined by birth, race, location, status, etc.

The only thing stopping you from being or accomplishing anything you want is—you. Therefore, if you believe that you can achieve it and dedicate yourself to the process of making it happen, then your success is inevitable... it's only a matter of time.

With belief, effort, and perseverance, you can conquer any mountain, slay any dragon, and achieve your wildest dreams.

ACTIVITY: Pros and Cons List

Think of a decision you're currently facing, whether choosing between two extracurricular activities, deciding on a weekend outing, or figuring out how to manage your time effectively.

Grab a pen and paper or open a note-taking app on your device. Create two columns: "Pros" and "Cons." Then, start brainstorming! List all the potential benefits or positive aspects of each option in the "Pros" column and all the drawbacks or negative elements in the "Cons" column. Be honest and thorough in your evaluation.

Once you've listed everything that comes to mind, take a step back and review your lists. This simple exercise can help you gain clarity, weigh your options more objectively, and make informed decisions that align with your aspirations.

Chapter 2

Communication Skills

Effective communication starts with listening.
—Catherine Pulsifer

Ever heard the saying, "It's not just what you say, but how you say it"? Well, get ready to step into the art of effective communication, where listening is just as important as speaking, if not MORE important. In this chapter, we'll explore the power of words, the magic of body language, and the importance of active listening.

Listening vs. Hearing

Hearing is like being at a party while someone is talking to you, but instead of being engaged in the conversation, you're half-heartedly bobbing your head to the music while eyeing the snack table. You might catch a few words here and there, but your brain is on vacation in a mythical place some refer to as "la-la-land," dreaming of the delectable treats that await you.

But listening? That's where the real magic happens! You're not just hearing their words; you're absorbing them like a sponge, trying to understand their thoughts, feelings, and experiences. When you truly listen, you're showing the other person that they matter, that their words have value. It's almost like *feeling the words* that another person is saying.

So, the next time someone starts talking to you, put down your phone, forget about that hilarious meme you saw earlier, stop eyeing the snack table, and give them your undivided attention. Trust me, it's a skill that will make you stand out in a world full of distracted zombies.

Active Listening

Picture this: you're chatting with a friend about their latest adventure, but instead of just nodding along, you're fully engaged in the conversation. You're making eye contact, nodding at the right moments, and maybe even throwing in a "Wow, that sounds amazing!" or two. That, my friend, is active listening in action!

Active listening is like giving someone the VIP treatment during a conversation. It's about showing genuine interest in what they're saying, asking follow-up questions, and really understanding their perspective.

Put your active listening skills to the test. Trust me, the folks you're conversing with will appreciate it, and your conversations will be ten times more meaningful. You'll be amazed at how much deeper your connections can become when you hear what the other person is saying AND the other person KNOWS they're being heard. It's a powerful combination.

Open-Ended Questions

Another element of truly effective communication is asking good questions. You see, asking questions isn't just about getting answers; it's about showing curiosity and opening up new avenues of conversation.

Think about it like this: If you ask someone a closed-ended question like "Did you have a good day?" you'll probably get a simple "yes" or "no" response, but if you ask an open-ended question like "What was the best part of your day?" you're inviting them to share more details and insights. So, try peppering your conversation with open-ended questions. It will keep the conversation flowing, and you'll learn much more about the people around you.

Remember, verbal communication is about building connections and understanding others, whether you're actively listening or asking questions. So, sharpen those listening skills and get in the habit of asking some thought-provoking questions!

Starting the Conversation

Ah, the age-old dilemma of starting a conversation without feeling like a deer in headlights! It can feel like being handed a microphone and told to entertain a crowd of strangers. But fear not, my friend, for I have a secret weapon: *open-ended questions*!

Instead of the classic "Hi, how are you?", try something like, "What's the coolest thing you've done lately? This not only shows that you're genuinely interested in getting to know the other person but also opens the door to a world of fascinating stories.

Another surefire way to get the conversation flowing is to find common ground. Maybe you both have a deep, unwavering love for a particular band or perhaps you've both recently discovered the joys of cooking. Sharing these common interests is like finding a secret handshake.

So, the next time you find yourself in a social situation, remember: open-ended questions and common ground are your trusty sidekicks. With these conversational tools at your disposal, you'll be navigating the treacherous waters of small talk like a seasoned captain. No longer will you be left stranded in the dreaded awkward silence!

Body Language and Non-Verbal Cues

Did you know that only 7% of communication is based on the actual words we say? That's right, a whopping 93% of our communication is nonverbal (Lindner, 2023)! Crazy, right?

So, what does this mean for you? It means that paying attention to body language and nonverbal cues is crucial for effective communication.

For example, imagine you're telling your friend about a hilarious joke you heard, but instead of laughing, they're staring blankly at their phone. Ouch, talk about a mood killer! In this case, their body language sends a clear message that they're disinterested and not engaged in the conversation.

On the flip side, if someone is leaning in, making eye contact, and nodding along as you speak, it shows that they're fully present and interested in what you're saying.

Tone Matters

Ever heard the saying, "It's not what you say, but how you say it"? When it comes to communication, your tone of voice, body language, and choice of words can make all the difference.

Picture this: you're asking your friend for a favor, but instead of saying, *"Hey, could you help me out?"* you snap, *"Ugh, why won't you just do this for me?"* It's essentially the same question, but the way you say something can completely change how it's received.

So, when communicating with someone, pay attention to your tone. Speak in a calm, respectful voice, use positive body language, like making eye contact and nodding, and choose your words wisely. It'll make your message much more effective and help you avoid unnecessary drama!

Speak Your Mind, Respectfully

Speaking your mind is like flexing a muscle—the more you use it, the stronger it gets! But here's the thing: While it's important to express your thoughts and opinions, it's equally important to do it respectfully.

Remember, everyone is entitled to their opinion, but that doesn't mean you should disrespect others or spread false information. So, before you speak your mind, take a moment to think:

Is what I'm about to say true?

Is it kind?

Is it necessary?

If the answer is yes, then go ahead and share your thoughts.

Remember to listen to others' perspectives and be open to respectful debate. And if you ever disagree, remember the golden rule: *treat others how you want to be treated.*

To take this a step further, let's touch on assertiveness. Being assertive means expressing your thoughts, feelings, and opinions clearly, confidently, and respectfully. It's like standing up for yourself without stepping on anyone else's toes. Now, let's not confuse assertiveness with aggression. Assertiveness is about being firm but fair, while aggression is more about being forceful and disrespectful.

With a bit of kindness and respect, you can speak your mind while maintaining healthy relationships with those around you. Trust me when I say this is a powerful skill that's highly underrated in today's society. Master the skill of speaking your mind respectfully, and you'll be lightyears ahead of your peers.

When you have something to say, speak up confidently, but remember to do it in a way that considers others' feelings.

Electric Etiquette

In today's digital world, communication doesn't just happen face-to-face. We've got phone calls, texting, emails—you name it! But here's the thing: Just because you're not talking in person doesn't mean manners go out the window.

Whether you're chatting on the phone, sending a text, or composing an email, it's important to remember the golden rule: Treat others with respect and courtesy. That means using polite language, responding promptly (but not too quickly—nobody likes a text bomb!), and thinking twice before hitting send.

Oh, and don't forget about tone! It's easy to misinterpret messages when texting or emailing, so always aim for a friendly and professional tone. And if you're ever unsure how to phrase something or whether it's appropriate to send, just ask yourself, "*Would I say this to my Grandmother's face?*" If the answer is no, then it's probably best to rephrase.

Trust me, a little digital etiquette goes a long way in building positive relationships and avoiding any communication mishaps!

Digital Communication Footprint

Ah, the internet—a magical place where your every move is immortalized for all eternity! It's like having a permanent record that follows you around like a relentless shadow. And trust me, that shadow has a knack for looming over you at the most inconvenient times!

Picture this: you're sitting in a job interview, feeling confident and ready to impress. Suddenly, your potential boss leans in and says, "*So, about that post you made five years ago...*" Cue the internal panic! It's in moments like these that you realize the true power of your digital footprint.

That's why it's crucial to ask yourself one simple question before hitting the "post" button: "*Would I want my parents, future boss, or college admissions officer to see this?*" If the mere thought makes you cringe harder than biting into a wasabi-filled donut, it's probably best to reconsider.

Remember, your online presence is like a digital tattoo—it's a reflection of who you are and can stick with you for a lifetime. So, before you unleash your inner keyboard warrior or share that questionable meme, take a moment to pause and ponder the long-term impact of your digital interactions. Leave a trail that you'll be proud to look back on—one that showcases your wit, wisdom, and impeccable judgment.

Cultural Sensitivity

In one corner of the world, a simple thumbs-up might be a friendly gesture, while in another, it could be as offensive as giving a random stranger a wet willie. And let's not even get started on the minefield of words that sound perfectly innocent in one language but could make a sailor blush in another!

That's why being culturally cognizant is so essential—it's like having a secret decoder ring for human interaction. By understanding and respecting these differences, you can navigate the world like a seasoned explorer without accidentally causing an international incident.

So, whenever you find yourself in a cross-cultural-communication conundrum, show genuine curiosity, ask questions, and be open-minded. Who knows, you might even learn a thing or two about your own culture in the process!

By embracing cultural sensitivity, you'll be able to build bridges instead of walls. You'll create connections with people from all walks of life, and your relationships will be richer and more colorful than a box of crayons.

Empathetic Communication

Picture this: You're chilling with friends, sharing stories, and the vibes are just right. But then, someone opens up about something heavy, something real. Suddenly, it's not just about hanging out anymore—it's about connecting on a whole other level. That's where empathy kicks in, a communication skill we all need in our toolbox.

Empathy isn't just about feeling for someone; it's about stepping into their world— feeling what they feel. It's when you dive deep into their emotions, see through their eyes, and show up with a heart full of understanding and compassion.

Listen—not just to the words they're saying but to the emotions behind them. Notice the way their eyes light up with excitement or how they hesitate when something bothers them. This isn't just about getting where they're coming from; it's about letting them know they're not alone.

Empathy transforms ordinary chats into deeply meaningful exchanges. It's the secret ingredient that strengthens bonds and builds trust. By being empathetic, you're not just hearing people out; you're making them feel heard. So, let's make empathy our go-to, not just because it's nice, but because understanding and supporting each other is what truly connects us.

Difficult Conversations and Conflict Resolution

Let's face it. Conflicts happen. Disagreements are a natural part of life, whether it's with friends, family, or classmates. But here's the good news: Conflicts don't have to be destructive! With the right approach, you can resolve disagreements peacefully and even strengthen your relationships. So, how do you do it?

First, stay calm. Take a deep breath and try to keep your emotions in check. Next, listen actively (like we talked about before). Hear the other person's perspective, and don't interrupt them or get defensive.

When it's your turn, express your thoughts and feelings respectfully, using "I" statements rather than "You" statements to avoid blaming or accusing.

Finally, work together to find a solution that satisfies both parties. Look for common ground, brainstorm ideas, and be open to compromise.

Remember, the goal isn't to "win" the argument like you're some kind of debate champion with a shiny plastic trophy. That's small-minded stuff. It's about finding a resolution that respects everyone's needs and feelings, even if it means admitting that maybe, just maybe, you might be wrong.

By approaching conflicts with empathy, understanding, and a willingness to find common ground, you'll become a pro at resolving conflicts peacefully—and that's definitely a skill worth having!

The Power Of Apology

Saying "I'm sorry" might seem like just two small words, but they pack a big punch when mending friendships and relationships that got a bit rocky. When you mess up or accidentally hurt someone's feelings, owning up to it shows you're mature enough to recognize your mistakes and care enough to set things right. It's about showing you're not too proud to admit you're wrong and that you're serious about keeping your relationships healthy.

An honest apology shows you're taking responsibility and not just brushing off what happened. It tells your friend or whoever you've upset that you get why they're hurt, and you're bothered about it too. Clearing the air can stop minor drama from blowing up into a bigger deal.

Ben Clardy

Remember, a genuine apology is more than just saying the words; it's about trying to change and not repeating the same mistakes. So, next time you slip up, a simple "I'm sorry" can go a long way. It can fix things you didn't even know were broken and make relationships stronger than they were in the first place.

Feedback

Giving and receiving feedback might not sound like the most exciting part of life, but it's super important for growing and improving at almost anything.

When it's your turn to give feedback, think about how you can help the other person improve. Be constructive, specific, and elaborate on details. It's also crucial to keep your tone friendly and understanding; make it clear you're on their side.

Now, flipping the script: when you're the one getting feedback, it can be tough not to take things personally or feel a bit defensive. The key is listening and seeing feedback as a gift, not a criticism. Someone is taking the time to help you level up. Show you appreciate their insights with a simple *"Thanks for the feedback!"* and think about how you can use their advice to do better next time.

Whether you're giving or receiving feedback, handling feedback well can lead to remarkable improvements and show everyone you're serious about being your best. It's all about using these moments to reflect, learn, and grow—not just in school or sports but in life.

Exiting Conversations Gracefully

All conversations will naturally run their course at some point. It happens, and it's totally okay. Knowing how to exit a conversation smoothly is a must-have skill, especially if you're at a party or just hanging out with friends.

Dropping a friendly "It was great talking to you, but I've got to head out now" or a casual "Let's catch up more later!" helps you make an exit without making things awkward or making anyone feel like they're being ditched.

Being good at talking to people isn't something you're just born with. It takes practice. Each conversation is a chance to get better. Being patient with yourself and willing to learn from each interaction is key. Maybe you'll notice that asking more questions makes people light up, or that keeping your phone in your pocket makes chats more engaging.

As you get the hang of these basic conversational moves, you'll find it way easier to handle any kind of social situation. Whether you're making new friends, talking to teachers, or just ordering pizza over the phone, knowing how to communicate well sets you up for success.

Keep at it, and soon you'll be chatting up a storm, starting and ending conversations smoothly, and rocking your interactions with complete confidence.

ACTIVITY: Active Listening Practice

- Pair up with a friend or family member.
- Choose a topic to discuss. It could be something lighthearted, like your favorite movie, or more meaningful, like personal goals.
- Take turns being the speaker and the listener.
- As the listener, your goal is to practice active listening. This means giving your full attention to the speaker, maintaining eye contact, nodding or using verbal cues to show understanding, and refraining from interrupting.
- As the speaker, share your thoughts on the chosen topic. Try to express yourself clearly and concisely.
- After each round, switch roles so both participants can practice active listening.
- Once both rounds are complete, take a moment to reflect on the experience. Discuss what you found challenging and what you found compelling.
- Encourage each other to continue practicing active listening in daily conversations.

This activity will enhance your active listening abilities and enrich your understanding of the significance of effective communication in fostering robust relationships.

Chapter 3
Money Skills

Financial peace isn't the acquisition of stuff. It's learning to live on less than you make so you can give back and have money to invest. You can't win until you do this.
—Dave Ramsey

Mastering money skills early on can set you up for a lifetime of financial success and freedom. Whether you're saving up for that gaming console that's been calling your name, buying your first car, or even investing in your future, understanding how to manage your money wisely is critical.

Throughout this chapter, we'll cover the basics of money management. How to earn it (legally, of course), save it (without resorting to a diet of ramen noodles), spend it (responsibly, not on that life-sized Yoda statue), and invest it (so you can watch your money grow like a magical beanstalk). By the end, you'll be ready to take on your financial future one dollar at a time.

Understanding the Value of Money

Money isn't just about the bills in your wallet or the digits on a screen. It's much more than that. *Money represents opportunities, options, and your ability to make things happen in life.* The more money you have, the more these things become available to you. Conversely, having less money can limit your choices and opportunities, making you feel trapped. *This is why money is an enormous source of stress for many people.*

Think of money as a tool that enables you to achieve your goals and live the life you want. Whether pursuing higher education, traveling the world, starting a business, or buying a home—money is crucial in making these aspirations a reality.

Achieving financial stability offers a sense of calm and the liberty to chase your interests without the constant concern of struggling to meet your needs. It empowers you to take calculated risks and invest in your future, knowing you have a safety net to fall back on if things don't go as planned.

On the other hand, struggling with financial challenges can be incredibly stressful and limiting. It can hinder your ability to seize opportunities and achieve your long-term goals. That's why it's essential to understand *the true value of money* and manage it wisely. We're going to talk a lot more about how to manage your money, but before you can manage it, first you have to earn it.

Ways To Put Cash In Your Pocket

This section is here to ignite your creativity and initiative, guiding you to identify potential earning opportunities that align with your passions and skills. Whether you're turning a hobby into a cash cow (moo-lah) or filling a need in your community (like becoming the neighborhood's go-to pet-sitter), this guide will inspire you to think outside the box for money-making opportunities.

- **Babysitting:** For those of you who are great with kids, babysitting is a tried-and-true method to earn some dough. This could be your go-to if you're responsible and enjoy hanging out with younger children. Start by watching neighbors' or family friends' kids. Word of mouth can really build your client base here.
- **Lawn Care or Snow Shoveling:** Do you have a knack for outdoor work? Many people don't have the time (or desire) to mow their lawns or shovel their driveways. Offering to take care of these chores can be lucrative, whether it's raking leaves, mowing lawns, or clearing snow. Plus, it's great exercise!
- **Tutoring:** If you're particularly good at a subject like math, science, or English or can play a musical instrument well, why not teach others? Tutoring younger students or peers can be a rewarding way to earn money. You can start with people in your neighborhood or spread the word at your school.
- **Pet Sitting and Dog Walking:** Animal lovers, unite! If you love pets, consider pet sitting or dog walking. Many pet owners need someone to

look after their furry friends while they're at work or on vacation. This job can be fun and relatively easy if you're an animal enthusiast.

- **Selling Crafts or Art:** Are you creative? You can make and sell your creations, whether jewelry, art, crafts or even digital designs. Platforms like Etsy or local craft fairs are great places to start turning your artistic talents into money.
- **Freelance Services:** For the tech-savvy, freelancing in graphic design, web development, or writing can be incredibly profitable. Sites like Fiverr and Upwork allow you to market your skills globally.
- **Social Media Management:** Many local businesses need help to maintain their social media presence. If you know your way around platforms like Instagram, Twitter, or Facebook, offer to manage social media accounts for some cash. It's a great way to use your online skills productively.
- **Part-Time Jobs:** Depending on your age, local businesses like grocery stores, cafes, or retail shops might be looking for part-time help. These jobs can offer regular paychecks, work experience, and sometimes even employee benefits.
- **Car Wash and Detailing:** If you can drive and access car-detailing supplies, offering car washing services can bring in good money. People love having a clean car but might not have the time, desire, or supplies to do it themselves.
- **Virtual Assistant Work:** As businesses move online, many entrepreneurs need help with tasks like data entry, appointment scheduling, and email management. If you're organized and can handle multiple tasks, this could be a perfect gig from the comfort of your home.

Earning your own money isn't just about the cash—it's about independence, responsibility, and learning to manage your finances. So pick one (or a few) of these ideas that sound fun to you and start sharpening those entrepreneurial skills.

Needs vs. Wants

Learning to identify your needs versus wants is like learning to tell the difference between a must-have, like oxygen, and a nice-to-have, like that fifth pair of sneakers. It's a crucial skill for anyone looking to make smarter money moves and keep their bank account in the green.

Needs are your non-negotiables. We're talking about the absolute basics here—food in your belly, a roof over your head, and clothes that prevent you from getting arrested for public indecency. These are the essentials that you really can't skip. Have to have them, can't do without them—these are needs.

Wants are all the extra things in life, vying for your attention and your dollars. This category includes the latest tech gadgets that make your friends go "ooh" and dining out at places where they put parsley on your plate. While these goodies can undoubtedly bring you joy and comfort, they're also the first thing you can ditch when your budget starts to look like a horror movie.

By being clear about what's essential and what's extra, you can manage your finances and stay on track. Cover your needs first, and then, if your wallet allows, sprinkle in some wants.

Impulse Buying

Ah, impulse buying—the art of acquiring something you hadn't planned on, often spurred by the irresistible call of a "limited-time offer" or a midnight shopping spree. Picture this: you're leisurely browsing your favorite online store, and, boom, a trendy jacket appears. It's sleek, it's stylish, and suddenly, you can't imagine life without it, despite a closet already bulging with jackets. Sound familiar? Yep, we've all had those moments.

But hold up before you smash that "buy now" button, take a beat to ponder, "Do I really need this, or is it just a shiny new want?" (remember our talk earlier?) If it's more about want than a need, consider hunting for a bargain or maybe waiting it out until your bank account is more, shall we say, "jacket-ready."

But, to really get control of your spending, what you need is a budget...

Budgeting Basics

A budget is a plan that helps you manage your income and expenses. It's made up of different components, kind of like pieces of a puzzle that fit together to give you a clear picture of where your money is coming from and where it's going.

The main components of a budget include your income, expenses, and savings. Your income is the money you earn, whether it's from a part-time job, an allowance, or any other source. Expenses are the things you spend your money on, like groceries, rent, transportation, and entertainment. And finally, savings are the portion of your income you set aside for future goals or emergencies.

Regarding prioritizing, it's important to cover your needs first — the essential expenses you can't live without, like food, housing, utilities, and transportation.

Once you've taken care of your needs, you can allocate some of your income toward your wants—the things that bring you joy and happiness, like dining out with friends or buying a new set of headphones.

Last but not least, remember savings! Setting aside a portion of your income for savings is crucial for building financial security and achieving your long-term goals, whether saving up for college, a car, or a dream vacation.

Building a Budget

One popular method that can help you structure your budget is called the 50/30/20 rule. Here's how it works (Whiteside, 2022):

- **50% for Needs:** Start by allocating 50% of your income toward your needs. These are the essential expenses that you can't live without, like rent or mortgage payments, utilities, groceries, transportation, and insurance.
- **30% for Wants:** Next, earmark 30% of your income for wants. These are the things that bring you joy and happiness but aren't necessary for survival. This category can include dining out, entertainment, hobbies, and shopping for non-essential items.
- **20% for Savings:** Finally, set aside 20% of your income for savings and financial goals. This could include building an emergency fund, saving for college or a car, investing for retirement, or paying off debt.

Start by listing all your sources of income, whether from a part-time job, an allowance, or any other source. Then, jot down all your monthly expenses, separating them into needs and wants. Once everything is laid out, do the math to see if your spending aligns with the 50/30/20 rule. If not, you may need to adjust your expenses or find ways to increase your income.

Utilizing Budgeting Apps

Budgeting apps are your digital sidekick for managing your money like a pro. These apps are like having a personal finance coach in your pocket, helping you stay on track with your spending and savings goals. For example, YNAB, Plan'it Prom, Mvelopes, and so on. Here's how they can level up your budgeting game:

Simplifying Expense Tracking

Say goodbye to manually jotting down every expense on paper. Budgeting apps make tracking your spending easy by automatically categorizing your transactions. Whether swiping your debit card at the grocery store or ordering takeout online, these apps record where your money is going. This way, you can see at a glance how much you're spending on essentials versus non-essentials and identify areas where you can cut back.

Goal Setting Made Easy

Want to save up for a new phone, a weekend getaway, or even college tuition? Budgeting apps make setting and tracking financial goals a breeze. Input your goal amount and target date, and the app will calculate how much you need to save each month to reach your target. You'll get real-time updates on your progress, motivating you to stay disciplined and stick to your budget.

The Envelope System

Here's how it works: You take your hard-earned money and divide it into different spending categories, like groceries (gotta keep the fridge stocked), entertainment (because Netflix isn't going to watch itself), or clothes (for when you outgrow your pair of lucky socks).

You put a designated amount of cash into each envelope, label them with the category, and boom! You're ready to take on the world, one purchase at a time. When it's time to buy something, you simply reach into the corresponding envelope and use that cash.

Now, here's the catch: once an envelope runs out of money, that's it. Finito. No more spending in that category. It's kind of like a game—and the name of the game is Financial Discipline.

The envelope system helps you stay on track and avoid overspending. It's a simple yet effective way to keep your money in check and make sure you're not blowing your budget on impulse buys.

So, grab some envelopes, label them with your spending categories, and get ready to get a better handle on your finances.

This method is a great way to visualize where your money is going and helps prevent overspending. Plus, it encourages mindful spending since you're using physical cash rather than swiping a card.

Applying Envelope System Principles Digitally

Many budgeting apps like Mvelopes offer a virtual envelope feature where you can allocate funds to different categories within the app. It works like the physical envelopes, but you use digital funds instead of cash.

The digital envelope system is convenient and customizable. It allows you to easily track your spending, set limits for each category, and adjust your budget on the go. Plus, it eliminates the risk of losing cash or dealing with bulky envelopes.

Smart Spending

We all love snagging a good deal, right? But sometimes, going for the cheapest option can cost you more in the long run. It's like this: not all bargains are created equal, and sometimes, splurging a bit on quality can be the more intelligent move.

Quality Over Quantity

Imagine you're trying to decide between 2 pairs of sneakers. One pair is cheap but flimsy, and another is pricier but sturdy. If you go for the cheap pair, you might return for new ones sooner than you think. But if you invest in the sturdy pair, your feet (and wallet) will thank you later when you're not shopping for replacements every few months. If you spend $100 on shoes that last two years instead of $30 on shoes that last three months, you're saving money and hassle in the long run.

Think Long-Term

It's not just about what you're buying; it's about considering the lifespan of what you buy. Take a backpack, for example. If you pick one that's more expensive because it's well-made and has a warranty, it could last through all your high school years and even into college. That's a lot of bang for your buck compared to replacing a cheaper one every year.

Invest in Experiences

Sometimes, the best thing you can spend your money on isn't a thing at all—*it's an experience*! Whether it's a concert, a travel adventure, or a class to learn a new skill, experiences can enrich your life in ways that a new gadget or outfit never will. These memories and skills don't lose value over time; they enhance your knowledge and expand your world!

So next time you're about to make a purchase, pause and consider: is this just a quick thrill, or is it something that will stand the test of time? Will it keep needing to be replaced, or will it last and last?

Sometimes, shelling out a bit more initially can be the move that saves you money and hassle, giving you better quality, longer-lasting satisfaction and, ultimately, more value for your hard-earned cash.

Remember, smart shopping isn't just about finding the lowest price. It's about understanding the true value of things and making good choices for now *and* later.

Financial Quicksand

Debt is when you owe money to someone else, and it can be a lot like quicksand— easy to get into but difficult to escape. While it's tempting to buy now and pay later, accumulating unnecessary debt can quickly spiral out of control, drowning you in interest payments and financial stress.

Whether through credit cards, loans, or installment plans, taking on debt should be carefully considered and reserved for essential purchases like education or a home. Avoiding unnecessary debt means being mindful of your spending habits, distinguishing between wants and needs, and resisting the temptation to overspend beyond your means.

One of the best ways to avoid debt and practice financial discipline is by setting realistic financial goals. Start by identifying what you want to achieve financially. Saving for a car, funding your education, or building an emergency fund. Then, break down these goals into smaller, manageable steps you can work towards over time.

For example, if your goal is to save $1,000 for a new laptop, you might set a target of saving $100 each month. By setting clear goals and creating a plan to achieve them, you'll be more motivated to stick to your budget, resist unnecessary spending, and prioritize saving for the things that matter most to you.

The Importance of Saving

Saving isn't just about setting money aside for unexpected expenses; it's also about planning for the things that bring you joy and fulfillment. Whether you invest in your education, buy a new gadget, or save for a special event, saving allows you to turn your aspirations into reality.

By setting aside a portion of your income for savings, you're preparing for the future and allowing yourself to enjoy life's experiences to the fullest. So, the next time you're tempted to splurge on something frivolous, think about how much more satisfying it will be to save up for something truly meaningful.

Luckily, you don't have to rely solely on guesswork when saving money. Plenty of online tools and calculators, such as Money Fit and My Doh, can help you visualize your savings goals and track your progress over time. These tools allow you to input information like your current savings, monthly contributions, and desired savings goal, then provide you with a clear projection of how long it will take to reach your target.

Whether saving for a short-term goal like a new phone or a long-term goal like retirement, using these tools can help you stay motivated and on track toward achieving your financial aspirations.

The Plastic Jungle

So, you're starting to handle your own money. Exciting, right? As you dive into the world of financial independence, you'll likely come across two main players: debit cards and credit cards. They may look the same, but they play different roles in managing your money.

Debit Cards: Your Direct Line to Your Money

Think of your debit card as a direct pipeline to your bank account. When you swipe or tap this card at the checkout, the cash you spend is pulled straight out of your account. There is no middleman, no borrowing, just your money paying for what you need right then and there. It's straightforward and great for keeping on track with your budget because you can only spend what you have.

Credit Cards: Borrow Now, Pay Later

Cue dramatic music Enter the world of credit cards, where the stakes are high and the temptations are plenty. Credit cards are like having a miniature loan shark in your wallet, except they wear fancy suits and go by names like "Platinum" or "Rewards."

When you use a credit card, you're essentially borrowing money from the issuer, who's fronting the cash on your behalf. It's like having a wealthy uncle who's always willing to lend you money, but with strings attached. You agree to pay back the amount you've borrowed, but here's the catch: if you don't pay off your balance in full each month, Ole Uncle Moneybags will slap you with interest charges faster than you can say "shopaholic."

If you're not careful, those interest charges can pile up faster than dirty laundry in a college dorm room. Suddenly, that $50 pair of shoes you bought on a whim ends up costing you $75 or more. It's like paying a tax for being forgetful or financially irresponsible.

So, while credit cards can be convenient and even rewarding (hello, cashback!), it's crucial to use them wisely. Treat them like a tool, not a toy, and always aim to pay off your balance in full each month.

Why Your Credit Score Matters

And then there's your credit score—a number that follows you around like a GPA for your financial behaviors. This score measures how well you manage debt and how risky it might be for a lender to lend you money. A high credit score can open doors to the nicer things in life, like reasonable rates on car loans, your first apartment, or more favorable credit cards. On the flip side, a low score can make these things harder and more expensive to obtain.

Investments and Compound Interest

You've heard people talk about investing, but what exactly does it mean? Investing is putting your money into something with the hope that it will grow over time.

There are different types of investments, like stocks, bonds, mutual funds, and real estate, each with its own level of risk and potential return. The idea is to choose investments that align with your financial goals and risk tolerance. For you, right now, I would recommend starting with a high-interest savings account. That way, you can start taking advantage of something called "compound interest".

Compound interest is like magic. It's the interest you earn on both your original investment and the interest that's already been earned. In simple terms, it's *interest on top of interest*. Over time, it can turn even a tiny amount of money into a substantial sum.

Example: Compound Interest Over 20 Years

Imagine you put $1,000 into a high-interest savings account and just left it there for 20 years. If the account has an interest rate of 5% per year, here's a simplified look at how your money would grow:

Start with: $1,000

After 20 years with compound interest:

Your initial $1,000 turns into approximately $2,653.30.

This growth happens because each year, you earn interest not just on your original $1,000 *but also on all the interest accumulated from previous years*. By the time you hit 20 years, your money has more than doubled, showing how powerful compound interest can be over time!

To take this example one step further, imagine if you were also to add $100 a month to that same account. Of course, this will be far more relevant once you're earning money regularly, but stay with me on this...

After 20 years of starting with an initial deposit of $1,000, adding $100 every month, and earning a 5% annual interest rate compounded yearly, your savings would grow to approximately $44,316.40.

Of that amount, $19,316.40 is from interest alone!

The key to harnessing the power of compound interest? Start early and be patient. By investing consistently over time and allowing your money to grow, you can take advantage of compounding to build wealth steadily. It's all about delayed gratification. Instead of spending all your money now, you're willing to wait and let it grow, knowing that your future self will thank you.

Wrap-Up

Managing your money wisely is a skill that will benefit you for a lifetime. Stay disciplined and focused, even when that sparkly new gadget is calling your name. And don't be afraid to seek guidance when needed—even the most successful people have mentors! With the right mindset and tools, you can take control of your financial future and build a solid foundation for the life you've always dreamed of.

ACTIVITY: Create Your Personal Budget Blueprint

1. Identify Your Income Sources: Begin by noting down all your income sources, including allowances, part-time jobs, and any other streams of income you might have.

2. List Fixed Expenses: Write out all your regular, recurring expenses, such as school fees, transportation costs, and monthly subscriptions or memberships.

3. Catalog Variable Expenses: Record your fluctuating expenses, which can vary from month to month, like entertainment, dining out, and shopping.

4. Calculate Net Income: Add up all your expenses and subtract the total from your income to determine whether you have a surplus or a deficit.

5. Manage a Surplus: If you find you have extra money after expenses, consider allocating a portion to savings or investing it.

6. Address a Deficit: If expenses exceed income, identify areas to reduce spending or explore options to increase your income.

7. Regularly Review and Adjust: Keep a regular check on your budget, updating and adjusting as necessary to ensure you stay aligned with your financial goals.

Chapter 4
Emotional Skills

When dealing with people, remember you are not dealing with creatures of logic but with creatures of emotion.
—Dale Carnegie

Emotions are like the unpredictable weather of our inner world, turning our days sunny or stormy without much warning. Ever felt butterflies doing aerobics in your stomach before a big event? Or maybe experienced the sensation of your heart taking the elevator straight to the basement when something goes wrong? Yep, those are your emotions showing up in full force. They're our body's dramatic way of responding to life's ups and downs—whether it's a surprise party, a horror movie, or just another day of bewildering plot twists in the ongoing story of our lives.

Understanding our emotions helps us make sense of what we're feeling and why we're feeling it. When we can name our emotions—like happiness, anger, sadness, or fear, it's like putting labels on different jars in our emotional pantry. When we can do that, it's the beginning of something called "Emotional Intelligence."

Emotional Intelligence

Have you ever heard the phrase "heart and mind"? Emotional intelligence is the magic that happens when your heart and mind work together. It's a powerful type of awareness that can guide our thoughts and actions.

Emotional intelligence comprises of four skills (Chefalo, 2023):

1. Self-awareness: Knowing how and why you feel that way.

2. Self-regulation: Managing your emotions, even when things get tough.

3. Social awareness: This involves recognizing and empathizing with the feelings and experiences of others.

4. Relationship management: Managing relationships involves leveraging your emotional intelligence to navigate social interactions and communicate proficiently.

These skills aren't just helpful—they're essential for getting along in the world. They help us build healthy relationships, make good decisions, and bounce back from challenges stronger than before.

So, by understanding our emotions and honing our emotional intelligence, we become the masters of our emotional universe!

Managing Emotions

Imagine you're at the movies, and suddenly, the music gets intense, your heart starts racing, and your palms get sweaty. What's happening? What you're feeling is a reaction to *stress*. So, the next time you find yourself swept up in a whirlwind of emotions, imagine you're watching a captivating movie starring none other than yourself. Take a step back, observe the storyline unfolding, and remember that you hold the power to influence the outcome.

Emotions can be pretty sneaky. Sometimes, they come on strong, like when you're excited about something extraordinary. Other times, they creep up quietly, like when you're feeling a little down for no apparent reason.

To get a handle on our emotions, we first need to recognize what we're feeling. Are you feeling angry, sad, happy, or maybe a mix of everything? Once we've identified our emotions, it's time to tackle them head-on. If you're feeling overwhelmed by stress, take a breather. Find a quiet spot, close your eyes, and take some deep breaths. Trust me, it works wonders!

Stress is like a little alarm bell going off in your brain, telling you something's up. But here's the thing: stress isn't always bad. Sometimes, it can motivate us to tackle challenges and get stuff done. The key is knowing when stress is helping us and when it's holding us back.

When stress starts to feel like a heavy backpack weighing you down, it's time to take action. It could be talking to a friend, going for a walk, or practicing mindfulness to calm your mind. And if stress starts to pile up, don't hesitate to reach out for help.

Coping Strategies

In the hustle and bustle of teenage life, stress can creep up on you like a ninja in the night. Before you know it, your mind is racing faster than a caffeinated squirrel, and you're wondering how you'll ever find a moment of peace. But fear not, dear reader, for mindfulness is here to save the day!

Mindfulness is the art of being fully present and aware of your thoughts, feelings, and surroundings without getting caught up in the drama. It's like pressing the pause button on the chaos and taking a step back to observe the madness with a sense of calm and clarity.

One of the simplest and most effective mindfulness techniques is deep breathing. Find a quiet spot where you can sit comfortably, close your eyes, and take a deep breath. Inhale slowly through your nose, hold the breath for a moment, then exhale slowly through your mouth—releasing all the tension and stress you've been holding onto. Repeat this process several times, focusing on the sensation of the breath moving in and out of your body. You might feel a bit silly at first, but trust me, your mind will thank you for the much-needed break.

If sitting still isn't your thing, don't worry! Exercise is a fantastic way to manage stress. When you get moving, your brain mixes up a potent cocktail of feel-good chemicals called endorphins, which can help you feel energized and ready to tackle any challenge. So, put on your favorite workout gear, crank up some motivating tunes, and get your sweat on. Whether you're running, dancing, or practicing martial arts, exercise is a surefire way to show stress who's boss. Embrace the power of physical activity, and you'll soon find yourself grinning from ear to ear, ready to take on the world.

For the creative souls out there, engaging in activities like drawing, writing, or playing music can be incredibly therapeutic. When you lose yourself in the flow of creation, it's like giving your mind a vacation from the daily grind. So, grab your tools of choice and let your imagination run wild. Who knows, you might just create a masterpiece that rivals the Mona Lisa (or at least a stick figure that could pass for abstract art).

So, take a deep breath, embrace the present moment, and remember that stress doesn't stand a chance against the power of mindfulness. And if all else fails, just remember: it's always okay to laugh at the absurdity of it all.

Building Emotional Resilience

Resilience is the ability to spring back from tough times like a champ. But guess what? It's not something you're born with; it's like a muscle that gets stronger with practice.

First, embrace challenges like a bear hug from your overly affectionate aunt. Instead of running away faster than a kid from a steaming plate of asparagus, face those obstacles head-on with a grin and a "bring it on" attitude. Every hurdle you encounter is a chance to grow, learn, and become more resilient.

By the way—being resilient doesn't mean you *never fail*—ha, who does that anyways? It means you fail so epically that your blooper reel could go viral on YouTube. But then you dust yourself off and give it another go... this time armed with better intel from your previous attempt. Remember, failure is just a stepping stone on the path to success.

Overcoming Fear

Fear—the sneaky little gremlin that loves to hold us back. But here's the secret: fear only has power if you let it. It's time to take back control and face your fears like a warrior.

Start by identifying your fears. What makes your palms sweaty and your heart race? Write them down and spotlight them. Sometimes, just acknowledging your fears can remove their power.

Next, separate rational fears from irrational ones. Sure, being afraid of jumping out of a plane without a parachute is pretty logical. *I feel sweaty just thinking about it.* But being terrified of speaking up in class? Not so much. Learn to distinguish between genuine danger and imaginary monsters under the bed.

And finally, take action. Don't let fear call the shots. Show it who's boss! Step out of your comfort zone, one tiny step at a time. With each brave move, you'll chip away at fear's armor until it crumbles away to nothing.

Coping With Loss

Whether it's saying goodbye to a loved one, a friendship, or a cherished dream, loss is a tough pill to swallow. But guess what? You're not alone, and there are ways to navigate the challenging emotions associated with grief.

First things first, give yourself permission to feel. Grief is messy, and it's OK to ride the emotional rollercoaster. Allow yourself to cry, scream, or even laugh. It's all part of the healing process.

Next, lean on your support system. Surround yourself with people who lift you up and provide a shoulder to lean on when times get tough. Whether it's family, friends, or a trusted adult, don't hesitate to ask for help.

And remember, healing takes time. There's no right or wrong way to grieve, so be gentle with yourself as you navigate the ups and downs. Take each day as it comes, and trust that with time, the pain will ease, and brighter days will come again.

Always remember this simple message:

You're stronger than you think you are!

You're also never alone on this journey. With love, support, and a sprinkle of resilience, you can weather any storm.

Self-Development & Forgiveness

Picture this: you muster up the courage to ask your crush to the school dance, only to hear a polite "no" in response. Ouch, right? Rejection stings, but here's the silver lining: it's not the end of the world. In fact, it's a golden opportunity for growth.

How so? Well, rejection teaches us resilience. It toughens our skin and strengthens our resolve to keep pushing forward, no matter the odds. So, dust yourself off instead of wallowing in self-pity, and hold your head high. Your worth isn't defined by one rejection. It's defined by how you bounce back from it.

Speaking of bouncing back, let's talk about forgiveness. Holding onto grudges is like carrying around a backpack full of rocks—it weighs you down and prevents you from moving forward. But forgiveness? It's like setting down that heavy burden and freeing yourself from its weight.

Forgiveness doesn't involve justifying someone's actions or erasing the memory of what occurred. It entails liberating yourself from the hold of anger and bitterness, creating room for healing and personal development. So, take a deep breath, let go of the past, and step into the future with a lighter heart.

Now, let's turn our attention inward and shine a spotlight on the most important relationship of all—the one we have with ourselves. Self-love isn't just about pampering yourself with bubble baths and chocolate (although those things are pretty great). It's about accepting yourself, flaws and all, and treating yourself with kindness and compassion.

So, next time you catch yourself criticizing your reflection in the mirror or doubting your worth, pause for a moment and challenge those negative thoughts. Replace them with affirmations of self-love and appreciation. Try this:

I am enough just as I am, and I have
the power to make my dreams a reality.
-You

Positive Outlook

Imagine yourself waking up in the morning, and instead of reaching for your phone to scroll through social media, you take a deep breath and think of three things you're grateful for.

It could be as simple as the warmth of sunlight streaming through your window, the fact that you have a soft bed to sleep in with a roof over your head, or maybe the deep gratitude for having been granted another day of life on this beautiful planet. As you can see, there are countless "ordinary" things surrounding us that we have to be genuinely grateful for. Taking the time to recognize them contributes hugely to our outlook on life.

Why bother with gratitude? Well, my friends, it's like hitting the reset button on your mindset. By focusing on the good stuff, you train your brain to see the silver linings, even on cloudy days. Plus, studies show that practicing gratitude can boost your mood, improve your sleep, and even strengthen your relationships (Reid, 2024). Talk about a win-win!

It's all too easy to get caught up in the comparison game—scrolling through social media, wishing you had someone else's life or possessions. But here's the truth: Comparing yourself to others is like trying to fit a square peg into a round hole. It just doesn't work.

Instead, focus on what you have, not what you lack. Savor the small joys in life, like sharing a laugh with friends, enjoying your favorite meal, or cuddling up with a good book.

Remember, happiness isn't about having more; it's about appreciating what you already have. So, let's raise a toast to the little things that make life oh-so-sweet!

Empathy and Integrity

These twin virtues, when cultivated and practiced, have the power to transform our relationships, our communities, and our world.

Empathy, at its core, is the ability to understand and share the feelings of another. It is the capacity to step into someone else's shoes, to see the world through their eyes, and to feel their joys and sorrows as if they were your own. When we empathize with others, we create a bridge of understanding that spans the gaps of difference and division.

Imagine a world without empathy. It would be a cold, harsh place where people are disconnected from one another, unable to relate to each other's experiences or emotions. In such a world, we would be trapped in our own narrow perspectives, unable to grow or learn from those around us.

But when we embrace empathy, we open ourselves up to the richness and diversity of human experience. We learn to listen deeply, to validate others' feelings, and to offer support and compassion without judgment. We recognize that everyone has their own unique struggles and triumphs, and we celebrate the common humanity that binds us all together.

Integrity, on the other hand, is the steadfast adherence to moral and ethical principles. It is the unwavering commitment to doing what is right, even when it is difficult or unpopular. When we act with integrity, we align our actions with our values and beliefs, creating a sense of inner harmony and purpose.

In a world that often seems to reward deception and self-interest, integrity can feel like a rare and precious commodity. It takes courage and strength of character to stand up for what you believe in, especially when faced with pressure to compromise your values.

But when we cultivate integrity, we build trust and respect with those around us. We become a beacon of honesty and reliability, someone that others can count on to do the right thing. We inspire others to hold themselves to a higher standard, creating a ripple effect of positive change in our communities.

Empathy and integrity are not just abstract ideals – they are essential skills for navigating the complexities of life. In our personal relationships, they help us to build deeper, more meaningful connections with others. In our professional lives, they enable us to collaborate effectively, resolve conflicts, and make ethical decisions that benefit the greater good.

When we bring empathy and integrity together, we create a powerful synergy that can transform the world around us. We become agents of compassion and justice, working to create a society that values the dignity and worth of every human being.

So listen with an open heart and mind. Act with courage and conviction. Be the change you wish to see in the world, one small act of kindness and one principled stand at a time. In doing so, you not only enrich your own life, but you help create a brighter, more compassionate future for all.

Encouragment VS Manipulation

Supportive encouragement is lifting others up, cheering them on, and helping them reach their goals. It's like being the wind beneath their wings, giving them the boost they need to soar to new heights. Imagine you're a gardener tending to a delicate plant. You provide the right environment, nourishment, and support, allowing it to grow and thrive at its own pace. That's the essence of supportive encouragement. It's about fostering growth, nurturing potential, and celebrating each individual's unique journey.

On the flip side, manipulative behavior is like trying to steer someone else's ship without their consent. It's about controlling or pressuring others to do what you want, even if it's not in their best interest.

For instance, let's say you have a friend who always insists on picking the movie every time you hang out, ignoring your preferences completely. They might use guilt-tripping tactics or subtle persuasion to make you feel like your choices don't matter. Instead of considering your feelings, they prioritize their own desires, leaving you feeling sidelined and unheard. That's an example of manipulative behavior, where someone tries to control the situation for their benefit without considering how it affects others.

So, instead of manipulating, let's focus on empowering others to make their own choices and supporting them every step of the way.

Self-Control and Responsibility

Imagine it's late at night, and you're 5 hours deep into a video game marathon, but that little voice in your head reminds you of the big test first thing in the morning. That's your opportunity to practice a bit of self-control.

Self-control is about resisting short-term temptations that can undermine long-term goals. It takes work, especially when what you want in the moment feels urgent and convincing.

But here's a trick:

1. Hit the pause button.

2. Take a deep breath.

3. Think about the consequences.

Choosing wisely in these moments might seem like a small thing, but it adds up. Every time you exercise self-control, you're not just avoiding a potential mess but *also building the mental muscle that makes you stronger in facing more significant future challenges.* And let's be honest: If you can trust yourself to make the right choice—that's a huge win!

So next time you're in a bind, remember: a moment of patience can save you a lot of stress and trouble down the line. Exercising self-control now will pay off big time, helping you steer your life in the direction you want to go.

No Excuses

Before we close out this chapter, let's get real about something we've all done before: *make excuses.* You know the drill—blaming the dog for chewing on your homework or insisting you're too swamped to take out the trash. Those might seem like little fibs, but here's the hard truth: making excuses doesn't fix anything.

It's like tossing your problems into a closet and slamming the door shut. Out of sight for now, but definitely not out of mind. Those pesky issues will keep banging on the door, demanding attention like a toddler who's just discovered the joy of pots and pans.

Rather than playing the blame game or crafting creative excuses, it's time to step up and own our actions. This means if you drop the ball, own up to it. Did you make a mistake? Apologize sincerely. Forgot to do your part of a group project? Don't point fingers or dream up reasons why. It's on you to make it right. Taking responsibility might feel tough at first, especially if you're used to deflecting with excuses, but it's a game-changer.

Owning up to what you've done shows real maturity. It proves you're strong enough to face the consequences and intelligent enough to learn from them. Plus, it builds trust. When people know you're someone who admits mistakes and tries to fix them, they respect and rely on you more.

So, as we wrap up, remember: ditching the excuses and embracing responsibility not only clears your conscience but also paves the way for genuine growth and stronger relationships. It's a bold move towards becoming the best version of yourself.

ACTIVITY: Emotion Journal

Grab a notebook and pen; it's time to start your emotion journal! Take a few minutes each day to jot down how you're feeling and why. Was it something exciting that happened at school? Or a frustrating moment with a friend?

At the end of the week, review your entries and look for patterns. Do certain activities or people tend to trigger specific emotions? Understanding these patterns can help you manage your feelings better in the future.

Plus, expressing your emotions through writing can be super therapeutic. So, as you embark on this journey of self-discovery, remember that your emotion journal is more than just a collection of words—it's a powerful tool for growth and healing. Embrace the process wholeheartedly, and let your journal guide you toward a deeper understanding of yourself and your emotions.

Chapter 5
Cooking Skills

Good food is very often, even most often, simple food.
— Anthony Bourdain

In this chapter, we'll dive into the magical world of cooking, where spatulas are your wands and aprons are your capes. We'll start by conquering simple recipes, like Boiled Water (it's a milestone for some, trust me).

Then, we'll graduate to creating *real* culinary masterpieces from proven recipes that will make your taste buds do a happy dance. You'll even learn how to experiment with various ingredients to create dishes of your very own design. Who knows, you might discover a method for turning a turnip into something edible!

But cooking isn't just about filling your belly; it's about the warm and fuzzy feelings that come with preparing healthy meals from scratch. By the end of this chapter, you'll be well on your way to becoming a master chef, or at least a master of not setting the kitchen on fire.

Why Cook?

Cooking is really about so much more than just filling your belly. It can be a fantastic way to bond with friends and family. Imagine hosting a dinner party or cooking a meal together. It's not just about the food; it's about the memories you create and about finding out which of your friends is brave enough to try your experimental dishes. But most importantly, learning to cook gives you a valuable life skill that you'll carry with you forever.

It's also a way to take charge of your health by cooking "from scratch"—because, let's face it, not all ingredients that go into processed foods are good for us—or even pronounceable. I mean, who really wants a side of zylophenitroxy-chlorolechantriphendrobenzamide.

Whether you're living on your own for the first time or just craving something tasty on a lazy Sunday afternoon, mastering the kitchen means you're always just a whisk away from a delicious, healthy meal.

Safety First

First things first, why is kitchen safety such a big deal? Well, think about all the things that could go wrong when cooking—burns, cuts, fires—you name it. Knowing how to stay safe in the kitchen can help prevent accidents and keep you and your loved ones out of harm's way.

So, how can you stay safe while cooking up a storm? Here are a few tips to keep in mind:

- Always wash your hands before and after handling food. This helps prevent the spread of germs and keeps your food safe to eat.
- Pay attention to what you're doing. It's easy to get distracted, especially when chatting with friends or listening to music while cooking.
- Use kitchen tools and equipment properly. That means knowing how to use knives safely, keeping pot handles turned away from the stove's edge, and using oven mitts when handling hot pots and pans.
- Last but not least, don't be afraid to ask for help if needed. Whether you're unsure how to use a particular kitchen gadget or feel overwhelmed by a recipe, there's no shame in asking for help.

Essential Kitchen Tools and Equipment

There are a lot of tools and utensils required for cooking.

Knives, cutting boards, mixing bowls, measuring cups, measuring spoons, whisk, spatula, ladle, tongs, saucepan, frying pan, baking sheet, colander, vegetable peeler, grater, kitchen shears, rolling pin, can opener, unicorn horn sharpener...

Just kidding about that last one, but you get the idea.

You might be thinking, "Do I really need all this stuff?" Well, the short answer is yes. Here are the basics and why you need them:

Knives

A good set of knives is like a chef's best friend. You'll want a chef's knife for chopping, slicing, and dicing; a paring knife for smaller tasks like peeling fruits and veggies; and a serrated knife for slicing bread and delicate items like tomatoes.

Cutting Boards

These are essential for protecting your countertops and food from germs. Opt for ones made of wood or plastic that are easily cleaned.

Pots & Pans

You'll want a few different-sized pots for boiling pasta, making soups, and cooking grains. Don't forget about frying pans for sautéing veggies, frying eggs, and searing meats.

Measuring Cups

Other must-have tools include measuring cups and spoons for accurately measuring ingredients, mixing bowls for combining ingredients, and a whisk for beating eggs and mixing batters.

Helpful Gadgets

Lastly, let's not forget about gadgets like ladles, tongs, and spatulas for flipping, turning, and serving food. Oh, and a can opener for, well, you know!

Understanding Cooking Methods

Cooking is like a science; each method brings out different flavors and textures in your food. Here are some of the most common techniques you'll encounter:

Grilling: Grilling is cooking over an open flame or hot coals. It's perfect for cooking meats, veggies, and even fruits like pineapple and peaches. Grilling gives food a smoky flavor and those beautiful grill marks we love.

Roasting: Roasting involves cooking food in the oven at high heat. It's great for meats, poultry, and veggies like potatoes and carrots. Roasting caramelizes the sugars in food, giving it a rich flavor and crispy texture.

Sauteing: Sauteing is a quick cooking method that involves cooking food in oil or butter over high heat. It's perfect for veggies, seafood, and thinly sliced meats. Sauteing gives food a golden-brown color and locks in flavor.

Boiling: Boiling is when you cook food in boiling water. It's great for pasta, rice, and veggies like broccoli and green beans. Boiling cooks food quickly and evenly, but be careful not to overcook!

Steaming: Steaming involves cooking food over boiling water without submerging it. It's perfect for delicate foods like fish, shellfish, and veggies. Steaming preserves nutrients and natural flavors without adding any extra fat.

Baking: Baking is cooking food in the oven surrounded by dry heat. It's perfect for bread, cakes, cookies, and casseroles. Baking creates a golden crust and soft interior, giving food that irresistible homemade taste.

Keep A Clean Kitchen

Firstly, cleanliness in the kitchen helps prevent foodborne illnesses. Bacteria love to hang out in dirty areas. If they get into your food, they can make you very sick. So, washing your hands before and after handling food and regularly cleaning countertops, cutting boards, and utensils can help keep those germs at bay.

Secondly, a clean kitchen makes cooking a lot easier and more enjoyable. Imagine chopping veggies on a cluttered countertop or cooking on a dirty stove. Not fun, right? Keeping your cooking area clean and organized gives you more space to work and less stress while preparing meals.

Now, here are some tips to help you maintain a clean kitchen:

Wash dishes as you go: Don't let dirty dishes pile up in the sink. Wash them or load them into the dishwasher as soon as you're done using them. It'll make cleanup a breeze!

Wipe up spills immediately: Spills happen, but leaving them to sit can lead to stains and sticky messes. Keep a clean cloth or sponge handy to wipe up spills as soon as they occur.

Empty the trash regularly: Nobody likes a smelly kitchen! Make sure to empty the trash bin regularly to keep odors at bay and prevent pests from making themselves at home.

Sweep and mop the floor: Crumbs and spills can accumulate on the floor, so give it a quick sweep and mop regularly to keep it clean and hygienic.

Reading and Following Recipes

Understanding a recipe is key to cooking success. Recipes lay out the ingredients you need and the steps you need to take to turn those ingredients into a tasty dish. So, before you start cooking, take a moment to read through the recipe from start to finish. Pay attention to the ingredients, measurements, and cooking methods. This will help you understand what you're about to make and avoid any surprises along the way.

Now, when it comes to following a recipe, accuracy is key. Here are some tips to help you follow recipes accurately:

Follow the steps in order: Recipes are like building blocks — each step builds upon the last. So, follow the instructions in the order they're given to achieve the best results.

Prep ingredients before you start: Chop, dice, and prep all your ingredients before cooking. This will make the process smoother and help you stay organized.

Measure ingredients correctly: Use measuring cups and spoons to ensure you add the right amount of each ingredient. Too much or too little can throw off the flavor and texture of your dish.

Pay attention to cooking times and temperatures: Keep an eye on the clock and set a timer to ensure you don't overcook or undercook your dish.

By taking the time to read and accurately follow recipes, you'll be well on your way to becoming a confident and skilled cook.

Substituting Ingredients

Inevitably, you'll eventually find yourself right in the middle of cooking up a tasty dish, only to realize you're missing a key ingredient. Don't panic! Ingredient substitutions to the rescue!

Here's the deal: ingredient substitutions involve swapping out one ingredient for another that serves a similar purpose in the recipe.

For example, if a recipe calls for buttermilk but you don't have any on hand, you can make your own by adding a tablespoon of lemon juice or vinegar to regular milk and letting it sit for a few minutes to curdle. Voila! Instant buttermilk substitute.

Now, when it comes to adapting recipes based on available ingredients, it's all about getting creative. Let's say a recipe calls for broccoli, but you have cauliflower instead. No problem! Cauliflower can easily step in for broccoli in many recipes, like stir-fries or casseroles.

Here are some tips for successful ingredient substitutions:

Understand the ingredient's role: Is it providing moisture, texture, flavor, or leavening? This will help you choose a suitable substitute.

Keep flavor profiles in mind: Choose substitutes that complement the other flavors in the dish. For example, if a recipe calls for rosemary but you're out, thyme or oregano could work well as substitutes.

Be flexible and experiment: Don't be afraid to get creative and try new things. Who knows, you might discover a flavor combination you love!

Simple Beginner Recipes

Let's whip up some magic in the kitchen and gain some valuable cooking experience with some easy-to-follow recipes!

Mac and Cheese

First, we have everyone's favorite comfort food: creamy mac and cheese (Gallagher & Gallagher, n.d.). Here's what you'll need:

Ingredients:

- 1 pound dried pasta (like elbow macaroni, shells, or penne)

- 5 tablespoons unsalted butter

- 1 pound white cheddar cheese (shredded)

- 5 cups milk (whole or 2% reduced fat)

- 4 ounces cream cheese (optional)

- 5 tablespoons all-purpose flour

- 1/2 teaspoon fresh ground black pepper

- 1/2 teaspoon fine sea salt (plus more to taste)

Instructions:

1. Cook the pasta according to package directions. Drain & set aside.

2. Now, let's make that creamy cheese sauce. Melt butter in a large pot over medium heat, then add flour and whisk until it's light brown and smells amazing.

3. Slowly pour in warm milk while whisking constantly until the sauce thickens and simmers.

4. Reduce the heat, then stir in cheddar and cream cheeses, salt, and pepper until smooth.

5. Add the cooked pasta to the sauce, stir well, and let it sit covered for 5 minutes. Then, it's ready to serve!

If you're feeling extra fancy, you can turn this into baked mac and cheese by transferring it to a baking dish, adding breadcrumbs and more cheese on top, and then baking it until golden brown and bubbly.

Chocolate Pudding Cake

Next on the list, we have a decadent chocolate pudding cake that's sure to satisfy your sweet tooth (Martha, 2014):

Ingredients:

- 1 1/4 cups granulated sugar

- 1/2 cup unsweetened cocoa powder

- 1 cup all-purpose flour

- 1/2 cup milk

- 2 teaspoons baking powder

- 1/3 cup unsalted butter (melted)

- 1/4 teaspoon salt

- 1/2 cup packed brown sugar

- 1 1/2 teaspoons vanilla extract

- 1 1/4 cups hot water

- vanilla ice cream (optional for serving)

Instructions:

1. Preheat your oven to 350°F and grease a 2-quart ceramic dish or a 9-inch square baking pan.

2. Combine granulated sugar, flour, baking powder, and salt in a mixing bowl.

3. Stir in milk, melted butter, and vanilla until smooth, then spread the batter in the prepared dish.

4. In another bowl, mix brown sugar and cocoa powder, then sprinkle this over the batter.

5. Pour hot water over the top of the batter, but don't stir.

6. Bake until set in the center, about 350°F for 40 minutes.

7. Let it cool for 15 minutes, then scoop into bowls, topping with ice cream if desired.

Classic Egg Salad

And last but not least, let's whip up a classic egg salad (Martha, 2020):

Ingredients:

- 4 quarts water

- 6 eggs

- 4 tablespoons mayonnaise

- 1 tablespoon white vinegar

- Pinch of salt

- Pinch of white pepper

Instructions:

1. Boil the eggs for 5 minutes, then let them sit in hot water for 13 minutes.

2. Peel and chop the eggs, then mix with mayonnaise, vinegar, salt, and pepper.

3. Chill in the fridge, then serve with lettuce and bread.

There, you have some simple yet delicious recipes to try out in your kitchen! Enjoy cooking, and don't forget to share your culinary creations with friends and family.

Keep in mind one of the most incredible things about cooking:

Cooking is the only art form where you get to eat your mistakes—so don't be afraid to try new things, experiment, and have fun. It's all part of the learning experience.

Planning and Organizing Meals

Trust me, meal planning is not as daunting as it sounds, and it can make your life much easier.

First things first, why is meal planning important? Well, think about it like this: When you plan your meals ahead of time, you're saving time and money and making healthier choices. Instead of scrambling last minute and settling for fast food or unhealthy snacks, you'll have nutritious meals ready to go.

Now, let's get into some tips for organizing your meals efficiently:

- Start by making a weekly meal plan. Sit down for a few minutes at the beginning of each week and jot down what you want to eat for breakfast, lunch, and dinner each day. Don't forget about snacks too!
- Take inventory of what you already have. Before heading to the grocery store, check your fridge, freezer, and pantry to see what ingredients you already have. This will help you avoid buying duplicates and save you money.
- Get creative with leftovers. Instead of letting leftover food go to waste, plan to incorporate it into future meals. For example, suppose you roast a chicken for dinner one night. In that case, you can use the leftover meat to make chicken salad sandwiches or add it to a pasta dish later in the week.
- Keep it simple. You don't have to make elaborate meals every night of the week. Stick to easy-to-make recipes that use simple ingredients, especially if you're short on time.
- Prep ahead of time. Spend some time on the weekends chopping vegetables, cooking grains, and marinating meats. This will make cooking during the week a breeze and help you stay on track with your meal plan.

Understanding Food Labels and Ingredients

So, why should you turn into a label sleuth? These little panels on every store-bought food item tell you what makes up the food inside the package. For instance, they tell you exactly how much sugar, fat, and sodium is hidden in your favorite snacks, helping you make choices that might even impress your doctor.

Sugar: Keep an eye out for added sugars in products like soda, candy, and packaged snacks. Too much sugar can contribute to weight gain and other health issues, so it's important to limit your intake.

Fat: Different types of fats have varying effects on your health. While fats from sources like nuts and avocados can be beneficial in moderation, trans fats, for instance, can elevate your chances of developing heart disease. Look for products with healthier fats and try to limit your intake of saturated and trans fats.

Sodium: High sodium levels can raise your blood pressure and increase your risk of heart disease. Try to choose lower-sodium options whenever possible, and be mindful of how much salt you add to your food when cooking at home.

Ingredients you can't pronounce: If you come across a long list of ingredients with names you can't pronounce, it might be a sign that the product is highly processed. PRO TIP: If it sounds more like a spell from Harry Potter than food, it's probably best to avoid eating it.

The Impact of Diet on Health

Have you ever heard the saying, "You are what you eat"? Well, there's a lot of truth to that! The food we put into our bodies significantly affects how we feel and function daily.

First, let's discuss how diet affects overall health. Eating a balanced diet that includes plenty of fruits, vegetables, whole grains, and lean proteins provides your body with the nutrients it needs to function properly. These nutrients help support energy levels, immune function, and even mood.

On the flip side, a diet high in processed foods, sugary snacks, and unhealthy fats can negatively affect your health. It can lead to things like weight gain, fatigue, and an increased risk of chronic diseases like diabetes and heart disease.

That's where cooking nutritious meals comes in. When you cook your own meals at home, you have control over what goes into them. Opt for fresh, whole ingredients to avoid added sugars, artificial additives, and unhealthy fats commonly present in processed foods.

So, next time you're thinking about what to eat, remember the impact that your diet can have on your health. You'll set yourself up for a happier, healthier life by cooking nutritious meals and making smart food choices.

Kitchen Emergencies

Cooking is all about crafting tasty dishes and having fun, but let's face it, it's also about perfecting your quick reflexes for when things go sideways. Being prepared for those unexpected kitchen mishaps is just as crucial. Whether it's a minor burn from a rogue splash of sauce or a serious grease fire that wants to audition for a spot in a disaster movie, knowing how to handle these emergencies can keep a small problem from turning into a dinner party anecdote that your friends will never let you live down.

Fire Safety: If you find yourself facing a grease fire, forget about using water. It could make things worse by spreading the flames. Instead, keep your cool and quickly smother the flames by covering the pan with a lid and turning off the burner. If the fire refuses to go out or grows too large, it's time to call 911 right away.

Dealing with Cuts and Burns: Accidents like cuts and burns can happen quickly. If you get a cut, rinse it under cool water and bandage it to keep it clean. For burns, cool the area under running water and gently cover it with a clean dressing. If the burn is really bad or covers a large area, don't hesitate to seek medical help.

First Aid Kit Essentials: Every kitchen should have a first aid kit that's easy to get to and stocked with essentials like bandages, antiseptic wipes, and burn cream. Make sure everyone knows where it is and how to use what's inside. Being prepared isn't just responsible—it's a pro move.

By being informed and ready for anything, you can keep your culinary adventures safe and focus more on the fun and creativity of cooking.

Kitchen Etiquette

When it comes to cooking, it's not only about following recipes and mastering culinary skills; it's also about being respectful and considerate in shared cooking spaces. Whether you're cooking with family, friends, or roommates, good kitchen etiquette can go a long way in creating a positive cooking experience for everyone involved.

First off, it's essential to clean up after yourself. Nobody likes to walk into a messy kitchen, so be sure to wash your dishes, wipe down countertops, and put away ingredients and utensils when you're done cooking. This helps maintain a clean and organized cooking environment for everyone to enjoy.

Next, be mindful of others' cooking preferences and dietary restrictions. If you're cooking for a group, take the time to ask if anyone has any food allergies or dietary restrictions – you don't want to accidentally serve your gluten-free friend a heaping plate of wheat spaghetti! If you've got a vegan in the mix, don't just hand them a head of lettuce and call it a day. Get creative and whip up some tasty plant-based dish that'll make even the most die-hard carnivores jealous.

Wrap-Up

Remember, conquering the kitchen is less about perfection and more about the journey of flavors, laughter, and occasional mishaps. Whether you're wrestling with your first complicated recipe or rescuing a dish on the brink of disaster, embrace each challenge with a dash of humor and a sprinkle of determination. So keep your spirit high and your curiosity alive; with each meal, you're not just filling plates but also crafting stories and honing a skill that will enrich your life in countless ways.

ACTIVITY: The Recipe Remix Challenge

Objective: Enhance your culinary creativity and technical skills by transforming a classic dish into something uniquely yours.

Materials List:

1. Classic Recipe: Choose a well-known dish to serve as the foundation. This could be something like spaghetti Bolognese, grilled cheese sandwich, or apple pie.

2. Additional Ingredients: Encourage creativity by selecting three to five ingredients not typically used in the classic recipe. These could include an exotic spice, an unusual vegetable, or a cheese you've never tried.

3. Timer: Give yourself a specific time frame to complete the challenge, such as one hour. This will encourage quick thinking and decision-making.

Make It Your Own:

Cook your remixed dish, focusing on integrating the new ingredients seamlessly with the old recipe. Once done, take a moment to plate your creation appealingly.

Reflection and Sharing:

- **Taste Test:** After cooking, sit down and taste your creation. Think about what worked and what could be improved.

- **Share Your Dish:** Share your dish with family or friends. Get feedback on your innovation and presentation.

- **Document It:** Take photos or even jot down the new recipe. Reflect on your cooking process and the flavors you created.

This challenge tests your ability to think outside the box and helps build confidence in your cooking abilities. It's a fun way to experiment with flavors and learn about balancing different ingredients in a dish. Plus, it's an excellent opportunity to add a personal touch to classic meals and discover a new favorite recipe!

Chapter 6
Personal Skills

Life is 10% what happens to us and 90% how we react to it.
—Charles R. Swindoll

This chapter is about setting you up with simple personal skills to help you better navigate life's twists and turns. From being punctual to taking responsibility, we'll dive into the skills that'll help you shine bright and achieve your dreams. First, let's get right to the core.

Understanding Core Values

Think of your core values as your compass in life, guiding you through tough decisions and helping you stay true to yourself.

Good vs. Bad

Imagine you're at a crossroads with a choice to make: cheat on an upcoming test to guarantee a good grade or hit the books and earn that grade through hard work. This isn't just about choosing between right and wrong; it's a decision that reflects the core of who you are. Your choice in this moment is a mirror to your values —those fundamental beliefs that guide your actions and decisions every day.

Values like honesty, integrity, and fairness aren't just abstract concepts; they're the principles that anchor you in life. When you choose to study hard and earn your grade honestly, you're not just preparing for a test; you're affirming your commitment to fairness and integrity. This choice might seem harder in the moment, but these decisions build your character and shape your future self.

Understanding what's truly important to you can make all the difference in navigating life's challenges. When you're clear about your values, every decision becomes easier. You're no longer swayed by peer pressure or tempted by shortcuts because you have a strong sense of self and an inner compass that guides you toward actions you'll be proud of.

Your values do more than influence your actions; they define who you are and who you aspire to be. They shape your interactions, affect your relationships, and determine how you fit into the world around you. By staying true to your values, you ensure that you grow into the kind of person who not only achieves goals but does so in a respectful, ethical, and genuinely rewarding way.

Self-Reflection

Self-reflection is like taking a step back and looking at yourself in the mirror, but instead of seeing your physical reflection, you examine your thoughts, feelings, and actions. Regular self-reflection helps you understand your strengths and areas for improvement.

Maybe you realize you're good at listening to your friends when they need someone to talk to, but you struggle with patience when things don't go your way. Recognizing these aspects of yourself can help you grow as a person.

So, what can you do? Take some time each day to think about your actions and how they align with your values. Ask yourself questions like, "Did I treat others with kindness today?" or "Did I stand up for what I believe in?" Doing this will make you more aware of who you are and what's important to you, paving the way for personal growth and development.

Understanding your core values and practicing self-reflection are like building blocks for becoming the best version of yourself. So, take some time to think about what truly matters to you and how you can use that knowledge to navigate life's ups and downs.

Taking Ownership

You know those moments in life when things don't go as planned? Maybe you forget to complete your homework or accidentally break something at home. Well, here's the deal: You've got a choice. You can either own up to your mistakes or start pointing fingers and making excuses. How you handle these situations says a lot about the kind of person you're becoming.

Taking responsibility isn't always easy, but it's a sign of maturity. It shows that you're willing to grow and learn from your slip-ups. When you admit your faults, people respect you more because they see that you're accountable for your actions.

On the flip side, constantly making excuses and shifting blame onto others doesn't do you any favors. Sure, it might feel like you've "gotten away with it" in the moment, but it's a weak move that keeps you stuck in a cycle of dissatisfaction and victimhood.

So, think about it: Do you want to be the kind of person who owns their mistakes and grows stronger from them? Or do you want to be the type who always finds someone else to blame and ultimately lives a life of constantly feeling like a victim?

The choice is yours, but remember, it's the act of taking responsibility that ultimately separates the fulfilled and capable from the weak and frustrated.

Taking Action and Perseverance

We will discuss two super important things here: taking action and perseverance. They're like the dynamic duo of success —they work together to help you achieve your goals and dreams. To greatly simplify the concept—to make things happen in life, you only have to:

1) Start

2) Keep going until you achieve what you want.

Let's break it down.

Action

So, you've got these big dreams, right? You may want to become a professional gamer, a lion tamer, start your own business, or get into a particular college. Whatever it is, just dreaming about it won't make it happen. You've got to take action! That means putting in the work, creating a plan, and doing the things that move you closer to your goals.

Sure, it might be tempting to take shortcuts or procrastinate, but trust me, those rarely lead to success. Instead, focus on taking meaningful action daily, even if it's just a small step forward.

Perseverance

Then there's perseverance, aka *grit*. It's all about sticking with something, even when it gets tough. Look, life will throw some curveballs your way—maybe you fail a test, get rejected from your dream college, or face setbacks in your personal life. But here's the thing: setbacks aren't the end of the road; they're just detours on the path to success.

Perseverance means staying focused on your long-term goals, celebrating your progress so far, and never giving up, no matter how hard things get. Remember, every obstacle you overcome makes you stronger and brings you one step closer to your dreams.

Therefore, take the initiative, maintain concentration, and continue moving forward, even during challenging times. With determination, you can achieve anything you commit to.

When The Going Gets Tough

When you're going after something in life, you will encounter challenges. What will help you endure when the going gets tough are things like:

Patience and Flexibility

Think about it: Life is full of unexpected twists and turns. Maybe you didn't get picked for the soccer team, or your plans for the weekend fell through at the last minute. It's easy to feel frustrated or stressed out in moments like these. But that's where patience and flexibility come in handy.

Instead of getting worked up over things you can't control, try taking a deep breath and rolling with the punches. Maybe that means being patient while you work to improve your soccer skills or being flexible and finding a new way to have fun on the weekend.

Whatever the situation, practicing patience and flexibility can help you stay calm, adapt to change, and keep moving forward, even when things don't go as planned.

Adaptability

Life is inherently unpredictable, and the ability to adapt to change is crucial to maintaining both sanity and success. For instance, imagine your disappointment when your favorite band suddenly cancels their concert or your school springs a last-minute schedule change on you. While it's natural to feel upset, reacting with frustration or anger won't alter the situation. Instead, try to embrace the unexpected change and explore how you can turn it into an opportunity.

Adaptability involves more than just making the best out of a disappointing moment. It's about actively seeking out alternatives and solutions. If a concert is canceled, you could spend that evening discovering a new band or exploring other genres of music. If your school schedule changes, see it as a chance to experiment with a new routine or study method that might be more effective.

Being adaptable means being able to pivot quickly and efficiently in the face of life's twists and turns. This might involve cultivating patience, exercising flexibility, or both. These qualities are not always easy to practice consistently, but the effort is rewarding. Over time, developing these skills will make you more resilient, more open to new experiences, and more capable of overcoming challenges.

With adaptability in your toolkit, you can be confident that no matter what changes come your way, you'll handle them gracefully and emerge stronger on the other side.

Embracing Failure and Follow-Through

Failure might seem scary, but it is actually super important. Yes, you heard me right. Failure is not the end of the world. In fact, with the right mindset, it's often just a bump in the road on the way to something amazing.

Failure Is Okay

Think about it this way: Every successful person you admire has faced failure at some point. Whether it's a botched test, a missed goal in a game, or a project that didn't quite turn out as planned, failure is a natural part of life. But failure isn't a sign that you're not good enough. It's a sign that you're trying, learning, and growing.

So, instead of beating yourself up over a failure, try to see it as an opportunity to learn and improve.

Ask yourself:

- *What can I learn from this experience?*

- *How can I do better next time?*

Embracing failure is all about having the courage to try, even if there's a chance you might fall short. Because, hey, it's far better to try and fail than to never try at all.

Follow-Through

Do you know that feeling when you start something with a lot of excitement but then hit a roadblock and suddenly lose interest?

Yeah, we've all been there.

But success doesn't come from starting something—it comes from finishing it. Whether it's a project, a goal, or even just a commitment to yourself, follow-through is key. It's about sticking with something even when it gets tough, staying focused on your goals, and maintaining a positive attitude, even in the face of challenges.

So next time you feel like giving up, remember why you started in the first place. Visualize your end goal, muster up some determination, and keep pushing forward.

Keep in mind that failure doesn't mark the end of the journey—it's merely a diversion on the path to success. So, when faced with obstacles, persevere and keep moving forward.

Stop Underestimating Yourself

Have you ever been plagued by thoughts that you're not good enough, smart enough, or talented enough? These feelings can be challenging, but here's something important to remember: you are far more capable than you might believe. You *truly* have the potential to achieve extraordinary things. The key is to believe it.

Self-doubt can be a significant barrier, silently undermining your efforts and dreams. But you can combat these negative thoughts by replacing them with positive affirmations. Next time you find yourself questioning your capabilities, pause and remind yourself of your strengths.

Say it out loud:

> *"I am capable. I am worthy. I am unstoppable."*

It's not just a mantra; **it's the truth**.

Regularly reinforcing these positive thoughts can transform how you view yourself and your abilities. Instead of being your own harshest critic, become your most supportive ally. By affirming your worth and capabilities, you'll start to see shifts not only in your self-perception but also in your actions and the outcomes you achieve.

Believing in yourself is more than an act of faith; it's a practical approach to unlocking your potential. So, embrace these affirmations and watch as you turn what seemed impossible into something perfectly achievable. Believe it.

Being Punctual

While some people think slipping into an event fashionably late is cool, it's really just another way of saying, "My time is more important than yours."

Showing up on time isn't just about not keeping others waiting—it also says a lot about your character. It shows you're reliable, responsible, and truly value others' time. Moreover, being punctual is a trait that sets you up for success across all aspects of life, from attending school to excelling in your future career, and even when you're just hanging out with friends.

So, how can you shift from "fashionably late" to 'impressively punctual'? It starts with planning.

Before your day kicks off, think about what you need to do and how much time each task will take. Set reminders on your phone—it's easy and can significantly help. Always aim to leave a little earlier than you think you should. Life is unpredictable—traffic jams happen, buses run late, and sometimes you can't find your keys. By leaving extra time for these unexpected delays, you'll arrive calm, collected, and on time.

Trust me, punctuality may seem like a minor thing, but it packs a significant punch in how others view you and your ability to meet and surpass your goals.

Once you make being on time a habit, you'll notice people will start seeing you as someone they can depend on, and doors you didn't even know existed might start opening up for you.

Cultivating Positivity

Ever noticed how negativity can spread like wildfire? It's like when one person starts complaining, suddenly everyone around them starts feeling down, too. It's as if the "Debbie Downer" zombie has bitten them, and now they're all part of the apocalyptic army of pessimism! But guess what? The same goes for positivity! When you choose to have a positive outlook, it can lift others up and create a better atmosphere for everyone.

Think of it this way: you can either be the dark rain cloud that ruins everyone's picnic, or you can be the sunshine that makes the whole day brighter. Plus, when you radiate positivity, it's like having a magnetic force field that attracts other positive people. Before you know it, you'll be surrounded by a squad of optimists ready to take on the world!

So, next time you're tempted to join in on a complaint-fest, remember that you have the power to change the narrative. Throw in a funny joke, share a silly meme, or just remind everyone of the good things in life.

Here are some quick tips for you to cultivate positivity:

Practice gratitude: Take a moment each day to think about what you're thankful for.

Surround yourself with positive influences: Spend time with friends who uplift and support you.

Focus on solutions, not problems: Instead of dwelling on what's going wrong, think about how you can make things better.

Stay active: Exercise releases endorphins, which can boost your mood.

Practice self-care: Take time to relax and do things you enjoy.

Challenge negative thoughts: Replace them with positive affirmations.

Help others: Acts of kindness can bring joy to both you and the recipient.

The Cherokee Legend Of The Two Wolves

There's a Cherokee legend about two wolves that live inside each of us. One wolf represents all the good things like kindness, love, empathy, and positivity. The other wolf embodies the negative aspects such as hate, anger, fear, and negativity. These two wolves are in a constant battle for control over our thoughts, feelings, and actions.

Now, here's the twist:

The wolf that wins *is the one you feed*.

This powerful parable teaches us that the thoughts and emotions we focus on grow stronger within us. If we feed our minds with positive thoughts, our lives will be filled with joy, kindness, and gratitude. But if we dwell on negativity, it will consume us, leading to bitterness, resentment, and unhappiness.

This story applies to every aspect of our lives, from the way we interact with others to the goals we pursue. By consciously choosing to feed the positive wolf within us, we can cultivate a mindset of optimism, resilience, and growth. It reminds us that we have the power to shape our reality by nurturing the thoughts and emotions that serve us best.

Choosing Empathy Over Judgment

Often, we make quick judgments about others or even ourselves, which can really skew our perception. It's like wearing blinders that block out everything except one narrow perspective. However, it's vital to remember that everyone has their own unique battles and struggles. We're all striving to navigate our challenges as best we can.

So, rather than quickly judging someone based on a single action or a bad day, why not try to foster a bit more empathy? Taking just a moment to consider where someone else is coming from can dramatically change how you see them. It opens up opportunities to connect on a deeper level and build more meaningful relationships.

Remember, your attitude and the way you treat others wield significant influence. Choosing to embrace positivity and understanding can transform your interactions and create a ripple effect in your community.

Adopting this approach isn't just a minor adjustment; it's a transformative shift that can enrich your life and those of the people around you. Let's strive to see the fuller picture and spread kindness wherever we go—it's a small change that can lead to profound impacts.

Finding Your Passion

Have you ever stopped to think about what genuinely excites you? Finding your passion might seem like a daunting task, but it can be as simple as trying out new things. Step outside your comfort zone and explore a variety of hobbies, interests, and activities. This could mean joining a photography class, learning a musical instrument, experimenting with different sports, or even delving into coding or gardening. The key is to engage with a wide range of experiences until you discover something that truly lights you up.

Whether it's art, music, sports, or something entirely unexpected, follow your curiosity wherever it leads. Each new activity opens up potential passions, creating opportunities to connect with like-minded individuals and communities that share your interests. This exploration is not just about finding a pastime; it's about discovering what makes you feel most alive and connected to the world.

Once you identify something that resonates deeply with you, throw yourself into it with enthusiasm and dedication. Pursuing your passion isn't just a hobby—it can transform your life, providing a source of joy, a means of expression, and a way to achieve personal growth. It's what makes life exciting and fulfilling. So, take the leap, follow your interests, and let them evolve into passions that color your life with happiness and satisfaction. Engage fully with what you love, and watch how it expands your horizons and enriches every aspect of your existence.

Finding Balance

Life can sometimes feel like you're in the center ring of a circus, juggling multiple balls in the air—school, extracurricular activities, family, friends, and your downtime. It's like each one demands a piece of you, but the trick to keeping all the balls in the air without dropping any is finding the right balance. Just remember, if you do happen to drop a ball or two, it's not the end of the world. The key is to pick those balls back up, dust yourself off, and keep on juggling. And if all else fails, just remember: at least you're not actually in a circus. (Unless you really are, in which case, *can I get some free tickets?*)

Seriously though—finding balance means making sure no single aspect of your life overshadows the others. Achieving this balance is about more than just splitting your time evenly; it's about managing your time wisely, setting priorities based on what really matters to you, and understanding that sometimes, you need to say no.

Let's paint a picture: Imagine you've got a major exam on the horizon that could really bump up your grades. But at the same time, your friends are planning something fun that you've been looking forward to for weeks. Striking a balance doesn't mean you have to choose one over the other. Instead, you might dedicate a solid chunk of your afternoon to study, then give yourself permission to relax and enjoy hanging out with your friends afterward. This way, you're not sacrificing your social life or your academic responsibilities; you're arranging them in a way that works to your advantage.

Remember, what balance looks like can vary widely from one person to another. For some, it might mean more time with books than at basketball practice, or vice versa. The key is to experiment and figure out a routine that aligns with your goals and values and also leaves room for spontaneous fun and relaxation.

Finding your unique balance is crucial because when you get it right, life feels a lot less overwhelming and a lot more fulfilling. So, take the time to assess your priorities, listen to your needs, and adjust as necessary. That's how you keep all the balls in the air, with a smile on your face and your feet firmly on the ground.

Wrap-Up

As we conclude this chapter on personal skills, take a moment to reflect on your growth thus far. You've honed your abilities to communicate effectively, sharpened your money skills, tackled problems head-on, and even learned how to cook up a decent meal without the assistance of the fire department. Whether you realize it or not, you're making great strides toward becoming a better version of yourself, and that's a pretty special thing!

As you prepare to turn the page to the next chapter of your journey, remember that you possess the resilience and determination to overcome any obstacle. So, step forward with confidence, knowing that you have the skills and mindset to navigate whatever life throws your way.

ACTIVITY: Values Exploration

1. Grab a piece of paper and divide it into two columns.

2. In the first column, write down five values that you believe are important in life. These could be things like honesty, kindness, responsibility, respect, or creativity.

3. In the second column, write down a brief explanation of why each value is important to you. For example, if you wrote "kindness," you might explain that being kind to others makes you feel good and creates a positive environment.

4. Once you've listed your values, take a moment to reflect on how they influence your decisions and actions in your daily life.

5. Share your values and reflections with a friend or family member, discussing how they align with your goals and aspirations.

6. Challenge yourself to live according to your values each day, making choices that reflect what's truly important to you.

This activity invites you, as a teen, to delve into your core values, grasp their significance, and ponder how they shape your actions.

Chapter 7

Practical Skills

A winner is someone who recognizes his God-given talents, works his tail off to develop them into skills, and uses these skills to accomplish his goals. —Larry Bird

In this chapter, we will explore practical skills that will help you navigate life more smoothly. These skills include keeping your car in tip-top shape, dressing sharply, dealing with a traffic stop, and even sending a traditional letter.

These skills might not sound super flashy, but believe me—they're the essentials you'll be glad to have in your toolkit. So, let's get our hands dirty and dive into learning how to handle these everyday tasks like a pro. Ready? Let's do this!

Mailing a Letter

Let's tackle a skill that might seem old-fashioned but is still super relevant, even in today's modern world—mailing a letter.

You may want to send a heartfelt birthday card to a friend who lives far away, or you may need to mail some important documents for school or work. Whatever the reason, knowing how to write, address, and send a letter is a handy skill.

First off, you'll need some paper and a pen. Yeah, the old-school way! But if you're not into handwriting, typing it up on your computer is fine—whatever feels right for you. Start with what you want to say. It could be a quick "hey" to a friend or maybe a longer catch-up for someone you haven't seen in a while. Just make sure to keep it clear and include all the key points.

Once your message is down, fold your paper up neatly and pop it into an envelope. Now, for the envelope: write the recipient's full address on the front center. That includes their name, street address, city, state, and ZIP code. Pro tip: double-check the ZIP to avoid any postal mishaps.

Then, add your return address in the top left corner of the envelope. This isn't just for show —it lets the post office know where to return the letter if it can't be delivered.

When sending a letter, as long as it weighs less than 1oz, which most standard letters will, you'll only need 1 "Forever" Stamp to cover postage. Pop a stamp on the top-right corner and your letter is ready to hit the mailbox.

That's all there is to it. A simple but very practical skill.

Practical Software

You might think, "I know how to use my phone and computer; what more do I need?" But trust me, there's much more to it than just scrolling through social media.

Let's chat about essential utility software like Word, Excel, and Calendar. Microsoft Word isn't just for writing essays; it's a versatile word processor that allows you to create professional-looking documents, from school assignments to resumes and cover letters. Plus, it has handy features like spell-check and formatting options to make your writing shine.

Now, onto the Calendar app. It's not just about marking down your dentist appointments or soccer practice; it's a powerful tool for time management. You can schedule reminders for important deadlines, set recurring events for weekly activities, and even color-code your events for better organization. With your schedule at your fingertips, you'll never miss a beat.

And then there's Excel. Sure, it might seem intimidating at first, but once you get the hang of it, you'll wonder how you ever lived without it. Excel is perfect for managing budgets, tracking expenses, and creating charts and graphs to visualize data. Whether planning a budget for your next shopping spree or analyzing data for a school project, Excel is your go-to tool for crunching numbers and organizing information.

So, don't underestimate the power of these seemingly mundane software programs. They may not be as flashy as the latest social media app, but when it comes to staying organized and productive, they're indispensable. Plus, mastering these tools now will set you up for success in college, your future career, and beyond.

Public Transportation

Now, this one doesn't apply to every teen, but for those of you in a big city, knowing how to navigate public transportation opens up a world of possibilities, allowing you to explore your city and beyond. But before you set off on your journey, it's crucial to do a little homework.

Naturally, ensure that your parent or guardian is on board to allow you to travel on the buses and trains running throughout your city. They'll be able to weigh in and provide insight on whether it's a good idea to travel by yourself. That's step #1, for sure.

Start by getting familiar with the routes and schedules of buses, trains, or subways in your area. Most transit agencies have user-friendly websites or mobile apps where you can easily access this information. Take some time to explore different routes and identify the ones that will get you where you need to go.

When planning your route, there are a few key factors to consider. Think about travel time—how long will it take you to reach your destination? Look for transfer points where you may need to switch buses or trains. And, of course, prioritize safety. Pay attention to well-lit stops and busy areas, especially if you're traveling alone.

If you are unsure about a particular route or stop, feel free to ask for help. Bus drivers and transit employees are usually more than happy to assist you. Remember, it's better to ask for guidance than to get lost along the way.

Also, always have a way of communicating with your home base while traveling on public transport. It's good practice to let them know where you're going and when you plan to arrive just so they can keep tabs on you and help ensure safe travels.

Stay in School

This one's a big deal: Finishing school is like building the ultimate foundation for whatever extraordinary future you've got in mind. There are days when school feels like a total slog—homework piles up, exams loom, and some lessons feel like they'll never end. But hang in there because every task you tackle is an investment in your future.

Now, don't get the wrong idea—I'm not saying it's all going to be a breeze. School is definitely going to toss some challenges your way. Maybe it's a brutal math assignment, a super strict teacher, or your own personal stuff that gets in the way. But guess what? During these challenging times, you really find out what you're made of. You learn a ton, not just about subjects, but about yourself too.

And hey, if the pressure ever gets too much, there's no shame in reaching out for some help. Whether it's confusion over a calculus problem or something personal getting you down, there's always someone around who's ready to help. Remember, asking for help isn't a sign of weakness—it shows you've got the guts to tackle your challenges head-on.

So keep at it, and don't be afraid to lean on others when necessary. School's not just about grades and graduation—it's a journey of growing into who you're meant to be.

Reading a Map

In today's digital age, GPS has become a go-to for navigation, but what if you're in a situation without a signal or battery? That's where map-reading skills step in.

Start by getting comfortable with the symbols and legends on the map. Landmarks are your friends. Use them to figure out where you are. Street names, intersections, and distance scales are crucial for accurately plotting your route. Oh, and don't overlook things like terrain and elevation changes. They can throw you off if you're not careful.

The more you practice reading maps, the better you'll get. Take every opportunity to hone your skills. Whether you're on a road trip, hiking in the great outdoors, or just wandering around your neighborhood. Not only will it sharpen your navigation abilities, but it'll also give you a sense of empowerment and self-sufficiency.

So, when your phone's GPS decides to take a break, you'll lead the way confidently, navigating like a seasoned explorer!

Dress for Success

Your appearance can make a big impression, whether you're heading to a job interview, meeting new people, or just going about your day. Dressing neatly and appropriately shows that you take pride in yourself and respect the situation you're in (and no, your favorite jammies don't count as "appropriate" for most occasions, no matter how comfy they are).

For boys, this might mean wearing clean, well-fitted clothes like a button-down shirt, trousers, and dress shoes for more formal occasions or a polo shirt and jeans for a casual look. Girls can opt for a blouse or dress paired with flats or heels for a polished appearance or a nice top and skirt for a more relaxed vibe.

Remember, dressing for success isn't about wearing expensive designer labels—it's about choosing clothes that fit well, are clean and wrinkle-free, and make you feel confident and comfortable. So, whether you're dressing up for a special event or just want to make a good impression, put your best foot forward and show the world what you're made of.

Know Your Rights

As a teen, it's essential to be aware of your fundamental rights. While these may vary slightly depending on where you live, here are some basic rights that every teen should know:

- **The right to education:** You have the right to access free, quality education that helps you develop your talents and abilities.
- **Freedom of expression:** You have the right to express your opinions, ideas, and beliefs as long as they don't infringe on the rights of others or promote hate or violence.
- **Privacy:** You have the right to privacy, which means you can control who has access to your personal information, both online and offline.
- **Protection from abuse and neglect:** You have the right to be safe from physical, emotional, and sexual abuse, as well as neglect.
- **Health care:** You have the right to access quality health care services, including mental health support.
- **Fair labor practices:** If you work, you have the right to fair wages, safe working conditions, and reasonable hours.
- **Equal treatment:** You have the right to be treated equally regardless of your race, gender, religion, sexual orientation, or disability.
- **Due process:** If you're accused of a crime, you have the right to a fair trial and legal representation.
- **Freedom of association:** You have the right to join clubs, organizations, or groups that align with your interests and beliefs.
- **Participation in decisions that affect you:** You have the right to have a say in decisions that impact your life, such as your education or health care.

Remember, knowing your rights is the first step in advocating for yourself and others. If you ever feel like your rights are being violated, don't hesitate to reach out to a trusted adult for help and guidance.

Learning to Drive

Learning to drive is a rite of passage that opens up a world of freedom and independence, and also the ability to impress your friends with your parallel parking skills. Still, it's also a responsibility that shouldn't be taken lightly. You don't want to be that person who thinks turn signals are optional and speed limits are just friendly suggestions. Beyond just understanding how to operate a vehicle, it's about developing the mindset and habits of a responsible driver who prioritizes safety.

Think of driving like a group project—everyone has to do their part to make it a success. It means always being aware of your surroundings, even if you're jamming out to your favorite tunes. It means following traffic laws, even when you're pretty sure you could totally beat that yellow light. And it means making intelligent decisions, like not texting while driving, no matter how hilarious that meme your bestie sent you seems.

So, when you're gearing up to hit the road, start by familiarizing yourself with the basics. Adjusting your mirrors, signaling properly, and obeying traffic laws seem like small details, but they're absolutely the building blocks of safe driving habits. And don't hesitate to ask questions or seek guidance from a trusted adult who can share their wisdom and experience with you.

Of course, practice is key to mastering any skill, and driving is no exception. Don't be afraid to log those hours behind the wheel, whether in an empty parking lot, on quiet neighborhood streets, or even on the highway with a seasoned driver by your side. Each experience behind the wheel will help build your confidence and competence as a driver.

But remember, safety always comes first. Buckle up, put away distractions like your phone, and always stay focused on the road ahead. Don't forget to watch for other drivers, pedestrians, and potential hazards. Defensive driving is a crucial skill that can help you avoid accidents and stay safe on the road.

Changing A Flat Tire

Imagine you're cruising down the road with your favorite tunes playing, and suddenly, you hear that dreaded flub-flub-flub sound. Yep, you've got a flat tire.

But no sweat. Changing a tire is a fundamental skill you can totally master, and it's your ticket to not being stranded on the side of the road.

Here's how to perform a tire change like a pro:

1. Safety First: Before doing anything, ensure you're parked safely away from traffic and on level ground. Turn on your hazard lights to alert other drivers, and if you have them, place reflective cones or triangles behind your vehicle.

2. Prep Your Tools: Pop the trunk and grab your spare tire, jack, and lug wrench. These are your new best friends. Make sure the spare tire is inflated and in good shape.

3. Loosen the Lug Nuts: Before you jack up the car, use the lug wrench to loosen the lug nuts on the flat tire. Turn them counterclockwise just enough to break their resistance. You'll completely remove them later, but it's easier to start when the tire is still on the ground, so it doesn't spin.

4. Lift the Car: Slide the jack under the car along the frame near the flat tire (your car's manual will show you the exact spot). Crank the jack to lift the tire off the ground. You need enough height to remove the flat and fit the spare.

5. Swap the Tire: Remove the loosened lug nuts and pull the tire off the hub. Slide the spare onto the hub, line up the holes, and screw the lug nuts on by hand. Then, snug them up with the wrench while the car is still lifted.

6. Lower and Tighten: Lower the car back to the ground. Give those lug nuts one last tighten, this time using your full strength to ensure they're super tight.

7. Pack Up: Put the flat tire and all your tools back in your trunk. Don't forget to turn off your hazards!

Congrats! You've just changed your tire and saved the day. Remember, this is a temporary fix —get that flat properly repaired or replaced ASAP to keep your chariot in prime condition.

DIY Car Maintenance

Think of DIY car care as giving your ride a little TLC. It's not just about keeping it looking good; it's about extending your four-wheeled friend's life, safety, and performance. Let's break it down into a few essential tasks that'll keep your car happy.

Wash Your Car Regularly: Getting out the hose, bucket, and soap isn't just about vanity—washing your car can protect its paint from dirt, grime, and rust, all of which can cause long-term damage if left unchecked. Plus, there's nothing quite like the feeling of cruising around in a car that shines like new.

Change Your Wiper Blades: Imagine driving in heavy rain, and your wipers are smudging water across the windshield. Not fun, right? Old, worn-out wiper blades can make driving in bad weather dangerous. Replacing them is simple, cost-effective, and ensures you can see clearly, regardless of weather. This small step can be a literal lifesaver.

Check and Change Your Oil: Keeping an eye on your oil level and color is crucial for your engine's health. Pull out the dipstick, wipe it clean, dip it back in, pull it back out again, and check where the oil sits. It should be within the marked areas and look relatively clean. Old or dirty oil can cause serious engine problems. Most car experts recommend changing your oil every 3000 miles or as specified in your owner's manual. Regular oil changes keep your engine running smoothly and can prevent costly repairs down the line.

Monitor Your Tire Pressure: Low tire pressure can lead to poor fuel economy, faster tire wear, and reduced safety. It's super easy to check: just use a tire pressure gauge on each tire, including the spare. Make sure the pressure matches the PSI recommended in your car's manual. Adjust as necessary using an air pump at most gas stations.

By managing these core aspects of car maintenance, you're not just caring for your car; you're ensuring a safer, smoother ride. Plus, getting hands-on with your vehicle is empowering. It builds confidence and knowledge, which are just as important on the road as a full gas tank. So, roll up your sleeves and take charge next time your car needs a little care. Your car (and your wallet) will thank you.

How To Act During A Traffic Stop

Picture this: you're cruising down the highway, singing along to your favorite song *(waaay off-key, but who's listening?)*, when suddenly, you see those infamous flashing red and blue lights in your rearview mirror. Your heart sinks as you realize you're being pulled over.

Now, before you panic and start crafting an elaborate story about how you were rushing to save a litter of kittens from a burning building, let's talk about how to handle this.

First, don't even think about pulling a fast one and trying to outrun the cops. This isn't a video game, and you're not invincible. Plus, let's be real, your mom's minivan isn't exactly built for high-speed chases. Instead, slow down, put on your turn signal, and carefully pull over to the right side of the road.

Once you've stopped, take a deep breath and remember that the officer is just doing their job. They're not out to get you (unless you've been driving like a maniac, in which case, you might want to rethink your life choices). Turn off the engine, roll down your window, and keep your hands visible on the steering wheel. No sudden movements, no reaching for your phone to live-tweet the experience, and definitely no sassy comebacks.

When the officer approaches, be polite and respectful. Address them as "Officer" and answer their questions honestly (but remember, you have the right to remain silent if you're unsure about something). If they ask for your license and registration, let them know where you're reaching before you do it. And if you do end up with a ticket, resist the urge to argue or make a scene. Save that energy for telling the story to your friends later (with a few embellishments, of course).

So, there you have it - the dos and don'ts of surviving a traffic stop. Just remember, a little bit of respect and common sense can go a long way in keeping the situation calm and drama-free. And who knows, if you play your cards right, you might even get off with a warning (but don't count on it, lead foot).

Voting

This one's specifically for those who are 18 and up, but stick around even if you're younger. This is important to understand because voting is your golden ticket to influencing the future.

You've probably seen loads of stuff about voting during significant elections, like when we're choosing the next president. But here's the scoop: voting is about much more than deciding who gets to sit in the Oval Office. It's your chance to weigh in on the decisions that shape your community, state, country, and even the world.

So, why should you care? Think of voting as the most direct way to make your voice heard in the government. It's how you get a say in what happens around you, from policies on education and healthcare to decisions on public transportation and environmental protection. Every single vote contributes to the outcome, shaping not just the present but the future as well.

So when you finally hit that age where you can cast your ballot, remember: your vote isn't just a right; it's a powerful tool to help steer our country in the direction you believe it should go. Don't let it go to waste. Even if you're under 18, get ready, get informed, and get excited. Your time to vote will come; when it does, you'll be prepared to make a difference. Your vote is your voice. It matters more than you think.

ACTIVITY: Perform An Oil Check

Learn how to properly check the oil level in a car under adult supervision and understand its importance for vehicle maintenance.

- With an adult's assistance, park the car on a level surface and turn off the engine. Let the car sit for 5-10 minutes to allow the oil to settle.
- Open the hood and locate the oil dipstick (consult the owner's manual if needed).
- Pull out the dipstick and wipe it clean with the rag or paper towel.
- Reinsert the dipstick fully, then pull it out again.
- Check the oil level on the dipstick. The oil should be between the minimum and maximum marks.
- If the oil level is low, consult with the adult to add the recommended oil gradually (as specified in the owner's manual) and recheck the level.
- If the oil level is above the maximum mark (this is seldom the case), some oil may need to be drained or there could be a larger issue. Ask the adult to help you consult a professional mechanic in this case.
- Reinsert the dipstick and close the hood.

Make it a habit to check your car's oil level at least once a month or before long trips to ensure your engine stays properly lubricated and to catch any potential issues early.

Chapter 8
Productivity Skills

The secret of getting ahead is getting started.
—Mark Twain

Ever feel like you've got a mountain of tasks staring you down, but you're not sure where to start? Sometimes, taking that first step is the hardest part, but once you do, you'll be amazed at what you can accomplish. Throughout this chapter, we'll explore practical strategies to help you manage your time effectively, stay focused on your goals, and tackle tasks with confidence.

Understanding Procrastination

Procrastination is the tendency to delay or postpone tasks, especially important ones, in favor of more pleasurable activities. It's like having a little devil on your shoulder, whispering sweet nothings about how much more fun it would be to watch cat videos or scroll through memes instead of tackling that essay or studying for that exam. Procrastination often stems from factors like fear of failure, lack of motivation, or feeling overwhelmed by the task at hand.

Procrastination is like the junk food of productivity—it feels good in the moment, but it doesn't do you any favors in the long run. And just like with junk food, the more you indulge in procrastination, the harder it becomes to break the habit.

So, how do you kick procrastination to the curb? Well, it starts with recognizing the problem and understanding why you're tempted to put things off in the first place. Is it because the task seems too daunting? Break it down into smaller, more manageable steps. Is it because you're not sure where to start? Try the "two-minute rule"—commit to working on the task for just two minutes, and chances are, you'll find yourself getting into a groove.

And remember, it's okay to take breaks and reward yourself for making progress. Just make sure your rewards don't turn into full-blown procrastination sessions (because that "quick" YouTube break can easily turn into a three-hour rabbit hole of rabbit videos because... I've been there).

Breaking the Habit

Want to kick an old habit to the curb and start fresh? Whether it's procrastinating on homework, spending too much time on your phone, or anything else you want to change, developing new habits is key. Here's how you can get organized and make your new habits stick. By following these steps, you'll build a routine that works for you, keeps you focused, and makes your goals achievable. Let's break it down:

- **Set clear goals:** Break tasks into smaller, manageable steps and set deadlines for each.

- **Create a schedule:** Utilize a planner or digital calendar to schedule dedicated time slots for each task.

- **Eliminate distractions:** Identify common distractions like social media, video games, or TV, and limit your exposure to them during work or study sessions.

- **Practice self-discipline:** Hold yourself accountable for sticking to your schedule and completing tasks on time.

- **Reward yourself:** Celebrate small victories along the way to reinforce positive behaviors and motivate yourself to keep going.

Benefits of Taking Action

Ever feel like you're stuck in a cycle of procrastination, stress, and last-minute panic? Breaking out of that loop starts with a straightforward step: *taking action*. When you start completing tasks proactively, you're not just ticking boxes—you're setting yourself up for a whole host of benefits. Here's what you can expect when you take charge and get ahead of your to-dos:

- **Reduced stress:** Completing tasks ahead of time eliminates the pressure of looming deadlines.

- **Increased productivity:** Promptly tackling tasks frees up time for other activities and prevents the accumulation of unfinished work.

- **Improved self-confidence:** Accomplishing goals boosts self-esteem and provides a sense of accomplishment.

Common Distractions for Teens

In today's digital age, distractions are just a click away, especially for teens who are trying to balance schoolwork, hobbies, and social life. These interruptions can make it difficult to focus and stay on task. Understanding what typically distracts you is the first step toward managing your time better and boosting your productivity. Here are some of the most common culprits that might be pulling your attention away:

- **Social media:** Constant notifications from apps like Instagram, Snapchat, and TikTok can disrupt focus.

- **Video games:** Engaging gameplay and multiplayer features can make it challenging to tear away from the screen.

- **Smartphones:** Text messages, calls, and browsing the web can lure attention away from more important tasks.

Strategies to Minimize Distraction

With a few intentional strategies, you can significantly reduce these interruptions and enhance your ability to concentrate on what truly matters. Whether it's homework, studying, or personal projects, applying effective methods to minimize distractions can make a substantial difference. Here are some practical strategies that can help you stay on track and maintain your focus:

- **Set boundaries:** Establish designated times for using social media and playing video games to avoid constant interruptions.

- **Use productivity apps:** Install apps or browser extensions that block distracting websites or limit screen time.

- **Create a distraction-free environment:** Designate a quiet, clutter-free workspace where you can concentrate without disruptions.

- **Practice mindfulness:** Stay present and focused on the task at hand, resisting the urge to multitask or switch between activities.

Knockout The Homework

Homework might not top your list of fun activities, but it's a key player in your academic journey. Yes, diving into assignments after a full day of school might seem like a drag, but think of homework as the secret sauce that boosts your understanding and retention of classroom material.

Now, let's talk strategy. Knocking out your homework early doesn't just free up your evenings—it also slashes stress and anxiety right out of your daily routine. Break down those big, scary projects into smaller, bite-sized tasks. This approach keeps you from feeling overwhelmed and helps you tackle each part with clear focus and determination.

And here's the real win: Finishing your homework ahead of time isn't just about getting it done—it's about setting yourself up for future triumphs. With your assignments out of the way, you've got extra time to dive into hobbies, hang out with friends, or just chill and recharge.

In the long run, managing your homework efficiently doesn't just boost your grades. It creates more space in your life for growth, relaxation, and exploration.

Prioritizing Tasks

Prioritizing tasks is all about knowing what needs to be done first and why. You might have a list of things to do, but not all of them are equally urgent or important. Here's how to tell the difference.

Weighing Importance & Urgency

You're hanging out and having fun, and suddenly, your phone lights up with a text message. This message demands your immediate attention, making it feel urgent, but there's a catch. The content of that message, usually a meme, a funny video, or a simple greeting—isn't actually important, especially not in the grand scheme of things. It feels urgent because it's immediate, but it lacks significant long-term impact.

Next, consider this scenario: You're preparing for an important presentation at school that counts significantly towards your final grade. It's scheduled for first thing tomorrow morning. Just as you're about to go to bed, you realize you've left your USB drive with the presentation files at a friend's house across town. This situation becomes truly urgent because retrieving the drive is essential for your presentation. Immediate action is required to ensure you have everything you need to avoid a significant impact on your grade. If you don't act quickly, you risk going unprepared and potentially facing significant negative consequences.

The next time you're interrupted by something that seems urgent, pause and ask yourself, "Is this as important as the other tasks I have?" If the answer is no, give yourself permission to postpone it.

By focusing on what's truly important, you're not only setting yourself up for success now but also developing essential prioritization skills that will serve you well throughout life.

Setting Daily Priorities

You're bombarded with things to do every day. It can be challenging to know when to do what, especially when everything seems to be screaming, *"Pick me! Pick me!"* like an overeager kid in class. Setting daily priorities helps you focus on what really matters and prevents you from feeling overwhelmed.

When you set daily priorities, you're not just randomly picking tasks to focus on like you're playing a game of "eeny, meeny, miny, moe." You're intentionally choosing the things that will move you closer to your goals or help you handle pressing responsibilities.

And remember, it's okay if your priorities shift throughout the day. Life has a way of throwing curveballs (like a surprise math quiz or a last-minute project), and sometimes you need to adjust your plan. The key is to stay flexible and keep your eye on the prize. With a bit of practice and a lot of determination, you'll be a daily priority-setting pro in no time!

Identifying Top Priorities

Identifying your top priorities means figuring out what tasks are the most important for you to accomplish each day. These are the things that absolutely need your attention and effort. For example, if you have a big project due at school or an important exam coming up, those would likely be your top priorities. Think about what tasks will have the most significant impact on your day or move you closer to your goals. By focusing on these top priorities, you can make sure you're using your time and energy in the most effective way possible.

Focusing on Daily Goals

Alright, now that you know your top priorities for the day, let's zoom in a bit and talk about focusing on your daily goals. Think of it as setting mini-milestones for yourself—little checkpoints that keep you moving forward.

So, let's say you've got a research paper broken down into sections. Each day, set a goal to tackle one or two of those sections. Maybe today, you'll knock out the introduction and outline the body paragraphs. Tomorrow, you'll dive into the research for those paragraphs and so on.

By setting these daily goals, you're giving yourself a clear roadmap for what you want to achieve each day. It's like having a little to-do list within your more enormous to-do list. Plus, crossing off those daily goals feels seriously satisfying. It's like a little victory dance every time you check something off. And before you know it, all those daily wins add up to some significant progress on your bigger tasks.

A Cool Trick For Prioritization

One way to sort and prioritize tasks visually is to use an "Eisenhower Box."

It looks like this:

	Urgent	Not Urgent
Important	Do	Decide
Not Important	Delegate	Delete

The thing about the Eisenhower Box is that it's designed to be used mentally, but for the sake of clarity, here's how it works visually:

In the upper/left box, you've got tasks that are both important and urgent, like if you have a deadline coming up or a sudden problem to solve.

The upper/right box is where tasks are important but not super urgent. This could be stuff like planning for a project or studying for a test that's still a few days away.

In the lower/left box is where you place tasks that are urgent but not that important. Think of things that pop up and demand your attention, like responding to non-urgent emails.

Finally, you've got the lower/right box, which is where you put tasks that are neither urgent nor important, like binge-watching a show.

By putting your tasks into these boxes, you get a clearer picture of what needs your immediate attention and what can wait. It's like having a roadmap for your day, helping you focus on what really matters and avoid getting sidetracked by less important stuff. So, give it a try next time you're feeling overwhelmed and need some help prioritizing things.

The Art Of "Saying No"

I know it might feel like you have to be a hero and save the day for everyone, but trust me, even superheroes need a break sometimes. Saying "no" doesn't make you selfish or lazy—it means you're taking care of yourself and your well-being.

Imagine this: you're already swamped with schoolwork, extracurriculars, and maybe even a part-time job. Then, out of the blue, someone asks you to help organize a fundraiser or join a new club. Before you jump in headfirst, take a moment to think about whether you can handle it without sacrificing your sanity. If the answer is no, don't be afraid to decline politely. It's better to do a few things well than to spread yourself too thin and end up feeling overwhelmed.

But let's say you do decide to take on a new challenge. Maybe it's something you're really passionate about or an opportunity to learn and grow. That's awesome! Just make sure it aligns with your priorities and goals. Will it help you reach your long-term objectives, or will it just add more stress to your plate? Be honest with yourself and choose wisely.

Rewarding Progress

Who doesn't love a little treat for crushing their goals, right? Let's say you've just finished a marathon study session without falling asleep on your textbook, aced that test, or completed a daunting assignment that was so long that you thought you might need a passport to reach the end. Now, it's time to celebrate your hard work!

Think about what gets you excited. Maybe it's a slice of your favorite pizza? Or perhaps a scoop of ice cream or two, or three – I won't judge. It could even be just a few minutes of scrolling guilt-free and enjoying some hilarious cat videos. Whatever it is, make it something that makes you smile and gives you a little pick-me-up!

And here's the best part: rewards aren't just about indulging in the moment, although that's definitely a bonus. They're also about giving yourself something to look forward to as you tackle your to-do list. Knowing that there's a yummy snack or a mini Netflix break waiting for you at the end can be seriously motivating. It's like having a little cheerleader in your brain, urging you on with pom-poms and promises of deliciousness.

So don't be afraid to treat yourself—you've earned it, champ! Just remember, moderation is key. Now go forth, conquer that homework, and enjoy your well-deserved reward.

Harnessing Habits For Productivity

Did you know that your habits can either make or break your productivity game? It's true! By establishing positive habits, you can automate certain behaviors and make getting stuff done feel like second nature.

For example, if you make it a habit to review your to-do list every morning or spend 10 minutes tidying up your workspace at the end of each day, you'll end up with a cleaner, more organized life.

Pretty self-explanatory, right?

Plus, once those habits are ingrained, you'll find yourself crushing tasks left and right without even thinking about it.

Creating Morning and Evening Routines

Alright, let's paint a picture here...

You open your eyes in the morning, feeling like you've just had the best sleep of your life. What's next? Maybe you start with a quick stretch, reaching for the sky and wiggling your toes to wake up your body. Then, it's time for breakfast—a hearty bowl of oatmeal topped with your favorite fruits, perhaps, or a smoothie packed with energy-boosting ingredients. While you munch away, you take a peek at your schedule for the day. What classes do you have? Any important deadlines or appointments? By checking in with your schedule first thing, you set yourself up for success and avoid any last-minute surprises.

Now, let's fast forward to the end of the day. You've conquered your classes, aced that test, and crushed your extracurricular activities. Now it's time to wind down and relax. Maybe you curl up with a good book. A thrilling mystery or an epic fantasy adventure. As you lose yourself in the pages, you feel the stress of the day melting away. Or perhaps you prefer to jot down any thoughts or tasks swirling around in your head in your trusty journal. By getting everything down on paper, you clear your mind and make space for a peaceful night's sleep. And hey, why not take a few minutes to pick out tomorrow's outfit? That way, you can hit the ground running when morning comes.

So there you have it. A morning and evening routine fit for a teen on a mission to conquer the world (or at least their homework). With a little structure and a whole lot of intention, you'll be well on your way to starting and ending each day on the right foot.

Adjusting Routines Over Time

Now, here's the thing about routines—they're not set in stone. As you grow and your priorities change, it's important to adjust your routines accordingly.

Maybe you used to be a night owl, but now you're more productive in the morning. Or perhaps you've discovered a new hobby that you want to make time for in your evening routine. Whatever it is, don't be afraid to tweak your routines to suit your evolving needs and goals.

Utilizing Task Management Apps

Task management apps can be a game-changer when it comes to staying organized and on top of your to-do list. Whether you prefer a simple checklist-style app or something more robust with features like deadlines, reminders, and categorization, there's a task management app out there for you.

First up, we've got Todoist. It's super user-friendly and perfect if you like to keep things simple with a basic checklist. Just pop in your tasks, set deadlines, and you're good to go. Plus, it syncs across all your devices, so you can stay on top of things no matter where you are.

If you're looking for something a bit more advanced, Trello might be right up your alley. It's like having a virtual bulletin board where you can organize your tasks into different boards and lists. You can add due dates, attach files, and even collaborate with friends on group projects. Talk about teamwork!

And, of course, let's not forget about calendars and scheduling tools. Digital calendars are a great way to keep track of appointments, deadlines, and important events. Whether you use Google Calendar, Apple Calendar, or another digital calendar app, having all your commitments laid out in one place can help you stay organized and ensure that nothing slips through the cracks.

Last but not least, let's talk about note-taking and idea-capture apps. Whether you're jotting down notes in class, brainstorming ideas for a project, or just need a place to keep track of random thoughts, having a reliable note-taking app on your phone or computer can be a lifesaver.

Apps like Evernote, OneNote, Notability, or even just the Notes app on your smartphone make it easy to capture ideas on the go and access them whenever you need them.

Goal Setting and Progress Tracking

Setting goals and tracking progress are pivotal for personal and professional growth. Together, these practices empower you to steer confidently toward your desired outcomes and manage your journey effectively.

Setting Long-Term vs. Short-Term Goals

Long-term goals are the big-ticket dreams that light up your future, kind of like the ultimate destinations on your personal road map. Maybe you see yourself tossing your graduation cap in the air, kicking off a killer career, or backpacking across Europe. These aren't just any goals; they're your hopes and aspirations that pull you forward through life's ups and downs.

On the flip side, short-term goals are like the signposts along the way. They're the manageable, bite-sized tasks that pave your path toward those big dreams. Think about taking that algebra test next week or saving a chunk of your weekend job earnings for a new laptop. These goals might seem small in comparison, but they're crucial. They keep you moving forward, one step at a time, and give you quick wins that boost your confidence and motivation.

Together, long-term and short-term goals work hand in hand. While your long-term goals give you a vision to strive for, your short-term goals offer daily or weekly focuses that make the big dreams feel achievable. They provide structure and momentum in your daily life, helping you stay on track and pushing you towards those bigger aspirations.

Understanding the difference between long-term and short-term goals and how they work together is the key to not just dreaming about the future you want but *actually making it happen*.

Visualizing Goals

Imagine yourself taking that big exam, landing that dream internship, or finally mastering that killer dance routine. What do you see? Are you celebrating with friends and family? High-fiving your future self? Take a mental snapshot of that moment and hold onto it tight.

Now, let's get practical. Break down that big, beautiful vision into bite-sized pieces. Maybe you create a vision board filled with inspiring images and quotes, or you jot down your goals in a journal every morning. Heck, you could even make a Pinterest board dedicated to your dreams. Who says goal-setting can't be stylish?

The key is to make it fun and personal. Find whatever gets your creative juices flowing—whether it's doodling in a notebook, creating a digital collage, or blasting your favorite tunes while you brainstorm. Remember, this is your dream world, so paint it however you like!

Monitoring Progress and Adjusting Goals

Checking in on your progress is like checking the map on a road trip. It helps you see if you're on track or if you need to make a U-turn. So, whip out your favorite method for keeping tabs on your goals. Whether it's ticking tasks off a checklist, updating a progress bar in an app, or scribbling in a journal, find what works for you and stick with it.

Now, here's the best part—adjusting your goals. If you find that your original plan isn't quite hitting the spot, don't sweat it! Take a step back, reassess the situation, and be open to trying a new approach. Maybe you need to break a big goal into smaller chunks, switch up your tactics, or even set a new goal altogether.

Remember, flexibility is your bestie on this journey, so don't be afraid to shake things up if you need to. The important thing is to keep moving forward, even if the path takes a few unexpected twists and turns.

ACTIVITY: Goal-Setting Challenge

Step 1: Set aside some quiet time to reflect on your goals, both short and long-term. Write them down in a journal or on your phone.

Step 2: Divide your objectives into more achievable tasks. Consider the necessary actions to progress towards each goal. Remember the part about long-term & short-term goals? This is it in action.

Step 3: Create a visual representation of your goals, like a vision board or a digital collage. Use pictures, quotes, and symbols that inspire you.

Step 4: Discuss your goals with a friend or family member. Sharing your goals can keep you responsible and driven.

Keep in mind that each step you take, regardless of its size, propels you nearer to your aspirations. Therefore, continue establishing goals, making steady progress, and persistently reaching for the stars.

Chapter 9
Social Skills

Your smile is your logo. Your personality is your business card. How you leave others feeling after having an experience with you becomes your trademark.
—Jay Danzie

In this chapter, we'll unpack the art of communication, the magic of making friends, and the finesse of handling tricky situations with grace. So buckle up, buttercup, and get ready to learn some life-changing skills that will help you become a master of your social world.

Social Etiquette and Manners

Social interactions can be a breeze when you know the ropes of etiquette and manners. It's all about treating others with courtesy and respect, which means being kind, considerate, and mindful of other people's feelings. Think about it—would you want someone to interrupt you while you're speaking or ignore you when you're trying to join a conversation? Of course not! So, be sure to listen actively, wait your turn to speak, and show genuine interest in what others have to say.

When you're at the table, remember to keep your elbows off it, chew with your mouth closed, and use your utensils like a pro. And if you're using your phone during a meal, try to keep it discreet—nobody likes feeling ignored or sidelined by someone scrolling through Instagram mid-conversation.

When it comes to socializing, a few simple tips can make a big difference. Remember to smile, establish eye contact, and extend a firm handshake when encountering someone for the first time. And don't forget the power of a genuine compliment or a simple "thank you"—it can greatly make others feel appreciated and valued.

So, whether you're at a party, a family gathering, or just hanging out with friends, remember to bring your A-game in manners and etiquette—it's the key to making lasting connections and leaving a positive impression wherever you go.

Social Radar

Personal protection is not just about physical safety, although that's important too. It's also about protecting yourself from situations and relationships that just aren't good for you. So, how do you do that? Well, it starts with recognizing the warning signs.

Think about it like this: Have you ever been in a social situation where something didn't feel right? Maybe you felt uncomfortable, pressured, or like something was off. Those are all warning signs that something might not be entirely kosher. Whether it's a sketchy party, a toxic friendship, or a relationship going south, it's crucial to trust your gut and make decisions prioritizing your well-being.

And speaking of decisions, let's focus on that for a second. Sometimes, it can be tempting to go along with the crowd or ignore our instincts to avoid conflict. But here's the thing: your safety and happiness are worth standing up for. Don't be afraid to assert yourself and say no when something doesn't feel right. Whether setting boundaries with friends, saying no to peer pressure, or walking away from a toxic relationship, remember that you have the power to protect yourself.

Being assertive doesn't mean being rude or aggressive. You just have to be confident, respectful, and firm in your decisions. And hey, it's okay to ask for help if you need it. Whether it's talking to a trusted adult, seeking guidance from a counselor, or reaching out to a hotline, there are people who care about you and want to support you.

Relationships

Friendships and relationships can be incredible, but they can also go bad sometimes. Unhealthy relationships can come in many forms, from friendships to romantic connections. Here are some signs to watch out for:

- **Lack of Respect:** If someone consistently disregards your feelings, boundaries, or opinions, it's a red flag. Respect should be mutual in any relationship.

- **Constant Criticism:** Constructive feedback is one thing, but constant criticism that makes you feel small or inadequate is another. Healthy relationships involve support and encouragement, not tearing each other down.

- **Control Issues:** Whether it's trying to control what you wear, who you spend time with, or how you behave, control issues can be a sign of an unhealthy dynamic.

- **Unbalanced Power:** In healthy relationships, power is shared, and decisions are made together. If one person always holds the upper hand or manipulates situations to their advantage, it's a warning sign.

- **Lack of Trust:** Trust is the foundation of any healthy relationship. If you constantly feel distrustful or betrayed, it's a sign that something isn't right.

Remember, it's OK to walk away from relationships that don't make you feel valued or respected.

Healthy Boundaries

Picture this: you're getting to know someone, and everything initially seems great. But as time passes, you start to notice little things that don't sit right with you. Maybe they're constantly monitoring you, invading your personal space, or pressuring you to do things you're uncomfortable with. That's where setting boundaries comes into play.

First, it's important to know what you're comfortable with and what you're not. Maybe you're okay with holding hands but not ready for anything more, or perhaps you need some alone time to focus on school or hobbies. Whatever it is, trust your instincts and communicate your boundaries respectfully.

When it comes to setting boundaries, honesty is key. It's okay to speak up and let the other person know how you're feeling. You might say something like, "Hey, I really enjoy spending time with you, but I need some space to focus on my studies right now." Remember, it's not about blaming or accusing—it's about respectfully expressing your needs and expectations.

Maintaining your personal health and well-being should always be a top priority. If someone makes you uncomfortable or doesn't respect your boundaries, it's okay to walk away. You deserve to be around people who respect you and treat you with kindness and understanding.

Dating Dynamics

Look, crushes and feelings are totally normal, but remember, there's no rush to dive headfirst into a relationship. Take your time, get to know the person, and most importantly, prioritize your safety and well-being.

When it comes to dating, safety should always be a top priority. Whether you're meeting someone new or going on a date with someone you know, let a friend or family member know where you'll be and who you'll be with. And trust your instincts. If something doesn't feel right, don't hesitate to speak up or remove yourself from the situation.

Now, let's move on to setting paces and making sound decisions. There's no rulebook for dating, and everyone moves at their own pace. Whether you're ready to take things slow or jump right in, it's important to communicate openly and honestly with your date about your boundaries and expectations. And remember, consent is key. Always ask for and respect your partner's boundaries.

If you ever find yourself in a situation where you're feeling pressured or uncomfortable, it's absolutely okay to say "no." Your priority should always be your own well-being, and a strong relationship is founded on mutual respect and empathy.

So, whether you're navigating your first crush or embarking on a new relationship, remember to prioritize safety, communicate openly, and trust your instincts. Dating should be a fun and exciting experience, so enjoy the journey and always put yourself first.

Making Friends

Friendship is one of the most important aspects of our social lives. So, what makes a healthy friendship tick? Healthy friendships are built on trust, respect, and mutual support. You know you've got a good friend when they're there for you through thick and thin, cheering you on during the highs and offering a shoulder to lean on during the lows.

Now, when it comes to meeting new people and forming friendships, it's all about putting yourself out there. Join clubs or extracurricular activities that align with your interests, strike up conversations with classmates or teammates, or attend social events in your community. Remember, making friends is all about finding common ground and shared interests, so don't be afraid to be yourself and let your personality shine.

But, sometimes friendships run their course, or you realize that a relationship is more toxic than supportive. You know what? It's alright. Terminating a toxic friendship is always challenging, but it's crucial to prioritize your well-being. Be honest and respectful with your friend about your feelings, and give yourself permission to walk away from relationships that no longer serve you positively. Remember, it's not about burning bridges but recognizing when it's time to let go and move on to healthier connections.

Peer and Social Pressure

We've all been there—faced with situations where our friends or peers might want us to do something that we're not entirely comfortable with. It could be anything from skipping class to trying drugs or alcohol. But here's the thing: It's okay to say no. In fact, it's more than OK—it's crucial to stand up for what you believe in and make decisions that align with your values and goals rather than letting other people call the shots for your life.

How can you withstand peer pressure and assert your autonomy in decision-making? Well, it starts with knowing yourself and what you stand for. Take some time to reflect on your values, interests, and goals, and don't be afraid to assert them when faced with peer pressure. Remember, true friends will respect your boundaries and support you in making decisions that are right for you.

Setting and upholding personal values is key to navigating social pressures. Whether it's sticking to your commitment to study, avoiding risky behaviors, or standing up for what you believe in, having a strong sense of personal values will guide you through tricky situations. And remember, it's okay to be different and go against the grain if it means staying true to yourself.

Lastly, don't be afraid to seek out friends who share your values and respect your boundaries. Surrounding yourself with like-minded individuals who support and uplift you can make all the difference when it comes to resisting peer pressure and staying true to yourself. So, stand tall, trust your instincts, and remember that you have the power to make choices that align with the person you want to be.

Building Supportive Networks

Having a supportive network of friends, mentors, and peers can be a game-changer in both your personal and professional lives. These are the people who have your back, offer guidance, and cheer you on through thick and thin. Whether you're facing challenges at school, navigating tough decisions, or pursuing your passions, having a strong support system can provide you with the encouragement and resources you need to thrive.

Now, let's discuss the value of teamwork and collaboration. Working together with others toward a common goal can lead to incredible outcomes. Whether you're collaborating on a group project, participating in team sports, or working on a community initiative, teamwork teaches you essential skills like communication, problem-solving, and compromise. Plus, it's a great way to learn from others, share ideas, and achieve things you couldn't accomplish alone.

And finally, let's talk about leadership. Leadership isn't just about being in charge--it's about inspiring others, guiding them toward a shared vision, and fostering a sense of unity and purpose. Whether you're leading a team project, organizing a volunteer effort, or serving as a mentor to others, leadership skills are essential for success in any endeavor. Plus, developing your leadership skills can help you become a more effective communicator, decision-maker, and problem-solver. All valuable qualities that will serve you well in all aspects of life.

Conflict Resolution

Conflict is a natural part of life. It happens when people have differing opinions, interests, or needs. Understanding the causes of conflict is the first step toward resolving it. It could stem from misunderstandings, competing priorities, or even personality clashes. By identifying the root cause of the conflict, you can better address the underlying issues and work toward a solution that satisfies everyone involved.

Now, let's move on to an effective resolution. One approach is active listening, where you genuinely hear and understand the other person's perspective without interrupting or judging. Another technique is finding common ground. Focusing on shared interests or goals can help bridge the gap between conflicting parties. Additionally, brainstorming solutions together and being open to compromise can lead to mutually beneficial outcomes.

However, perhaps the most important aspect of conflict resolution is empathy. Empathy is about putting yourself in the other person's shoes, understanding their feelings and experiences, and showing compassion. By embracing empathy during conflicts, you increase the chances of discovering mutual understanding and achieving a resolution that honors the needs and emotions of all parties involved.

For example, let's say you and your friend disagree about which movie to watch. Instead of arguing or insisting on your choice, you could practice active listening to understand why your friend prefers a different movie. Then, you might suggest a compromise. Maybe you watch one movie this time and the other next time. By showing empathy and being willing to find a solution together, you can resolve the conflict without damaging your friendship.

So, remember, conflict is normal, but how you handle it makes all the difference.

Mentorship

Mentorship can be an absolute game-changer when it comes to your personal and professional growth.

A mentor is someone who can offer guidance, support, and valuable insights based on their own experiences. They can help you navigate challenges, set goals, and make important decisions.

So, how do you find a mentor? Start by identifying someone you admire and respect. Maybe it's a teacher, coach, family friend, or professional in your field of interest. Reach out to them, express your admiration, and ask if they'd be willing to mentor you. Remember, mentorship is a two-way street, so be respectful of their time and expertise and show gratitude for their support.

As you grow and learn, don't forget to pay it forward. Share your knowledge, skills, and experiences with others who may be seeking guidance. Whether it's offering advice to a younger student, volunteering in your community, or mentoring someone who's just starting out in your field, giving back not only helps others but also enriches your own life.

One of the most significant benefits of mentorship is the chance to gain insights from someone who has already traveled the road you're about to embark on. Mentors can offer practical advice, share lessons learned from their successes and failures, and provide encouragement during difficult times. This guidance can be invaluable as you navigate the ups and downs of life and work towards achieving your goals.

ACTIVITY: Reflection and Growth

Take some time to reflect on your social interactions over the past week. Write down an instance where you felt your social skills were particularly effective and helped you navigate a situation successfully. Then, jot down an instance where you thought you could have handled a social interaction better and consider how you might approach similar situations differently in the future. Finally, identify one new social skill you'd like to work on developing and brainstorm some actionable steps you can take to improve in that area. It could be anything from setting healthy boundaries to conflict resolution or assertiveness.

Chapter 10
Safety Skills

By failing to prepare, you are preparing to fail.
—Benjamin Franklin

In a world full of uncertainties, one of the most empowering things you can do as a teen is to master the art of safety and preparedness. This chapter delves into the crucial life skills that help you anticipate potential challenges and effectively mitigate risks. From personal safety tips to emergency preparedness, we'll explore strategies to keep you confident and secure in various situations.

Online Security

You've heard the terms "hackers" and "online scams" thrown around, right? But what do they really mean for you? Well, it means that there are bad people out there who wish to harm or steal from you. Yeah—that's the honest truth. It's up to you to keep your personal info safe while you're surfing the web, gaming, or just hanging out online. The good news is that there are some simple skills you can use to stay safe.

Let's break it down: First, your passwords are like the keys to your digital kingdom. Make them strong and unique for each account—mix up letters, numbers, and symbols to create a fortress that's tough to crack. Using the same password everywhere? It's not cool because if one site gets hacked, all your accounts could be at risk.

Next up, be super skeptical about emails or messages that seem off. You know the type—strange links, promises of free stuff, or someone claiming to need your help transferring money. These are classic bait for scams. If something feels weird, trust your gut and don't click.

When it comes to your personal details, think before you share. Social media can seem like fun and games until someone uses your info in ways you never intended. That awesome vacation pic or your phone number might seem harmless to post. Still, they can actually make you a target for identity theft or even online bullies. Ask yourself: "Who really needs to see this?" before you hit share.

And remember, knowledge is like your secret weapon when it comes to tech safety. Get to know the tools and apps you use. Check out their security settings and use them. Not sure about something or feeling uneasy about a message or an online interaction? Reach out for help. Talk to someone you trust, like a parent or a teacher, or look up reliable tech advice online.

Staying safe online isn't just about dodging hackers—it's about making smart choices and knowing how to protect yourself in the digital world. Stay curious, stay cautious, and keep your digital life locked down tight!

Roadside Emergencies

Roadside emergencies can be unpredictable, ranging from minor mechanical issues to major accidents. Imagine you're driving, and suddenly your engine starts making a strange noise, steam begins billowing from under the hood, or worse, you're involved in a collision. In any roadside emergency, knowing how to react swiftly and safely is crucial.

When trouble strikes, the first step is *always to prioritize safety*. If it's possible and safe to do so, guide your vehicle to the side of the road, well away from moving traffic. Turn on your hazard lights immediately to signal to other drivers that you need assistance, and they should proceed with caution around you.

Once you're safely parked, assess what's happening. If you see smoke or steam from the engine compartment, it could indicate an overheating problem or a fluid leak—do not attempt to open the hood until the engine has cooled, as this could cause injuries. If there's a strange noise coming from the engine, it could suggest a serious mechanical failure that might need professional attention.

In scenarios where you're involved in an accident, check for any injuries to yourself or passengers first. If medical attention is needed, call 911 right away.

Even in minor collisions where everyone seems fine, it's wise to contact the police to file a report for insurance purposes.

If the situation is beyond your ability to fix, like engine failure or significant vehicle damage, calling for roadside assistance is a sensible next step. They can provide towing, technical support, or even just more robust tools to help manage the situation.

Remember, the key to handling any roadside emergency effectively is to stay calm. Panic can cloud judgment and lead to poor decisions. By staying composed, you'll be able to think more clearly, evaluate the situation better, and decide the best course of action. Whether you end up needing to fix a minor issue yourself or require professional help, knowing you have a plan and can remain calm will make all the difference.

Learn to Swim

Swimming isn't just about having a good time in the water; it's a valuable skill that can keep you safe in any aquatic environment. Whether you're chilling at the beach, splashing around in a pool, or even out on a lake adventure, knowing how to swim means you're equipped to handle yourself in the water, reducing the risk of accidents and giving you the freedom to fully enjoy water-based activities.

Now, when it comes to learning how to swim, we're talking about more than just doggy paddling or doing cannonballs. It takes mastering fundamental skills like floating effortlessly, treading water like a pro, and getting comfortable with basic strokes like freestyle and backstroke. Once you've got these down, you'll be ready to tackle more advanced techniques like breaststroke and butterfly or even try your hand at cool water sports like surfing or diving.

But here's the thing—learning to swim isn't a one-and-done deal. It's a skill that you can keep honing and refining throughout your life. That means considering things like taking swimming lessons to brush up on your technique or joining a swim team to push yourself and improve your endurance. And, of course, regular practice is key to maintaining your skills and feeling confident in any water scenario.

So, whether you're a newbie or a seasoned swimmer, there's always something new to learn and explore in the world of swimming!

Extinguish A Fire

So, you find yourself staring down a fire. Your heart's racing, time is doing that weird slow-mo thing, and suddenly you're the lead in an action movie—except this isn't Hollywood, it's your kitchen.

Knowing how to deal with a fire isn't just for the pros; it's crucial for any teen who might need to step up as the hero in their own home drama. Here's your quick guide to handling those flames, whether it's time to bust out a fire extinguisher, smother the fire, or grab the phone for a potentially life-saving chat with 911.

We're going deep on this one because knowing this stuff can potentially make the difference between a little stove-top fire and your house being burnt to the ground. Stay sharp, stay safe, and let's keep things cool (literally) when things start heating up. Let's get into it.

Recognizing the Type of Fire

Before you act, it's crucial to identify what kind of fire you're dealing with. Fires involving everyday materials like wood and paper require different handling than those fueled by grease or electrical issues. Knowing the source can dictate whether to use a fire extinguisher or another method to douse the flames.

Smothering the Flame

If a fire breaks out from a small source, like a pan on the stove, smothering the flames might be your best bet, especially if you don't have an extinguisher handy.

1. Cover the Flames: For a pan fire, use a metal lid or a cookie sheet to cover the pan completely. This cuts off the oxygen and smothers the flames. Do not use glass, as it can shatter from the heat.

2. Turn Off the Heat: Once covered, turn off the burner. Do not move the pan; let it cool completely to avoid reigniting the fire.

3. Avoid Water: Never throw water on a grease fire. It can cause the oil to splash and spread the flames even more dangerously.

Using a Fire Extinguisher

1. Select the Correct Extinguisher: Ensure you have the correct type of extinguisher. A multi-purpose extinguisher labeled "ABC" is suitable for most fires you'll encounter at home.

2. PASS Technique: Once you have the proper extinguisher, remember the PASS technique:

- **Pull:** Pull the pin to break the tamper seal.

- **Aim:** Aim low, pointing the extinguisher nozzle at the base of the fire.

- **Squeeze:** Squeeze the handle to release the extinguishing agent.

- **Sweep:** Sweep the nozzle from side to side, covering the area of the fire until it's completely out.

Using an extinguisher can be effective, but it requires calm and precision. Practice this technique in advance so you're ready if the need arises.

When to Call 911

Sometimes, the best action is to retreat and call for help. Here are scenarios when you should dial 911:

1. The Fire Grows: If the fire is getting out of control control, it's time to call 911.

2. No Extinguisher Available: If you don't have access to a fire extinguisher or the fire is not smotherable, get out and call for help.

3. Smoke Becomes Excessive: Too much smoke can be hazardous to breathe. If you see heavy smoke, it's safer to leave the area and let professionals handle the situation.

Preventative Measures

Prevention is your best defense against fires:

- Regularly check smoke detectors and replace batteries as needed.

- Keep flammable materials away from stoves and heaters.

- Never leave candles unattended.

Learning how to put out fires is not just about saving your stuff—it's about potentially saving lives, maybe even your own. Getting the skills necessary for dealing with flames means you're ready for action if things get fiery. Stay cool under pressure, make smart moves, and don't forget—sometimes the hero move is to call 911 and get out. Remember, safety first, heroics second!

First Aid Skills

Picture this: you're chilling with your friends, having a grand old time, when suddenly, someone takes a spill and scrapes their knee. It may seem minor, but knowing how to handle the situation calmly and quickly can make all the difference.

First things first: PANIC!!!

Only kidding, c'mon!

Seriously, in these moments, it's easy to get caught up in the moment and add unnecessary stress to the situation. Take a deep breath and *calmly* spring into action!

Grab your trusty first aid kit and assess the situation. Is it a minor scrape that just needs a little TLC, or is it something more serious that might require a trip to the doctor? In technical terms, if it's what one would call a "boo-boo", then break out the antiseptic wipes and get to work.

Clean the wound gently but thoroughly, making sure to get rid of any dirt or debris. Then, apply some antibiotic ointment to help prevent infection and speed up healing.

Finally, cover the wound with a bandage or gauze, depending on its size (and your friend's preference for cartoon characters or superheroes). Give your friend a pat on the back for being such a trooper, and then get back to your regularly scheduled fun!

See? With a bit of know-how and a dash of humor, you can handle any minor first-aid situation. Just remember, if it's something more serious, don't hesitate to call for help.

But what about being prepared for emergencies on the go? That's where a simple first aid kit comes in handy. You don't need anything fancy.

Here are the 10 basic components of a simple first-aid kit:

- Bandages
- Antiseptic wipes
- Antibiotic ointment
- Gauze pads

- Medical tape
- Scissors
- Tweezers
- Instant cold pack
- Instant hot pack
- Disposable gloves

Keep your kit in a readily accessible spot, whether it's in your backpack, car, or even your bedroom, so you can grab it quickly when needed. And don't forget to check and replenish your supplies regularly to ensure everything's up-to-date and ready for action.

Disaster Preparedness

When the skies darken and the winds howl, the world can go from mundane to menacing in a heartbeat. Whether it's a fierce hurricane, an earth-shaking quake, or a tornado that threatens to send everything flying, being prepared isn't just wise—it's essential. Here's how you can stand strong and stay smart when nature decides to go off-script.

Know Your Enemies

First of all, understand the types of disasters most likely to visit your area. Hurricanes? Tornadoes? Earthquakes? Each villain has its own playbook, so your battle plan will depend on who's most likely to knock on your door. Get to know these forces of nature—what triggers them, how they behave, and how to tell when they're about to crash your party.

Emergency Kits: Your Disaster Day Pack

Think of your emergency kit like your go-to-the-beach bag—except instead of snacks and sunblock, this one's stocked with survival essentials. Here's your packing list:

• **Water:** One gallon per person per day for at least three days.

• **Food:** A stash of non-perishable items that could last you through a weekend music fest.

• **Lights and Power:** Flashlights, extra batteries, maybe a solar-powered charger if you want to stay really connected.

• **First Aid Kit:** Because sometimes the party gets rough, and you need to patch up a friend—or yourself.

- **Personal Documents:** Keep copies of key documents like your ID and insurance. Digital copies in a waterproof case can be a game-changer.

- **Extra Clothes and Blankets:** Because weather doesn't always follow the forecast, staying warm and dry isn't just comfortable; it's potentially life-saving.

Make a Plan

Choreograph your moves before the chaos starts. Where will you meet your family if your house becomes the next blockbuster disaster scene? How will you get in touch if cell towers decide to take a day off? Plan your escape routes, designate a meeting spot, and have a backup for your backup.

Stay Informed

Keep an ear to the ground—or, more accurately, an eye on your phone. Apps and alerts from reliable sources like the National Weather Service can give you the heads-up you need to either buckle down or bounce before things get hairy. Knowledge is power, and in this case, it's also safety.

Practice Makes Prepared

Run drills like they're dress rehearsals. The more you practice, the less likely you'll freeze if the big show happens when you least expect it. Earthquake drills, tornado drills, or even just a fire drill at home can make the difference between panic and poise.

Community Connections

Connect with your community for larger disasters. Neighbors looking out for neighbors can create a network of helpers because sometimes, the cavalry you're waiting for is just next door.

With your emergency kit packed, your strategies set, and your drills dialed in, you're not just sitting tight for the storm to clear—you're well-prepared to handle whatever comes your way safely and confidently.

ACTIVITY: Disaster Preparedness Kit

Building a simple disaster preparedness kit is easy and essential, especially for people who live in areas prone to natural disasters such as hurricanes, earthquakes, or tornados.

Start by picking a sturdy backpack or bin to store your items. Pack a bottle of water and some non-perishable snacks like granola bars or dried fruits. Include a flashlight with extra batteries and a first aid kit with basic supplies such as band-aids and antiseptic wipes. Don't forget a change of clothes and sturdy shoes suitable for your climate. Add personal items like a toothbrush, toothpaste, and any medications you might need. It's also smart to have copies of important documents like your ID in a waterproof bag. Lastly, throw in a few small bills for cash and a book or game to keep you occupied.

Store your kit in an easy-to-reach place so you can grab it quickly in an emergency. This kit will help you stay prepared and safe if a disaster strikes.

Chapter 11
Household Skills

Everyday acts within the home are more powerful than you might think. –Rod Dreher

In this chapter, we'll explore the essential tasks and responsibilities that keep a home running smoothly. From chores to basic maintenance, mastering these skills not only improves the functionality of your living space but also fosters independence and self-sufficiency.

We'll explore various aspects of household management, providing practical tips and strategies to confidently tackle common tasks.

Make Your Space Ship Shape

Having a well-organized space is a personal haven where you can think clearly and feel at ease. Keeping things tidy can seriously boost your mood and productivity, whether it's your bedroom, study area, or even your digital spaces.

Here's how to get things ship shape:

1. Start with a Clean Sweep: Begin by decluttering. Take everything off your desk, out of your drawers, and off your floor. Sort through it all. Do you really need six different blue pens or that t-shirt from a 5th-grade field trip? It might be time to say goodbye if it doesn't serve a purpose or bring you joy.

2. Designate Spaces: Once you've whittled down your possessions, decide where everything should go. Assign specific spots for your books, clothes, gadgets, and everything else. This way, you'll know exactly where to find things when needed and where to put them back after using them.

3. Get Storage-Smart: Utilize boxes, baskets, and organizers to keep your things tidy. Clear storage containers are great because you can see what's inside without digging through them. Use drawer dividers for smaller items like socks or stationery to avoid becoming a jumbled mess.

4. Keep a Routine: Make tidying a regular part of your routine. Spend a few minutes each day putting things back in their places. This will prevent clutter from building up and keep your space looking neat without needing major clean-up sessions.

5. Personalize Your Organization: Make your space yours. If you're into tech, set up a charging station for all your devices. If you're a fashion enthusiast, organize your closet in a way that makes it easy to pick your outfits. Are you a musician, photographer, or skateboarder? Your space should reflect your interests and make them easier to manage.

6. Digital Clean-Up: Don't forget about your digital spaces. Organize your study files into folders, keep your desktop clutter-free, and unsubscribe from emails you never read. A tidy digital space can enhance your focus just as much as a physical one.

7. Regular Reassessments: Every once in a while, take a step back and assess your space. As your interests and activities change, so might your organizational needs. Reevaluate what's working and what's not, and make adjustments to keep your space functional and refreshing.

Creating and maintaining an organized space can transform it from a chaos zone into your personal command center. It's not just about cleanliness; it's about crafting an environment where you can flourish. So take charge, get organized, and enjoy the calm and focus that comes with a well-laid-out space.

Laundry Basics

Unless you're a big fan of pink T-shirts, you should keep those red socks away from your white clothes. Separate your laundry into piles—whites, darks, and colors. Easy-peasy.

Check those clothing labels to see if they're machine washable and what temperature they can handle. Nobody wants their favorite shirt shrinking in the wash! Use the appropriate detergent and set your machine to the appropriate cycle. And remember, cold water is usually best for preserving colors and preventing shrinking.

When it comes to drying, air drying is your friend for delicate items like sweaters or jeans that you want to keep looking fresh. But for things like towels and sheets, the dryer works like a charm. Just toss in a dryer sheet to keep things smelling nice and static-free.

Last but not least, folding. Trust me, a little folding goes a long way in keeping your clothes looking neat and tidy. Take your time, fold along the seams, and voilà! Your clothes are ready to go back in the drawers or closet, all nice and organized. And hey, if you need a little extra help, there's no shame in watching a YouTube tutorial or two.

Surface Cleaning

Keeping your space clean is more than a chore; it's about crafting a sanctuary where you can unwind, focus, and have fun. Let's explore the key cleaning tasks that can transform your room, apartment, or home into a refreshing retreat.

Begin by sweeping. Grab a broom and clear away any dirt or debris on hard flooring surfaces like tile or wood. This is your initial move to prepare the area for a more thorough cleaning. After you've swept up the larger particles, it's time to switch to vacuuming. Vacuuming is essential for removing finer dust and particles embedded in carpet fibers or hidden in corners. Be sure to vacuum those tricky spots under the bed and behind furniture where dirt tends to accumulate.

Next up, dusting. Armed with a duster or a simple microfiber cloth, go over all surfaces. Begin with higher items like shelves and work your way down to tables and chair legs. Remember, dust can be sneaky, so keep an eye out for less obvious places like the tops of doors and picture frames.

When it comes to wiping surfaces, an all-purpose cleaner is your best friend. Spray and wipe down everything from countertops to desks, not forgetting light switches and door handles, which can collect germs.

I saved the best for last...

Next, let's dive into the glamour of bathroom cleaning! Arm yourself with a trusty scrub brush and your bravest smile—it's time to battle the germs in their natural habitat. Tackle the toilet with the enthusiasm of a knight in shining armor, conquer the tub like a pirate seizing a ship, and polish that sink until it sparkles like your personality. Armed with your disinfectant of choice, leave behind a trail of fresh scents and slain germs.

Clothing Maintenance

Nobody likes wrinkly clothes, right? Grab your iron, set it to the appropriate heat setting for your fabric, and start smoothing out those wrinkles. Just focus on button-down shirts, dresses, slacks, etc. No need to iron your undies, but hey—if you prefer knowing that underneath it all you're sporting crisp, wrinkle-free bloomers, then by all means, knock yourself out.

Next, stains. Whether it's spaghetti sauce or grass stains from your latest soccer game, stains happen. But fear not! With a bit of know-how, you can banish those stains like a pro. Treat stains promptly with a stain remover or a bit of dish soap before tossing them in the wash. And don't forget to check the care label first to ensure you're using the correct method for your fabric.

Ah, the noble art of button reattachment—a rite of passage for every teen! It's simple: grab a needle and choose your thread, ideally in a shade that doesn't scream, "*I did this myself in semi-darkness.*" Secure that rogue button while taking care not to perforate your paw. Not only re-attaching a button save your favorite shirt from an untimely farewell, but you'll also feel like a DIY superhero. Who knew such a tiny task could boost your street cred in the world of practical life skills?

Packing a Suitcase

Nothing to it, right? Toss in 2 heaping arm-fulls of random clothes from the floor - far too much for the lid to close without a liberal application of brute force—place your full body weight on the lid like a human pancake to just baaaaarely get the latch to catch—and VOILA...

A *"packed"* suitcase.

That's one way to do it, but here's another:

Jot down all the essentials you'll need based on where you're going, how long you'll be there, and what the weather will be like. This way, you won't forget anything important.

Instead of folding your clothes, try rolling them up. This saves a ton of space and helps prevent wrinkles, too. You can also stuff smaller items, like socks and underwear, inside your shoes to maximize space.

While you're packing your suitcase, think about what you'll need easy access to during your trip. Stuff like chargers, toiletries, and any important documents should go in a separate compartment or on top so you can grab them quickly.

And don't forget about being prepared for anything! Pack a small first-aid kit with essentials like Band-Aids, lip balm, and allergy medicine, just in case. Oh, and always remember to leave a little extra room in your suitcase for any souvenirs you might pick up along the way.

Saving on Utilities

Little changes can add up to big savings over time. So, remember to turn off lights when you leave a room, unplug electronics when you're not using them, and try to use natural light during the day instead of turning on lamps.

Now, when it comes to your appliances, there are a few things you can do to be more efficient. For starters, make sure your fridge and freezer are set to the right temperature—not too cold, not too warm. Also, try to run your dishwasher and washing machine with full loads to make the most of each cycle. And if you've got air conditioning, consider setting it a few degrees warmer in the summer and using fans to help circulate the cool air.

These might seem like small changes, but they can really add up when it comes to saving on your utility bills. Plus, it's good for the environment too!

Yardwork

Taking care of your yard might not sound like the most exciting task, so I'll do my best to spice things up a bit...

- Depending on your local climate and the mood of your grass, you might need to mow every week to keep your lawn from turning into a suburban jungle. Make sure to adjust your lawnmower height based on the type of grass you have and the time of year.
- Grab those hedge clippers and style those bushes like you're the barber of the burbs. Overgrown bushes can make your yard look messy, so grab some hedge trimmers and give them a good trim to keep them in shape.
- Now, for the delightful task of weeding. These sneaky green intruders can overrun your yard faster than teens raiding the fridge after school. Arm yourself with a weeding tool, or go old school and yank those weeds with your hands—just pretend you're pulling out the vegetables you don't like from your dinner plate.
- The finishing touch: yard cleanup! Sticks, debris, and those leaves from last autumn that thought they could stay forever? Time to break out the leaf blower and go full hurricane on that mess. Aim to make your yard so

pristine that it could feature on the cover of "Impeccable Lawns Monthly" or at least win a nod of approval from nosy neighbors.

Basic House Maintenance

Getting the hang of some basic DIY home repair skills can be a total game-changer. You know, the little things—like sorting out a leaky tap, unblocking the sink, or even patching up the elbow-shaped hole in your bedroom wall after that epic Nerf battle went south. Handling these repairs on your own can be quite empowering and often more straightforward than you might think.

It's important to have a basic toolkit. Essentials like a hammer, screwdriver set, adjustable wrench, pliers, and a tape measure can make a big difference. With these tools in hand, you're ready to tackle most of the common household issues that might pop up.

Don't forget to use YouTube as a resource. It's filled with how-to videos that can guide you through almost any household repair. Just search for what you need, like "how to fix a leaky tap" or "how to patch drywall," and you'll find detailed tutorials that can help you step-by-step. It's a great way to build your skills and confidence.

However, know your limits. For repairs that involve electricity, gas, or anything that feels beyond your skill level, it's safer to call in a professional. Also, if you attempt a repair and it doesn't go as planned, don't hesitate to seek help. Sometimes, it's wiser to call in an expert rather than risk making a problem worse.

Owning a Pet

Now, having a pet can be super rewarding, but it's also a big responsibility. First off, there's the daily stuff like feeding, exercising, and grooming. You've got to make sure your pet stays healthy and happy, just like you would for yourself.

But, hey, it's not all work and no play! Pets bring tons of joy and companionship into your life. They're always there to cuddle up with or play fetch when you need a break from studying. Plus, having a pet can even boost your mood and reduce stress. It's like having a built-in best friend!

Now, here's the real talk. Pets aren't just a short-term commitment—they're in it for the long haul. You'll need to plan for their care and well-being for years to come. That means regular vet check-ups, vaccinations, and maybe even unexpected medical bills. And let's not forget about the cost of food, toys, and other supplies.

So, before you bring home that adorable ball of fur, or feathers, or scales, or... whatever a hedgehog has—make sure you're ready for the responsibility and the financial commitment that comes with it.

Recycling

Recycling is a vital practice that transforms used materials like paper, plastic, glass, and metal back into valuable resources, thereby conserving natural materials and reducing environmental strain.

To truly make a difference with recycling, it's crucial to properly sort your recyclables, ensuring they are placed in the appropriate bins as determined by your local waste management guidelines. Effective sorting maximizes the potential for these materials to be processed and repurposed, playing a significant role in promoting sustainability.

By adopting and advocating for diligent recycling habits, you help sustain an ongoing cycle of reuse that benefits both the environment and society. This proactive approach not only aids in reducing landfill waste but also lessens the greenhouse gas emissions that come from manufacturing new products.

Engaging in recycling is a straightforward yet impactful way to contribute to environmental conservation and encourage a culture of sustainability among your peers and within your community.

Composting

Composting is a highly effective eco-practice that benefits both the environment and your garden. It involves the natural breakdown of organic materials such as fruit and vegetable scraps, eggshells, coffee grounds, and yard waste like leaves and grass clippings. By collecting these items in a compost bin or simply heaping them in a designated spot in your yard, you set the stage for nature to do its work. Over time, these organic materials decompose and transform into a nutrient-rich soil additive.

This natural process results in a potent compost that acts as an organic fertilizer, enriching the soil and promoting robust plant growth without the use of chemical fertilizers. Engaging in composting not only reduces the amount of waste that ends up in landfills but also returns valuable nutrients to the soil, enhancing its quality and fertility.

Once your compost is ready, it can be used in a variety of ways to boost the health and vitality of your garden. You can mix it into garden beds to improve soil structure and nutrient content, use it as a top dressing for lawns and flower beds, or incorporate it into potting mixes for container gardening. The rich, organic material helps retain moisture in the soil, supports root development, and fosters overall plant health.

Starting a composting routine is a straightforward way to contribute positively to environmental sustainability. It's rewarding to see everyday waste repurposed into something that can dramatically improve the soil of your garden. Composting is a smart, sustainable choice that benefits the planet and helps you cultivate a greener, more vibrant garden.

ACTIVITY: Create a Household Chore Chart

Creating a household chore chart is a practical way to ensure everyone contributes to maintaining the home. Here's how you can make this activity manageable and even enjoyable:

1. Gather The Fam: Bring all family members together for a meeting. This ensures everyone has a say and understands their responsibilities.

2. List Tasks: Write down all the chores that need to be done regularly, such as laundry, dishes, vacuuming, and taking out the trash. Don't forget less frequent tasks like cleaning windows or organizing the garage.

3. Assign Chores: Divide the chores among family members according to their abilities and schedules. Be fair and considerate—some tasks may be easier for some than others.

4. Schedule Days: Assign specific days for each chore. This could be daily, like dishes, or weekly, like vacuuming. Having a set schedule helps prevent any confusion about who needs to do what and when.

5. Create the Chart: Use a large poster board or a digital app if everyone is tech-savvy. Mark the chart with colorful markers, stickers, or digital icons to make it visually appealing and easy to read.

6. Decorate and Display: Let everyone decorate the chart with markers, stickers, or drawings. This makes the process fun and gives the chart a personal touch. Then, place it in a common area where it's easily visible to all family members.

7. Review and Adjust: After a few weeks, review the chart together. This is a good time to make any necessary adjustments based on what's working or not. This can keep the system fair and flexible.

A chore chart isn't just a way to keep your home tidy; it's also a tool for learning responsibility and boosting teamwork. It's about more than just chores—it's about working together to make your home a better place for everyone.

Chapter 12
Health and Well-Being Skills

Your body is your most priceless possession; take care of it. –Jack Lalanne

We're about to begin a journey that's all about feeling fantastic inside and out. From fueling your body with the right foods to finding ways to relax and recover, I've got you covered. So, let's get right into it and explore how you can live your best, healthiest life.

Breaking Bad Habits

First up, let's unpack something quite surprising: about 40% of what you do every day isn't the result of active choices but habits—those little routines you hardly think about (Lindner, 2023b). This means a big chunk of your life runs on autopilot. So, it's super important to hone in on ditching those not-so-great habits that might be dragging you down. You know the ones I'm talking about—staying up way too late, caught up in endless social media feeds, or constantly reaching for a bag of chips instead of an apple or some carrots.

Initially, these habits might not seem like a big deal. What's a little late-night scrolling or a few extra chips, right? But here's the kicker: over time, these small choices accumulate, gradually taking a toll on both your physical and mental health. That's why recognizing these habits is the first crucial step.

The next step? Actively replacing them with positive ones. Instead of mindless scrolling, why not try winding down with a book or planning your next day to boost productivity? Swap out junk food for healthier snacks that leave you feeling energized rather than sluggish.

Breaking habits doesn't just mean stopping something; it's about transforming your routine to support a healthier, happier you. It's like upgrading your system software—you're enhancing how you operate on a daily basis, which can lead to significant improvements in how you feel and perform.

So, take the reins on those 40% of your actions that are habitual. Make them count for something good, and you'll start to see just how much better life can be when you're in control of your habits rather than them controlling you.

Establishing Healthy Habits

Have you heard of habit stacking? This clever technique, which involves linking a new habit to an existing one, can significantly boost your chances of making the new habit stick (Seaver, 2024).

For instance, if you're looking to start journaling every day, consider doing it right after your morning cup of tea or just before you hit the hay at night. By anchoring this new activity to a part of your routine that's already well-established, you effectively make the new habit part of your daily flow without much extra effort.

It's important to note that when trying to build new habits, you'll inevitably encounter setbacks. They're a natural part of trying to change or introduce new habits—no one gets it right all the time! The important thing isn't to dwell on the slip-ups or get down on yourself. Instead, see each setback as an opportunity to learn and refine your approach.

Maybe your timing needs tweaking, or perhaps your goals need to be a bit more attainable. Whatever adjustments you need to make, remember that setbacks are not roadblocks but merely bumps along the path.

Keep your spirits up and your focus forward. With persistence and a bit of strategic planning, these new healthy habits will soon weave seamlessly into the fabric of your daily life, becoming as natural and unconscious as any of your old habits. Before you know it, you'll be living a healthier, more intentional life with ease.

Sleep

You might think that sleep is just something you do at the end of the day to recharge, but it's so much more than that. Getting enough sleep is crucial for your physical health, mental well-being, and overall performance in everything you do.

Here's a little tidbit that might make you think twice about skimping on your sleep: people who clock in less than six hours of shut-eye each night are up to four times more likely to catch a cold than those who get a solid seven hours or more. Crazy, huh?

It turns out that skimping on sleep can really affect your immune system, not to mention your overall health. And when your health isn't up to snuff, your performance—whether at school, work, or in life—takes a hit, too. Moreover, when you're running low on sleep, it's not just your body that suffers.

Research shows that being sleep-deprived can mess with the mind to a similar level as someone who is intoxicated. Yeah, this is serious stuff! So, if you want to keep on top of your game, both mentally and physically, making sure you get enough sleep is pretty crucial. It's not just about feeling rested; it's about keeping your performance on point.

So, how do you establish healthy sleep routines? Well, it starts with setting a consistent bedtime and wake-up time, even on weekends. This assists in regulating your body's internal clock, making it simpler to drift off to sleep and wake feeling rejuvenated.

Establishing a soothing bedtime ritual can also indicate to your body that it's time to relax. This might involve activities such as reading, enjoying a warm bath, or engaging in deep breathing exercises.

Here's something worth mentioning—if you struggle with insomnia, trouble falling asleep, or waking up throughout the night, there are some simple solutions that might help. For example, limiting screen time before bed can reduce the blue light exposure that can interfere with your sleep cycle. Cutting back on caffeine and heavy meals close to bedtime can also make it easier to drift off. And if you find yourself tossing and turning, try getting out of bed and doing something relaxing until you feel sleepy again.

Move It, Move It

It's no surprise that exercise is beneficial to our physical and mental health, but sometimes, it can be hard to get started. So, let's tackle those barriers together.

One significant barrier to exercise is a lack of time. Between school, homework, and hanging out with friends, it can feel like there's no time left for a workout. But here's the thing—you don't need hours in the gym to reap the benefits of exercise.

Even just 10 minutes a day of moderate activity can make a big difference. So, find activities you enjoy, whether it's dancing to your favorite tunes, going for a bike ride, or playing a pickup game of basketball with friends. The key is to make it fun!

Speaking of fun, there are a variety of exercise options out there. From cardio and strength training to yoga and dance, there's something for everyone. Don't be afraid to try new things keep it interesting. Who knows, you might discover a new passion along the way!

Now, let's address those sedentary activities that can sneak into our daily routines. Whether it's binge-watching Netflix, scrolling through social media for hours, or playing video games non-stop, these activities can take up a lot of our time and keep us glued to our seats. But remember every minute spent sitting is a missed opportunity to move your body and feel amazing. So, try to limit screen time and find ways to incorporate more activity into your day, like taking a walk during breaks or doing some stretches while watching TV.

Grooming and Hygiene

Grooming and hygiene: the unsung heroes of self-care. So, why is staying squeaky clean so crucial? Well, besides the obvious perks like not being the person everyone subtly scoots away from on the bus, good hygiene is your body's best defense against sneaky germs looking to throw a sick-day party. Plus, taking the time to scrub up and look sharp can boost your confidence. It's about feeling fabulous, staying healthy, and rocking that "*I definitely showered today*" glow.

So, what does a healthy grooming routine look like? It's all about finding what works for you and sticking to it. For example, make sure to brush your teeth at least twice a day and floss regularly to keep your smile bright and your mouth healthy. When it comes to bathing, aim to shower or bathe daily, especially after sweaty activities like sports or exercise. And don't forget to wash your hands frequently throughout the day to prevent the spread of germs—especially important during cold and flu season!

Everyone's routine will look a little different depending on their needs and preferences, but there are a few basics that everyone should have on hand. Things like deodorant to keep you smelling fresh, nail clippers to keep your nails neat and tidy, and toothpaste and a toothbrush to keep your smile sparkling. And let's not forget about skincare. A gentle cleanser, moisturizer, and sunscreen can go a long way in keeping your skin healthy and glowing.

Remember, taking care of yourself isn't just about looking good on the outside; you need to feel good on the inside, too. So, make sure to prioritize your grooming and hygiene routine as part of your overall self-care regimen.

Body Changes

This topic can be a bit like bringing up who put the empty milk carton back in the fridge—it's awkward, but someone's got to address it. Puberty, that wild ride every human signs up for without actually signing anything, is as normal as pineapple on pizza (a little controversial, but definitely a part of life). You grow taller seemingly overnight. Boys get muscles, girls get curves. Not to mention, hair starts auditioning for new roles all over your body. Yes, puberty is basically your body's own extreme makeover: teenage edition!

But every single one of these changes is entirely normal and nothing to be embarrassed about. We all go through it! Embracing your body's natural changes is an essential part of growing up and becoming comfortable in your own skin. Sure, it might feel a bit awkward at times, but remember that everyone around you is going through the same thing—even if they don't always show it.

In a world inundated with images of "ideal" bodies on social media and in magazines, it's common to feel inadequate. However, it's essential to understand that there's no such thing as a perfect body, and beauty manifests in various shapes, sizes, and forms.

Rather than fixating on outward appearance, it's beneficial to appreciate our bodies' *incredible capabilities*. Whether it's the ability to run, dance, or simply reading this book...

Think about it:

Your miracle of a body is able to understand the thoughts in MY HEAD by looking at thousands of little squiggly lines of ink on a sheet of paper. Isn't that just *insane*?

So, instead of worrying about whether you have the "right" body type, focus on keeping your body healthy and strong. Eat nutritious foods, get regular exercise, and make time for self-care activities that make you feel good about yourself from the inside out.

Skewed Media Reality

We all know that scrolling through Instagram or TikTok can be a lot of fun, but it's important to be aware of the impact that overexposure to social media can have on your well-being.

We've touched on this a little already, but one big thing to watch out for is the messages that social media sends us about what we should look like, how we should act, and what we should have. You've probably seen tons of posts showing people with perfect bodies, flawless skin, and seemingly perfect lives, right? It's *extraordinarily important* to remember that these images are seldom realistic.

Constant exposure to these kinds of images can make us feel like we're not good enough or like we're missing out on something. It can also lead to unhealthy comparisons with others and even feelings of anxiety or depression. That's why it's so important to be mindful of how much time you're spending on social media and to take breaks when you need to.

Now, I'm not saying that social media is all bad—far from it! It can be a great way to stay connected with friends, share fun moments, and even learn new things. The key is to cultivate healthy social media habits that prioritize your mental and emotional well-being.

So, how can you do that? Well, start by setting boundaries around your social media use. Maybe limit yourself to checking your accounts for a certain amount of time each day or take regular breaks from social media altogether. You can also curate your feed to include accounts that inspire and uplift you rather than ones that make you feel bad about yourself.

Remember, it's okay to unfollow accounts or take a break from social media if it's not making you feel good. Your mental health is far more important than likes or followers.

Substance Abuse Awareness

Even though teens should avoid being involved in such matters, it's crucial to acknowledge the possibility and know how to respond if needed.

Substance abuse refers to the harmful or excessive use of drugs or alcohol, and it can have severe consequences for your health, relationships, and future opportunities.

It's important to be aware of the signs of substance abuse, whether in yourself or others. These signs might manifest as changes in behavior, sudden shifts in mood, significant changes in weight, or neglecting usual responsibilities or interests. If you notice any of these signs in yourself or a friend, don't hesitate to seek help. Speaking up and reaching out for support is the first step toward getting the assistance necessary.

Living a substance-free life isn't just about saying no to drugs or alcohol—it's about making positive choices that support your health and well-being. Surround yourself with friends who share your values and support your decision to stay substance-free. Find healthy ways to cope with stress and pressure, like exercising, practicing mindfulness, or pursuing your passions.

It's also important to educate yourself about the dangers of substance abuse and how it can impact your life. Take the time to learn about the risks associated with different substances, and don't be afraid to ask questions or seek guidance from trusted adults.

Remember, you are in control of your choices and your future. By staying informed, seeking support when you need it, and making positive choices that align with your values, you can live a happy, healthy, and substance-free life.

Digital Detox

We all love scrolling through our feeds, checking out the latest memes, and staying connected with friends online. But have you ever stopped to think about how all that screen time might be affecting your mental health and real-life relationships?

It's like that moment when you realize you've been staring at your phone for so long that you've forgotten what the sky looks like. Spending too much time online can sometimes make us feel like we're not measuring up to the perfectly curated lives we see on our screens.

That's where the digital detox comes in. It's all about taking a break from social media and other digital distractions to give our minds a chance to reset and recharge (and maybe even remember what our friends look like in person). Whether it's for a few hours, a day, or even a whole week (gasp!), disconnecting from our devices can help us reconnect with ourselves and the people around us.

So, go ahead and unplug for a bit. Take a walk outside, hang out with friends in person, or pick up a hobby that doesn't involve screens, like knitting or extreme ironing (yeah—it's a thing).

Environmental Awareness

The environment we live in has a profound impact on our physical and mental health. Everything from the air we breathe to the food we consume plays a critical role in shaping our well-being.

Take air quality, for instance. Breathing in polluted air isn't just unpleasant—it can trigger a host of health issues, including asthma, allergies, and even more serious conditions like heart disease. This makes it clear why we each need to contribute to maintaining clean air.

How can we make a difference? Simple everyday actions can significantly reduce our environmental footprint. Opting to walk or bike instead of driving is a great start. It's not only good for the planet but also our health. Using energy-efficient appliances and reducing reliance on single-use plastics are other effective strategies. For instance, switching to a refillable water bottle instead of buying bottled water not only cuts down on plastic waste but also saves money in the long run.

By making these changes, we don't just improve our immediate surroundings, but we also contribute to a healthier planet. And a healthier planet means a healthier us. It's all interconnected, and every small action counts.

You Are What You Eat

Eating a diet packed with fresh fruits, vegetables, whole grains, and lean proteins does wonders for your health—it's not just about maintaining a healthy weight but also about enriching your body with essential nutrients.

When you choose foods that are grown locally and sustainably, you often get the added benefit of enhanced freshness. Such foods haven't been transported across vast distances, which usually means they retain more of their nutritional value by the time they reach your plate. This translates into more vitamins, minerals, and antioxidants in your diet—elements crucial for maintaining energy, boosting your immune system, and overall wellness.

But there's more to our daily consumption than just food; water plays an equally crucial role. Staying hydrated is essential for everything from cognitive function to digestion. Yet, access to clean drinking water is not a given for everyone. This makes it especially important for those of us who do have access to manage it responsibly.

Mindful practices like reducing shower times, promptly repairing leaks, and being careful not to overwater lawns can significantly minimize wastefulness. Such habits not only help preserve this vital resource but also contribute to a broader effort to ensure there's enough clean water available for all, promoting health and equity across communities.

ACTIVITY: Healthy Habit Tracker

Grab a piece of paper or use an app on your phone to create a simple chart with the days of the week listed horizontally and healthy habits listed vertically.

For example, you could include habits like drinking enough water, getting at least 30 minutes of exercise, eating a serving of fruits and veggies, getting enough sleep, and practicing self-care. Each day, check off or mark the habits you've completed.

At the end of the week, take a look at your tracker. Celebrate the habits you've consistently stuck to and reflect on any areas where you might want to improve. Maybe you notice that you're not getting enough sleep or that you could use a little more exercise. That's okay—use this insight to set goals for the upcoming week and keep working towards building healthier habits.

Remember, progress takes time, so be patient with yourself and celebrate every small victory along the way!

Chapter 13
Conclusion

Throughout this book, you've explored dozens of practical life skills that aren't taught in school but are crucial for navigating the journey into adulthood. By embracing and honing these skills, you're not just preparing for the future—*you're actively shaping it.*

So, as you step forward, do so with confidence, knowing that you possess the tools and knowledge to thrive in whatever challenges life may bring. And if one of those challenges happens to be folding a fitted sheet, well, just remember, *nobody actually knows how to do that one.*

As you close this book and prepare to set off on the next phase of your journey, remember that learning doesn't end here. Keep this book within reach, ready to revisit its pages whenever you encounter new challenges or need a refresher.

In closing, I want to leave you with this: ***You are capable, resilient, and ready to face what challenges lie ahead.*** With the life skills you've acquired, you have the tools to navigate the path to adulthood with confidence and grace.

You've got this!

With gratitude and admiration,

Ben Clardy

PERSONAL FINANCE FOR TEENAGERS

The Fast Track to Financial Literacy with Teen-Tailored Money Management Skills - Hands-On Activities for Earning, Saving, Budgeting, Spending, and Investing

PERSONAL FINANCE
for TEENAGERS

Fast Track To Financial Literacy With Teen-Tailored Money Management Skills

HANDS-ON ACTIVITIES FOR EARNING, SAVING, BUDGETING, SPENDING, AND INVESTING

BEN CLARDY

Chapter 1
The Basics Of Money

Money is not everything...
...but it ranks right up there with oxygen.
—Zig Ziglar

Money. It's a concept that touches every aspect of our lives, from the daily necessities we buy to the long-term dreams we save for. But how much do you really know about this powerful force that shapes our world?

The History Of Money

Money is so much more than colorful pieces of paper we exchange for goods and services. It's a reflection of human civilization itself. It's a tale of ingenuity, advancement, and necessity that has shaped our world in ways we often overlook. By the end of this chapter, you might just find yourself looking at those bills in your wallet with a newfound appreciation for the history they carry.

Bartering

Picture this: you're a young farmer in ancient Mesopotamia, and you've got a bunch of goats that are the envy of the village. Your neighbor, a skilled potter, has been eyeing those goats for weeks, and it just so happens that you've been admiring their beautifully crafted clay pots.

One day, you strike up a conversation and realize that you've got a perfect opportunity for a trade. You offer up two of your finest goats in exchange for a set of pots that would be the pride of any household. Your neighbor jumps at the chance, and just like that, you've both received something you wanted without a single coin changing hands.

Bartering was the go-to way of doing business for thousands of years, from ancient civilizations like the Babylonians and Egyptians to indigenous tribes around the world. It was a simple, effective way to exchange goods and services without the need for a standardized currency.

Of course, there must have been plenty of awkward moments when someone tried to trade a handful of turnips for a new loincloth, or when a particularly stubborn goat refused to be bartered away without a fight. But hey, that's just part of the charm of the barter system – it wasn't always pretty, but it got the job done!

Currency

Now imagine that you're strolling through an ancient Lydian marketplace around 600 B.C. — perusing the wares and trying to score a sweet deal on the latest in toga fashion. Suddenly, you spot the perfect one – it's stylish, it's comfy, and it's just the right shade of purple to make you stand out at the next chariot race. There's just one problem: *you're fresh out of goats*.

In centuries past, this would have been a major bummer, but thanks to those clever Lydians and their newfangled *electrum coins*, you can now simply plunk down a few standardized tokens and walk away with your snazzy new outfit.

This revolutionary concept caught on like wildfire, and soon enough, everyone was trading in their cumbersome bartering goods for shiny, uniform coins. It streamlined commerce, made transactions more efficient, and paved the way for the development of more advanced currency systems.

From there, money continued to evolve. Pure gold and silver coins became the norm, offering even greater standardization and stability. And then, in a move that would have blown the minds of those ancient Lydians, we started using *paper money* – a concept that probably would have seemed about as crazy to them as the idea of carrying around a tiny computer in your pocket that can access the sum of human knowledge.

So the next time you're out shopping and you hand over a crisp bill, take a moment to appreciate those innovative Lydians and their game-changing electrum coins. Without them, you might still be trying to procure sustenance with a slightly confused goat in tow.

Banking

The prototypes of modern banking began in medieval Italy during the 12th and 13th centuries. These early financial institutions were not just places to store gold or silver; they changed the game by introducing fundamental banking services such as lending money at interest. These critical developments fueled economic expansion across Europe, forming the backbone of what would evolve into the intricate, global financial systems we rely on today.

Banking is a big deal. Just imagine daily life without banks—no ATMs for quick cash withdrawals, no online banking services for easy transactions, no safe havens for your hard-earned money. The very thought underscores the profound impact of banking on society. Yet, intriguingly, even in an age dominated by financial technologies, some individuals still opt for traditional methods of saving, like tucking away cash under a mattress, burying repurposed mayo jars in the backyard, or depositing coins into a trusty ceramic swine. To each their own!

Digital Currency

In the 21st century, the concept of money is undergoing yet another radical transformation. The digital era has not only reshaped how we interact with the world but also how we manage and perceive currency. Cryptocurrencies, such as Bitcoin and Ethereum, are reshaping the very foundations of modern banking systems and forcing us to re-evaluate our understanding of money.

The emergence of cryptocurrencies has also introduced a new paradigm in financial transactions, where speed, decentralization, and digital security converge in a powerful trifecta. With a few taps on a smartphone, individuals can now transfer funds across the globe faster than sending an email. It's a compelling era where financial power is quite literally in the hands of the masses, democratizing access to wealth creation and management in ways that were once unimaginable.

Key Financial Terms

Now seems like a good time to lay out some terminology because no matter what form money takes – whether it's a goat, a coin, a bill, or a string of digital code – it's essential to understand how it works.

Income

First up, let's talk about income. This is the money you earn, whether it's from a part-time job, an allowance, or even a side hustle like selling handmade crafts online.

Income can be further broken down 3 different ways:

- **Earned income:** This is money you make from working a job or providing a service. If you babysit on the weekends or work a part-time job, that's earned income.
- **Passive income:** This is money you earn without actively working for it, like earning interest on a savings account or earning royalties from a book you've written.
- **Portfolio income:** This is money you earn from investments, like stocks or bonds. If you own stock in Apple, Coke, or Nike then you'd receive this type of income.

Expenses

Next is the flip side of income: *expenses*. These are all the things you spend money on, from necessities like food and clothing to fun stuff like concert tickets and video games.

There are two main types of expenses to keep in mind:

- **Fixed expenses:** These are costs that generally stay the same each month, like rent, car payments, or a Netflix subscription.
- **Variable expenses:** These are costs that can fluctuate from month to month, like eating out, buying new clothes, or going on a weekend road trip with friends.

Assets vs. Liabilities

Another key concept to understand is the difference between *assets* and *liabilities*. An asset is something you own that has value and can potentially produce an income, like money in a savings account, a piece of real estate, or even a rare collectible item. A liability, on the other hand, is something that costs you money, like a credit card balance, a car payment, or a student loan.

To build long-term wealth, it's important to focus on acquiring assets and minimizing liabilities. Think of it this way: every dollar you save and invest is like a little seed that can grow into a big, beautiful money tree over time. But every dollar you spend on liabilities is one less seed you have that has the potential to grow—it's gone forever.

Perceived Value Of Currency

Money, in essence, has value because we all buy into the belief that it does. This is what's known as *"perceived value"*—the notion that something is worth whatever everyone thinks it's worth, rather than any real, tangible value.

Consider the humble $100 bill. In simplest terms, it's a paper rectangle with a picture of a dead guy on it. Is it *actually worth* $100? Not even close. Unlike a gold coin or a diamond, a dollar bill doesn't have any tangible value beyond perhaps that of a makeshift bookmark. But because we all agree to treat this fancy paper as something precious, we can wield its mighty "perceived" power to buy groceries.

This concept is crucial because it reveals that money's value can swing like a pendulum based on the whims of economic and social trends. So next time you hold a bill, remember, it's not just paper—it's a collective pinky promise within our society!

Economic Principals

Now that we've covered some of the key concepts related to money and financial literacy, let's zoom out a bit and talk about how larger economic principles can impact your personal finances. Don't worry – we're not going to get too bogged down in academic jargon or complex graphs. Instead, we'll focus on only two concepts that are essential to understand as you navigate your financial journey.

Supply & Demand

This fundamental concept dictates that the price of a good or service is determined by its availability (supply) and how much everyone is clamoring to get it (demand).

Picture this: when there's a mountain of something and no one's particularly desperate for it, the price is as low as a limbo stick at Bilbo Baggin's beach party.

On the flip side, when something is scarce, and everyone wants a piece, prices climb faster than an orangutan on Red Bull.

Inflation

One of the sneakiest villains in the world of money is inflation, a silent beast that creeps into your wallet and plays havoc with the purchasing power of your hard-earned cash.

Here's how it works:

As the price of goods and services rises, the value of money falls.

Suppose you've got $10 tucked away in your wallet. Today, that crisp tenner could net you a couple of those overpriced lattes or maybe a shiny new paperback to add to your collection. But give inflation a few years to do its thing, and watch what happens. That same $10 might barely purchase a single latte or, at best, snag a dog-eared novel from the bargain bin.

This creeping currency conundrum is why it's crucial to put your money to work by purchasing assets or investing! Think of it as training your dollars to fight off inflation and protect their purchasing power.

Investing wisely, whether in stocks, bonds, or mutant squirrel farms *(just seeing if you're paying attention)*, helps ensure that your money grows muscles, keeping pace with or even outrunning inflation. That way, your future self can enjoy more than just half a coffee and a faded cover!

ACTIVITY: "Basics-Of-Money" Quiz

1. What is the difference between earned income and passive income? a. Earned income is money you make from working, while passive income is money you earn without actively working for it. b. Earned income is money you earn from investments, while passive income is money you make from a job. c. There is no difference between earned income and passive income.
2. Which of the following is an example of a fixed expense? a. Buying a new pair of shoes b. Going out to dinner with friends c. Paying your monthly car insurance bill
3. What does it mean when we say that money has "perceived value"? a. Money is backed by a tangible asset, like gold or silver. b. Money is worth what people collectively agree it's worth, rather than having any inherent value. c. Money has no real value and is just a social construct.
4. How can inflation impact your purchasing power over time? a. Inflation makes your money more valuable over time, so you can buy more with it. b. Inflation has no impact on your purchasing power. c. Inflation can decrease your purchasing power over time, as prices rise while the value of your money stays the same.
5. What is an example of an Asset? a. A brand new smartphone b. Your Netflix subscription c. A silver coin.

Answer Key: 1a, 2c, 3b, 4c, 5c

Chapter 2

Earning Your Own Money

The only place success comes before work is in the dictionary. —Vince Lombardi

When you earn your own money, you're taking a big step towards financial independence and responsibility. You're also learning valuable skills that will serve you well throughout your life, like time management, communication, and problem-solving.

So, what are some ways to earn money as a teenager? We'll talk about many different options, ranging from simpler jobs for younger teens to more advanced opportunities for older, more experienced teens. There's a smorgasbord of opportunities for everyone, so let's get right into it.

Household Responsibilities & Earning Opportunities

Ah, the illustrious teenage years! A time of growth, rebellion, and... learning how to load a dishwasher properly. Yes, dear young compatriot, as you navigate the treacherous waters of teendom, you'll find yourself embarking on the noble quest of household chores. Fear not, for these tasks are not mere drudgery, but stepping stones on your path to adulthood *(and perhaps a well-organized sock drawer)*.

Picture, if you will, the humble abode you call home - a veritable kingdom of dust bunnies and misplaced remote controls. As a junior member of this domestic realm, your charge is to aid in its upkeep. Why, you ask? Well, beyond the obvious goal of preventing your living space from being mistaken for a post-apocalyptic wasteland, these responsibilities serve a greater purpose.

By mastering the art of vacuuming and tackling the enigma that is folding fitted sheets, you're doing more than just sprucing up your living space—you're actually building a toolkit of life skills that'll come in handy long after the dust settles. Think of it as a crash course in teamwork, time management, and the subtle science of laundry preservation. Who knew that learning to rescue your favorite t-shirt from a dryer-induced miniaturization could be so valuable?

Now, here's where things get tricky: what constitutes a standard family duty versus an opportunity to line your pockets?

In the Johnson household, young Timmy might be expected to feed the family's pet iguana as part of his regular duties. Meanwhile, across the street, the Smiths might consider iguana-feeding an exotic task worthy of monetary compensation. The key is to engage in that most ancient and revered of family traditions: the household negotiation. Approach your parental units with the grace of a diplomat in order to gain clarity on what tasks represent income earning opportunities.

Regular chores might include:

- Keeping your bedroom clean
- Participating in the daily ritual of washing dishes
- Feeding and watering the family pet(s)
- Maintaining shared living spaces

Tasks that might fatten your piggy bank:

- Taming the jungle that is your backyard
- Washing & detailing the family car
- Cleaning and organizing the garage
- Pressure-washing the driveway

Now, before you start seeing dollar signs every time you pick up a broom, let's talk about the elephant in the room *(which, by the way, you should probably dust)*. Not every household task should come with a price tag. If they did, you'd be missing out on some pretty crucial life lessons.

Contributing to your household without expecting payment is part of being in a family. It's about pulling your weight, showing appreciation for the roof over your head, and learning to be a responsible human being. If you got paid for every dish you washed or every sock you paired, you'd be learning the wrong lesson—that you should only help out when there's something in it for you.

It's all about finding the right balance. Maybe routine chores are your family contribution, but bigger projects or extra efforts could be opportunities to earn some dough. The key is to approach it with the right attitude—one of willingness to help and contribute, not just for your own, personal benefit.

Remember, the skills and values you're developing—responsibility, work ethic, time management—are worth **far more** than a few bucks here and there. They're the foundation for your future success, whether you're aiming to be the CEO of a Fortune 500 company or the world's greatest dog walker.

So, as you navigate the world of chores and responsibilities, keep this in mind: sometimes, the most valuable rewards aren't the ones that jingle in your pocket. They're the ones that shape you into a capable, responsible, and considerate adult. That's a payoff that'll keep on giving long after you've mastered the art of loading a dishwasher.

Part-Time Jobs

One of the most traditional ways for teens to earn money is through part-time jobs. Whether it's slinging hash at a local diner, selling the latest fashion at a retail store, or surviving the chaos of summer camp—part-time jobs offer a fantastic way to gain work experience and earn a steady paycheck without totally ruining your social life.

But how do you find these mythical part-time jobs? Start by considering your interests and skills. Fancy yourself a future tech mogul? Look for opportunities at electronics stores or IT support centers. Have a knack for keeping two-year-olds entertained? Consider applying for a job at a daycare center. What do you enjoy? What are you good at?

Don't forget to scour online job boards like Indeed or Snagajob, which often feature sections dedicated to teen jobs. And tap into your personal network— inform your friends, family, and teachers that you're on the hunt. They might know someone, who knows someone, who knows someone else who's looking for the next great part-time, teenage employee.

Finally, walk right into local businesses and see if they're hiring. Many small businesses love to hire teens, especially those who demonstrate the initiative to actively seek out work.

Filling Out An Application

When you find a job that interests you, it's time to start the application process. Even if you don't have much work experience, you can still create a strong resume and cover letter.

Focus on highlighting your strengths, like your academic achievements, extracurricular activities, or volunteer work. If you've helped out with any school projects or community events, be sure to mention those, too!

Here are a few tips to make your application stand out:

1. Tailor your resume and cover letter to the specific job you're applying for. Show how your skills and experiences match what the employer is looking for.
2. Use action verbs to describe your achievements, like "led," "organized," or "created."
3. Double-check your spelling and grammar, and ask a trusted adult to review your application before you submit it.
4. If possible, include a reference or two, like a teacher or coach who can speak to your work ethic and character.

Once you land an interview, it's essential to prepare. Research the company and think about how your skills and experiences align with the job requirements. Practice common interview questions with a friend or family member, and don't forget to dress professionally and arrive on time.

During the interview, be sure to:

- Make eye contact and offer a firm handshake.
- Listen carefully to the questions and take a moment to think before answering.
- Provide specific examples of times when you've demonstrated the skills or qualities they're looking for.
- Ask questions of your own to show your interest and enthusiasm for the job.

Remember, every interview is a learning opportunity, even if you don't get the job. Ask for feedback on how you can improve, and stay positive – the right opportunity will inevitably come your way.

The Gig Economy and Freelancing

If traditional part-time jobs aren't your thing, don't worry – there are plenty of other ways to earn money as a teenager. One option that's become increasingly popular in recent years is the gig economy and freelancing.

So, what exactly is the gig economy? Essentially, it refers to a labor market characterized by short-term contracts or freelance work, as opposed to permanent, full-time jobs. Thanks to the internet and digital platforms, it's easier than ever for people to find and offer freelance services.

By the way, in 2023, the global value of the gig economy was estimated to be $455.2 billion dollars and is only expected to continue growing in value. What that means is that there's *a lot of money* to be made by those who have the necessary skills and know-how, so let's explore this in more detail.

Freelance Platforms

Some popular gig and freelance platforms for teens include Fiverr, Upwork, and TaskRabbit. On these sites, you can create a profile showcasing your skills and services, whether it's graphic design, writing, or even doing odd jobs like assembling furniture or running errands.

Let's say you're a whiz at social media and have a knack for creating engaging posts. You could offer your services on Fiverr as a social media manager for small businesses or entrepreneurs. Or maybe you're a talented artist who could design custom logos or illustrations on Upwork. The opportunities are virtually endless.

Building A Portfolio

To be successful in the gig economy, it's important to build a strong portfolio that showcases your work and attracts potential clients. Start by taking on a few small projects and asking for testimonials and reviews from satisfied customers. As you gain more experience and positive feedback, you can start to raise your rates and take on more significant projects.

Here are a few tips for creating a standout freelance profile:

1. Choose a clear, professional profile picture and username.
2. Write a compelling bio that highlights your skills, experience, and unique selling points.
3. Include samples or links to your best work, and make sure they're up-to-date and relevant to the services you're offering.

4. Set competitive rates based on your experience and the market demand for your services.
5. Be responsive to client inquiries and maintain clear communication throughout each project.

Of course, managing gig work can be a bit different than a traditional part-time job. You'll need to be proactive about finding and applying for gigs, and you'll also need to manage your own time and workload. It's important to set realistic deadlines, communicate clearly with clients, and deliver high-quality work to build a positive reputation.

Learning Valuable "Gig" Skills

With online learning platforms like Udemy, you can take a variety of courses that can teach you valuable gig skills. There are near-countless courses to peruse and take, but here are some general ideas of valuable skills you may want to look into that will come in handy if you'd like to start taking on some gigs.

Word Processing: Young scholars can learn the ins and outs of Microsoft Word and Google Docs. These aren't just nifty skills for acing that English paper—they're also in hot demand in the freelance market.

Picture this: You, the master of fonts, the ruler of margins, the sultan of spacing. Your skills are in high demand, and local publishing houses are practically begging for your expertise. They need someone who can wrangle those pesky formatting issues and make their documents look like a million bucks. And guess what? That someone could be you!

Graphic Design: Ever judged a book by its cover? Well, buckle up, buttercup, because now you can be the one behind those covers, pulling the strings and making the magic happen!

Enter the dazzling world of graphic design, where you'll transform from a mere mortal into a visual virtuoso. With the power of Adobe Photoshop at your fingertips, you'll be turning bland into brand faster than you can say "CMYK."

Whether you're crafting the next iconic logo that'll be plastered on everything from billboards to t-shirts, or simply trying to make your mom's bake sale flyer look less like a ransom note, these skills will have you stacking the aesthetic deck in your favor.

With great design power comes great responsibility. Use your newfound abilities wisely, and soon you'll be the one everyone turns to when they need a visual makeover.

Digital Marketing: In the vast and ever-expanding digital kingdom, marketing reigns supreme as the queen, with content as her trusty king. And guess what? You, my young friend, can become a key player in this royal court!

Digital marketing is all about mastering the art of advertising for businesses on the wild, wild web—and driving sales with your trusty tools of SEO talent and social media savvy.

And let's be real, you teens are practically born with smartphones in your hands. You've been tweeting, sharing, and liking since you could crawl. Why not put those skills to work and turn them into a lucrative gig or even launch your own digital marketing empire?

Coding and Web Development: Listen up, digital dynamos! It's time to unveil the true power behind our online realm: *code*.

With coding skills, you're not just another face in the digital crowd—you're the mastermind, the architect, the wizard wielding a secret language that makes computers bow to your will.

These days, coding isn't just a skill; it's a superpower. Imagine creating websites so slick they make users weep with joy or apps so addictive people forget their basic human needs. And the best part? It pays, and pays very well.

So, what are you waiting for? Dive into coding and unlock the secrets of our digital domain. Who knows? You might just create the next big thing that takes the internet by storm.

Video Editing and Production: Lights, camera, action! In the wild world of social media, video content is the undisputed king of the jungle. And you, my friend, can be the one sitting pretty in the director's chair with the power of video editing at your fingertips.

With video editing skills, you're not just another content creator; you're a visual alchemist, mixing and matching clips, adding special effects, and weaving together narratives that make people laugh, cry, or gasp in awe. You have the power to create videos that go viral faster than a cat playing the piano, a cat eating snow, or a cat scared of it's reflection... really almost any cat video.

In today's attention economy, video is the currency that rules them all. From YouTube to TikTok, Instagram to Facebook, video content is what keeps the masses glued to their screens. Why settle for being a mere spectator, watching viral videos from the sidelines, when you can be the one behind the camera, pulling the strings and making the magic happen?

Entrepreneurship for Teens

For some teens, the ultimate dream is to be their own boss and start a business. While it might sound intimidating (*gulp), entrepreneurship can be an exciting and rewarding way to earn money and gain valuable experience.

The first step in starting a business is to generate and validate your idea. What products or services are you passionate about? Is there a need or demand for them in your community? Do some market research to see what similar businesses are out there and how you can differentiate yourself.

Let's say you're an avid baker and have always dreamed of starting your own cookie delivery service. You could start by surveying your friends, family, and neighbors to gauge interest and get feedback on your product. You might even offer free samples to get people hooked on your delicious treats!

Once you have a solid idea, it's time to start business planning. This means outlining your product or service, identifying your target market, developing marketing strategies, and creating financial projections.

Don't worry if this sounds overwhelming – there are plenty of resources and templates available online to help guide you through the process.

One helpful tool is the Business Model Canvas, which is a simple template that helps you visualize and plan the key components of your business. It includes sections for your value proposition, customer segments, revenue streams, and more. You can find free templates online or even create your own using a spreadsheet or slide presentation.

As you develop your business plan, be sure to think about your start-up costs and how you'll fund your venture. Will you need to purchase equipment or supplies? Will you need to rent a space or hire employees? How much will you charge for your products or services, and how many units do you need to sell to break even?

It's also important to think about your marketing and sales strategies. How will you get the word out about your business? Will you use social media, flyers, or word-of-mouth referrals? How will you process orders and payments, and deliver your products or services to customers?

Now, I know this sounds like a lot to figure out — *and it is*, but starting your own business can be incredibly rewarding. Not only will you have the opportunity to earn money doing something you love, but you'll also gain valuable skills in leadership, problem-solving, and communication. Plus, you'll have a unique story and experience to share with future employers or college admissions officers.

A Teen Entrepreneur

Take the example of Jordan, a 17-year-old who started his own lawn care business last spring. He began by mowing lawns for his neighbors on weekends, but quickly expanded his services to include landscaping and yard clean-up. With the help of his parents, he invested in some basic equipment and created a simple website and social media pages to promote his business.

Within a few months, Jordan had a steady stream of clients and was earning enough money to save for college and even hire a few friends to help with bigger projects. He learned how to manage his time, communicate with customers, and handle the financial aspects of running a business. Now, he's considering studying entrepreneurship in college and dreams of owning his own full-fledged commercial landscaping company one day.

The sky's the limit when it comes to entrepreneurship, so don't be afraid to dream big and take risks. With hard work, creativity, and a willingness to learn, you can turn your passions into a profitable business.

ACTIVITY: Create A Business Plan

Now that we've explored some different ways to earn money as a teenager, it's time for you to put these ideas into action! Here's a fun activity to get you started:

Choose a small business idea that aligns with your skills and interests. This could be tutoring, pet-sitting, lawn care, washing cars, or anything else you're passionate about.

Create a simple business plan that includes:

1. A description of your service (mowing lawns, baking cookies, etc.)
2. Your target market (who will your customers be?)
3. Your pricing strategy (monthly service, pay per product, etc.)
4. A basic marketing plan (Door flyers, newspaper ad, etc))
5. A goal for your earnings (how much do you hope to make?)

By creating this basic plan, you'll gain practical experience in thinking like an entrepreneur and setting financial goals. Who knows – this activity could be the first step towards starting your own successful business!

Chapter 3
The Art Of Budgeting

A budget is people telling their money where to go instead of wondering where it went. —John Maxwell

Imagine this: Your friend Alex has been saving up for months to buy a new phone and she's finally got enough to make the purchase, but on her way to the store, her car breaks down. It's an unfortunate event, but one that she's ready to handle because Alex has a budget.

As part of her budget, she set aside $20 a month from her part-time babysitting job as an *"emergency fund"*. It's because she planned ahead and maintained a budget that she was able to dip into her emergency savings, fix her car, and carry on with her plan to purchase a new phone.

This would have been a different situation if she had not budgeted her money well. Without her emergency fund, she would have needed to pay for repairs rather than get her new phone, which would have been a real bummer. Not Alex though — she was prepared and armed with a budget that helped her easily navigate life's inevitable twists and turns.

Why Budgeting Matters

If your money were a car, budgeting would be the GPS that helps you navigate to your destination. Without a GPS, you're just driving aimlessly, hoping you'll end up somewhere good.

But with a well-planned budget, you have a clear sense of direction to your financial goals, whether that's saving up for a new laptop, starting a college fund, or even planning for your future dream home.

Budgeting gives you the power to decide where your money goes, rather than wondering where it went.

Budgeting isn't just about reaching your goals. It's also about reducing financial stress and anxiety. When you have a clear picture of your income and expenses, you're less likely to be caught off guard by unexpected bills or run into debt trouble. You can plan ahead, save for emergencies, and even treat yourself occasionally, all without worrying that you're jeopardizing your financial future.

Think about it this way: when you're in school, you probably have a planner or calendar to keep track of your assignments, exams, and extracurricular activities. You wouldn't just wing it and hope for the best, right? The same goes for your money. By creating a budget and sticking to it, you're setting yourself up for success both now and in the future.

Understanding Income

The first step in creating a budget is to get a clear picture of your income. This might include:

- Allowance from your parents or guardians
- Money from a part-time job or online gig
- Birthday or holiday cash gifts
- Cash earned from washing cars

Take a moment to list out all your income streams and add them up to determine your total monthly income. If your income varies from month to month (like if you work odd hours at your part-time job), try to estimate an average monthly amount.

It's important to be honest and realistic about your income. Don't inflate the numbers or count on money that you don't actually have coming in. The goal is to create a budget based on your real financial situation, not an idealized version of it.

Tracking Your Expenses

Now that you know how much money you have coming in each month, it's time to take a look at where that money is going. This is where tracking your expenses comes in.

Start by listing out all your regular monthly expenses, like:

- School lunches or supplies
- Clothing or personal care items
- Transportation costs (like gas money or bus fare)
- Phone or internet bills
- Subscription services (like Netflix)
- Entertainment expenses (like movie tickets or video games)

Don't forget to include any irregular expenses that come up throughout the year, like birthday gifts for friends or family, vacations, or school trips.

Categorizing Expenses

Once you have a complete list of your expenses, try categorizing them into "*needs*" (essential expenses, like school supplies), "*wants*" (non-essential expenses, like eating out or buying new clothes), and "*savings*" (money you set aside for future goals or emergencies).

This categorization process can help you identify areas where you might be overspending and opportunities to cut back. For example, if you notice that you're spending a lot of money on fast food or coffee shops, you could try packing your own lunches or brewing your own coffee at home to save money.

Remember, tracking your expenses isn't about judging yourself or feeling guilty about your spending. It's simply a way to bring awareness to your financial habits and make informed decisions about where you want your money to go.

Setting Financial Goals

One of the key benefits of budgeting is that it allows you to set and achieve financial goals. These could be short-term goals, like saving up for a new phone or a summer road trip, or long-term goals, like saving for college or a car.

Take some time to think about your financial goals and write them down. Be specific and realistic – instead of just saying "*save money,*" set a concrete goal like "*save $500 for a new laptop by the end of the year.*"

Once you have your goals in mind, incorporate them into your budget. Determine how much money you need to save each month to reach your goal, and treat that savings amount as a non-negotiable "expense" in your budget.

Having clear financial goals can help you stay motivated and focused when it comes to budgeting. Instead of feeling like you're depriving yourself, you'll know that every dollar you save is bringing you one step closer to achieving your goals.

Choosing a Budgeting Method

Now that you have a clear picture of your income, expenses, and financial goals, it's time to choose a budgeting method that works for you. Here are a few popular options:

1. **The 50/30/20 rule:** This method suggests allocating 50% of your income to needs *(like rent, utilities, and that pesky expense called "food")*, 30% to wants *(like those new shoes you've been eyeing or that fancy dinner out with friends)*, and 20% to savings and debt repayment *(because your future self will thank you)*. It's a simple and effective way to ensure you're covering your essentials while still leaving room for fun and future planning.
2. **The envelope system:** With this method, you physically divide your cash into different envelopes labeled with each expense category (like "groceries," "entertainment," or "savings"). Each category is allowed a specific dollar amount of your choosing. This system can be especially helpful if you tend to overspend in certain areas. Just be sure to keep your cash-filled envelopes in a safe place. You wouldn't want your "grocery fund" mysteriously disappearing before your next trip to the supermarket.
3. **Budgeting apps and spreadsheets:** There are tons of digital tools available to help you track your income and expenses, set goals, and monitor your progress. Some popular options include Mint, YNAB (You Need a Budget), and PocketGuard. You can also create your own simple budget spreadsheet using Google Sheets or Microsoft Excel.

Ultimately, the best budgeting method is the one that you'll actually stick with. It may take some trial and error to find a system that works for you, and that's okay! The most important thing is to choose a method that aligns with your personality, lifestyle, and financial goals.

Sticking to Your Budget

Creating a budget is one thing – sticking to it is another. It takes discipline, commitment, and a willingness to make tough choices sometimes. But trust me, the rewards of living within your means and achieving your financial goals are so worth it!

Here are a few tips for sticking to your budget:

1. **Track your spending:** Keep a close eye on where your money is going. You can use a budgeting app, a spreadsheet, or even a simple notebook to log your purchases.
2. **Review and adjust your budget regularly:** Set aside time each month to review your budget and see how you're doing. If you notice that you're consistently overspending in one category or have extra money left over in another, make adjustments as needed.
3. **Celebrate successes & learn from your setbacks:** Budgeting is a skill that takes practice – don't beat yourself up if you make mistakes along the way. Instead, celebrate your wins (like hitting a savings goal or staying within your budget for a whole month) and use your setbacks as opportunities to learn and improve.

Remember, sticking to a budget isn't about depriving yourself of all joy and fun. It's about being intentional with your money and using it in a way that aligns with your values and goals.

Dealing with Unexpected Expenses

No matter how well you plan, life has a way of surprising us at the most unexpected of times. Whether it's a car repair, a medical bill, or a last-minute school expense, unexpected costs can put a serious strain on your budget.

That's why it's so important to have an emergency fund — a separate savings account that you can tap into when the unexpected happens. Aim to save up at least $500 to $1,000 in your emergency fund, or enough to cover one to two months' worth of expenses. Think of it as a financial safety net, ready to catch you when life decides to give you a shove off the trapeze.

If an unexpected expense comes up and you don't have enough saved in your emergency fund, don't panic. See if you can adjust your budget temporarily to accommodate the extra cost. Just remember, a little sacrifice now can save you from a world of financial pain later.

If the expense is too big to handle on your own, talk to your parents or a trusted adult about your options. They might have some wisdom to share or be able to offer some short-term assistance to get you back on your financial feet.

The key is to anticipate the unexpected as much as possible and have a plan in place to handle it. That way, when life throws you a financial curveball, you'll be ready to swing for the fences. With a little forethought and preparation, you'll be able to handle whatever comes your way.

Budgeting Tips for Teens

Budgeting as a teenager comes with its own unique set of challenges and opportunities. Here are a few tips to help you make the most of your budgeting journey:

Involve your parents or guardians

If you're still living at home, it's helpful to involve your parents or guardians in your budgeting process. They can offer valuable guidance, help you track your expenses, and even provide incentives for achieving your financial goals. Plus, being open about your finances now can set the stage for healthy money conversations in the future.

Find ways to increase your income

If you're struggling to make your budget work, consider looking for ways to boost your income. This could mean taking on additional shifts at your part-time job, starting a side hustle (like tutoring or pet-sitting), taking on some online gig projects, or selling items you no longer need.

Identifying "Needs" vs. "Wants"

It's all too easy to get caught up in the latest trends or feel pressure to keep up with your friend's spending habits. But learning to distinguish between "needs" (things you can't live without) and "wants" (things that are nice to have but not essential) is a key part of successful budgeting. Before making a purchase, ask yourself – is this something I truly need, or just something I want in the moment?

Avoiding Common Budgeting Mistakes:

To wrap up this chapter, here are a few common pitfalls that can derail even the best-laid budgeting plans.

These include:

- Not tracking your expenses regularly
- Not setting clear financial goals
- Not adjusting your budget as your circumstances change
- Not having an emergency fund for unexpected expenses
- Comparing yourself to others or trying to keep up with unsustainable spending habits

By being aware of these potential mistakes and taking steps to avoid them, you'll be well on your way to budgeting success.

ACTIVITY: Create Your Budget

Now that you've learned the basics of budgeting, it's time to put your knowledge into practice! Follow these steps to create your own personal budget:

Step 1: Income

- List all your sources of income (allowance, part-time job, birthday gifts, etc.)
- Calculate your total monthly income.

Step 2: Expenses

- List all your monthly expenses (needs, wants, and savings).
- Categorize each expense as a need, want, or savings.
- Add up your total expenses for each category.

Step 3: Compare

- Subtract your total expenses from your total income.
- If you have money left over *(cha-ching!)*, allocate it to your savings or financial goals.
- If your expenses exceed your income *(fear not!),* look for areas to cut back or ways to increase your income.

Step 4: Choose a Budgeting Method

- Decide on a budgeting method that works for you (50/30/20 rule, envelope system, or digital tools).
- Allocate your income to each expense category based on your chosen method.

Step 5: Set Goals

- Write down your short-term and long-term financial goals.
- Determine how much you need to save each month to reach your goals.
- Incorporate your goal savings into your budget.

Step 6: Review and Adjust

- Track your income and expenses throughout the month.
- At the end of the month, review your budget to see how you did.
- Make adjustments as needed based on your progress and any changes in your financial situation.

Remember, your budget is a dynamic system that *absolutely should* adapt to your changing circumstances, so don't be afraid to make adjustments as needed. The goal is to find a balance that works for you and helps you achieve your financial objectives.

Chapter 4
Saving For The Future

Compound interest is the eighth wonder of the world. He who understands it earns it; he who doesn't pays it.
— Albert Einstein

Every dollar you save today is a gift to your future self. It's a promise that you'll have the resources you need to chase your dreams, weather unexpected challenges, and live life on your own terms. But here's the most important thing I can tell you about saving — *the earlier you start, the better.*

Take the story of Wyatt; he's 26 now, but when he was 14 years old, he started saving $50 a month from a part-time job. At first, it wasn't easy – he had to cut back on spending, and that meant saying *"no"* when it would have felt so much better to say *"yes"*. Fast forward 10 years, and Wyatt's savings have grown to over $9,000, thanks to the power of *compound interest*. His savings allowed him to pay cash for his first car and eventually put a downpayment on his first house — all because he made the choice to *start saving early.*

The Power of Compound Interest

Compound interest is the interest you earn on **both** your initial savings **and** the interest those savings have already earned.

Let's break it down with a few examples that build on each other using an easy-to-calculate interest rate of 5%:

$100 at 5% for 1 year

Say you put $100 into a savings account that earns 5% interest per year. After the first year, you'll have $105 – your original $100, plus $5 in interest. Nothing to get too excited about, but that's just the beginning...

$100 at 5% for 10 years

Now, imagine that you leave $100 in your savings account for 10 years. Compound interest will turn that $100 into about $163. That's over 63% growth, without you having to lift a finger! Now we're getting somewhere, but it gets much better...

$100 at 5% for 10 years with contributions

Instead of simply leaving $100 in your savings account all by its lonesome, *imagine that you faithfully contribute $50 each month.*

In ten years, your initial $100 investment would quietly swell to about $7,836. Of that amount, $1,736 is from interest alone! This tidy sum reflects not just your consistent monthly contributions but also the sneaky power of compound interest working its magic in the background, proving that regular savings, even in small doses, can grow impressively over time.

Types of Savings Accounts

Now that you understand the power of compound interest, let's talk about where you can put your savings to maximize its growth potential. There are several different types of savings accounts, each with its own pros and cons.

Vanilla Savings Account

This is probably the account you think of when you hear the word "savings". It's a simple account where you can deposit money and earn a small amount of interest. These accounts are easy to open and give you quick access to your cash when you need it. However, their interest rates tend to be pretty low, often much less than 1%.

High-Yield Savings Account

If you're looking for a bit more bang for your buck, you might consider a high-yield savings account. These accounts typically offer much higher interest rates than traditional savings accounts – sometimes 10 or 20 times higher! The catch is that they often require a larger minimum balance and may have restrictions on how often you can withdraw funds.

Say you have $1,000 to put into savings. If you put that money in a traditional savings account earning 1% interest, you'd earn $10 over the course of a year. But if you put that same $1,000 in a high-yield savings account earning 5% interest, you'd earn $50 in a year – *that's 5x the yield just by choosing a different savings account!*

Certificate of Deposit

Another option is a certificate of deposit, or CD. With a CD, you agree to leave your money in the account for a set period of time, usually anywhere from a few months to a few years. In exchange, you'll typically earn a higher interest rate than you would with a regular savings account. The interest rate is often around 3%. The downside is that if you need to access your money before the CD term is up, you'll likely face a penalty.

CDs can be a great option if you have a chunk of money that you know you won't need for a while. By locking in a higher interest rate for a set term, you can maximize your savings growth without the temptation to spend the money prematurely.

One strategy to maximize the benefits of CDs while maintaining some flexibility is called "CD laddering." This involves spreading your money across multiple CDs with different maturity dates. For example, instead of putting $5,000 in a single 5-year CD, you might put $1,000 each in 1-year, 2-year, 3-year, 4-year, and 5-year CDs. As each CD matures, you can either withdraw the money if needed or reinvest it in a new 5-year CD, potentially at a higher interest rate. This approach allows you to take advantage of higher long-term rates while still having regular access to a portion of your funds.

How to Choose?

So, which type of account is right for you? It really depends on your individual savings goals and circumstances. If you need easy access to your money and aren't too worried about maximizing interest, a basic savings account might be the way to go. If you have a larger sum to save, want to earn more interest, and know you won't need access to the money for a while, then a high-yield account or CD could be the smart choice.

The key is to do your research and shop around. Compare interest rates, fees, and minimum balance requirements from different banks and credit unions. And remember, you don't have to put all your eggs in one basket. You can use a combination of different accounts to meet your various savings needs and goals.

For example, you might keep your emergency fund in a high-yield savings account for easy access and higher returns, while putting your car savings in a CD to lock in a good rate. The point is to be strategic and intentional with where you stash your cash.

Setting Savings Goals

Let's talk about how to set effective savings targets. After all, saving money is a lot easier when you have a clear idea of what you're saving for and why.

One popular framework for goal-setting is the SMART criteria. This stands for **S**pecific, **M**easurable, **A**chievable, **R**elevant, and **T**ime-bound.

Let's break down each of these components:

- **Specific:** Your savings goal should be clearly defined and focused. Instead of saying, "*I want to save money*," try something like, "*I want to save $500 for a summer road trip.*"
- **Measurable:** Your goal should be quantifiable so you can track your progress. "*Save $500*" is much more measurable than "*save some money.*"
- **Achievable:** Make sure your goal is realistic and attainable, given your current financial situation. If you're working part-time and have a lot of expenses, saving $10,000 in a year might not be feasible.
- **Relevant:** Your savings goal should be meaningful and aligned with your values and priorities. If travel isn't important to you, saving for a big road trip might not be the most motivating goal.
- **Time-bound:** Finally, your goal should have a clear deadline. This helps create a sense of urgency and accountability. "*Save $500 by June*" is much more powerful than "*save $500.*"

If your savings goal fits within the SMART framework, you're far more likely to achieve the goal. Let's put this into action with a real-life example.

Meet Liam, a 15-year-old who loves photography. Liam's dream is to buy a high-quality camera to take his hobby to the next level. Using the SMART framework, Liam sets his savings goal:

"I will save $750 to buy the Canon EOS Rebel T7 camera bundle within 8 months, by December 31st. I will do this by saving $94 per month from my part-time tutoring job and birthday money."

See how specific and actionable Liam's goal is? He's not just saving for a vague "camera" – he's identified the exact make and model he wants, along with a clear price target and timeline. By breaking his goal down into monthly increments, he's created a roadmap for success that is perfectly achievable.

Staying On Track

Of course, setting a goal is just the first step. To stay on track, you'll need to regularly monitor your progress and make adjustments as needed. One helpful strategy is to visualize your savings growth using charts or graphs. Many banking and budgeting apps have built-in tools for this, or you can create your own using a spreadsheet.

Saving For Multiple Things

Another key to successful saving is balancing multiple goals. Let's face it, you probably have more than one thing you want to save for – maybe you're eyeing a new phone, planning for college, and dreaming of a post-graduation trip all at the same time. The key is to prioritize your goals based on importance and timeline and to allocate your savings accordingly.

One approach is to divide your savings into different categories for each goal. For example, you might have a "car fund," a "college fund," and a "fun fund." Each month, you'll allocate a portion of your savings to each category based on your priorities and timeline.

This not only helps you stay organized and motivated, but it also ensures that you're making progress on all your goals, not just the most pressing or exciting ones. And remember, it's okay to adjust your goals and priorities as your life changes. The key is to stay flexible and keep saving, no matter what.

Emergency Funds

In addition to saving for specific goals, there's one type of savings that everyone should have: *an emergency fund*. This is a stash of cash set aside specifically for unexpected expenses or financial setbacks, like a car repair, medical bill, or job loss.

Having an emergency fund is like wearing a seatbelt – you hope you never need it, but if you do, it could save you from serious harm. Without an emergency cushion, you might be forced to rely on credit cards or loans to cover sudden costs, which can quickly spiral into debt. Or, you might have to raid your other savings goals, setting you back on your financial journey.

Let's look at a real-world scenario. Consider Sophia, a 19-year-old college student who got into a fender bender and needed to pay a $500 insurance deductible to get her car fixed. If Sophia didn't have an emergency fund, she would have needed to put that $500 on a high-interest credit card. That $500 credit charge could eventually amount to hundreds more in interest if she were only able to make the minimum payment. Thankfully, Sophia planned ahead and set up an emergency fund, which allowed her to tap into savings to cover the deductible without going into debt or sacrificing her other financial goals.

How much to save?

So, how much should you have in your emergency fund? A good rule of thumb is to save enough to cover 3 to 6 months' worth of essential living expenses. This includes things like rent/mortgage, food, utilities, transportation, and insurance – basically, the bare minimum you need to get by.

To calculate your emergency fund target, add up your essential monthly costs and multiply by either 3 or 6, depending on how much of a cushion you prefer to have. For example, if your core expenses are $1,000 a month, you'll want to aim for an emergency fund of $3,000-$6,000.

I know that might seem like a daunting number, especially if you're just starting your savings journey. But remember, you don't have to build your emergency fund overnight. Start small, with whatever you can afford to set aside each month, and make it a priority to contribute regularly to your emergency fund over time.

How to fund it?

One strategy is to treat your emergency fund like an expense, just like rent or utilities. Include it in your budget and automate your contributions so you're saving without even thinking about it. And when you get a windfall, like a tax refund or birthday cash, consider putting a portion directly into your emergency stash.

Where to keep it?

As for where to keep your emergency fund, you'll want to choose an account that's safe, accessible, and earns at least a little bit of interest. A high-yield savings account is usually a good bet, just avoid accounts with high fees or minimum balance requirements, and make sure you can access your money quickly if needed.

The key is to build your emergency fund consistently over time and resist the temptation to dip into it for non-emergencies. You don't want to be like the trapeze artist who, on a whim, decided to trade in their safety net for a fancy new sequin leotard. Sure, they looked fabulous soaring through the air in dazzling fashion, but if a slip occurred...

Savings and Technology

In today's digital age, technology has made saving easier and more convenient than ever before. From budgeting apps to online savings accounts, there are countless tools at your fingertips to help you reach your financial goals.

Automatic Savings

As mentioned in the last chapter, apps like Mint and YNAB (You Need A Budget) help you create and stick to a budget by tracking your income, expenses, and savings goals. They offer features like bill reminders, spending alerts, and personalized recommendations to keep you on track.

Another handy tool is spare change investing apps, such as Acorns or Stash. These apps round up your purchases to the nearest dollar and invest the spare change into a diversified portfolio. Over time, these small investments can add up to significant savings without you even noticing the money leaving your account.

Tracking Progress

Another benefit of technology is the ability to track your progress in real-time. With just a few taps on your phone, you can see exactly how much you've saved, how much you have left to reach your goal, and how your savings have grown over time. This can be a huge motivator to keep saving and stay on track.

Gamify Saving

There are also apps that gamify the savings process, turning it into a fun challenge. For example, the app Digit analyzes your spending habits and automatically transfers small amounts of money into your savings account when you can afford it. The app Qapital lets you set rules for your savings, like rounding up each purchase to the nearest dollar and saving the change.

Saving and Discipline

Picture this: You're standing at the crossroads of your financial destiny. On one path, you see the glittering temptations of instant gratification. On the other, you see the steady, reliable route of saving – not as flashy, but it leads to a future of financial stability.

The choice is obvious... *but difficult!*

Choosing the path of saving takes real discipline. It's like being on a diet and walking past a donut shop. You know that sugary goodness is tempting, but sticking to your goals will pay off in the long run. And let's be real, watching your savings grow is just as sweet (*well, almost*).

Developing the discipline to save consistently is like building a muscle. At first, it might feel like a strain, but the more you flex that savings muscle, the stronger it becomes. Soon enough, saving will be as natural as brushing your teeth.

Delayed Gratification

There's always going to be a new shiny object vying for your attention and your hard-earned dollars. That's why you need to build the habit of *"delayed gratification"*. Here it is in action:

So you're walking through the mall, minding your own business, when suddenly, a shiny new gadget catches your eye. It's the iPhone 57, complete with a built-in espresso machine and a holographic display that projects your favorite memes. Your quivering hand involuntarily reaches for your wallet, ready to make it rain, but then you remember: *you're supposed to be saving for something more important.*

So, you take a deep breath, put on your best *"responsible near-adult"* face, and walk away from the sparkling iPhone 57. It's not easy; in fact, it very well may be one of the most difficult decisions you've made thus far in your young life, but you now understand that delayed gratification is the key to unlocking a better future.

So, the next time you're tempted to blow your cash on something frivolous, just remember: delayed gratification is your secret weapon. It might not be as exciting as buying a jetpack or a lifetime supply of gummy bears, but it's the financial equivalent of putting on your superhero cape and doing what's right.

Continue practicing delayed gratification, and you'll look back on many more moments like these and have thankful thoughts such as, *"Wow, I'm so glad I didn't buy that toaster that burns motivational quotes onto my bread."*

Build the habit

Another way to stay disciplined with saving is to make it a habit. Just like brushing your teeth or doing your homework, saving should become a regular part of your routine.

Set a schedule for when you'll transfer money into your savings account, and stick to it like glue. Whether it's every week, every paycheck, or every time you find a dollar in the laundry (*cha-ching!*), make saving a non-negotiable part of your financial plan.

At first, it might feel like a chore, but over time, saving will become second nature – something you do automatically without even thinking about it. You might even start to look forward to those regular transfers, watching your savings grow like a well-watered plant.

And if you ever feel your resolve wavering, just remember: every dollar you save is a step closer to your goals. Whether it's a new laptop, a down payment on a house, or maybe you're just really, *REALLY* set on the motivational quote toaster— your future self will thank you for the sacrifices you make now.

Accountability

It can also help to have an accountability partner on your savings journey. This could be a parent, sibling, or friend. Share your goals with your accountability partner and check in with each other regularly to stay motivated and on track. You can even make it a friendly competition—see who can save the most each month, with the winner getting bragging rights (*or maybe a small prize, like a homemade origami trophy crafted from dollar bill*s).

Knowing that someone else is rooting for your success can be a powerful motivator to stay disciplined. When you're tempted to splurge on something you know good and well that you don't need, just picture your accountability partner's disapproving face. Plus, having someone to celebrate your wins with makes the whole savings process a lot more fun—who doesn't love a good high-five or happy dance?

So find yourself an accountability buddy and start saving together. With a little teamwork and a lot of determination, you'll be unstoppable in your quest for financial success!

ACTIVITY: Savings Goal Roadmap

Now, it's time to put your savings knowledge into action! Let's create a roadmap for one of your savings goals.

1. **Define Your Goal**: Choose what you're saving for. Define your goal using the SMART criteria: Specific, Measurable, Achievable, Relevant, and Time-bound.
2. **Set Monthly Milestones**: Decide how much money you need to save each month to meet your goal by your target date. Sketch out a timeline of these monthly savings amounts.
3. **Identify Challenges**: Think about possible obstacles, such as needing to

cut back on expenses or upcoming events that might impact your savings. Plan ways to overcome these challenges.

4. **Incorporate Windfalls**: Factor in any expected extra money, like birthday money or those accidentally laundered dollar bills (*so fresh*), which could help boost your savings ahead of schedule.

5. **Commit and Motivate**: Write down why this goal matters to you and what achieving it would mean. Place your roadmap where you can see it daily to keep motivated.

6. **Review and Adjust**: Remember, your roadmap can change as needed. Update your plans as you progress to stay on track toward your goal.

Remember, this roadmap is a living document. As you progress on your savings journey, feel free to adjust your timeline, tactics, or even your goal as needed. The key is to stay flexible, stay focused, and keep moving forward.

Chapter 5
Smart Spending

The bitterness of poor quality remains long after the sweetness of low price is forgotten. —Benjamin Franklin

Imagine this: you've just received your first paycheck from your part-time job, and you're feeling pretty good about yourself. You've worked hard, and now you have some cold-hard cash to call your own. You might be tempted to celebrate by buying those limited-edition sneakers you've been eyeing or treating your friends to a gourmet pizza party, *but hold on there, moneybags!*

You see, many people fall victim to the siren song of frivolous spending. It's like their feelings hijack their wallet and go on a wild shopping spree without inviting their brain along for the ride. In the next section, we'll dive into some of the most common emotional triggers that can lead you to overspend so that you can learn to stay grounded and in control of your finances.

The Psychology Behind Spending

Have you ever found yourself browsing online shopping sites when you're feeling stressed or down, only to end up with a cart full of items you don't really need? Or have you ever gone out with friends and felt pressured to keep up with their spending habits, even if it means stretching your budget too thin?

If you answered yes to either of these questions, don't worry—you're not alone. In fact, there are a variety of psychological triggers that can lead us to make impulsive or emotional spending decisions, even when we know better.

Emotional Spending

One common trigger is emotional spending. When we're feeling stressed, anxious, or down, it's easy to turn to "*retail therapy*" as a way to cope. That new pair of shoes or the latest gadget might give us a temporary boost of happiness, but it's often short-lived and can lead to feelings of guilt or regret later on.

The thing is, emotional spending is totally normal, and we all do it from time to time. The key is to recognize when it's happening and find healthier ways to cope with those feelings. Instead of turning to spending, try calling up a friend to vent, going for a run to clear your head, or busting out your favorite hobby to get your mind off things. Your wallet will thank you and you'll feel better knowing that your money is going to more productive uses.

Social Pressures

Another big influence on our spending habits is social pressure. It's like there's this unspoken competition to see who can have the coolest stuff, the most epic experiences, and the most Insta-worthy moments. And when you're constantly bombarded with images of your peers rocking designer labels, jetting off on lavish vacations, and brunching at the trendiest spots in town, it's hard not to feel like you're missing out if you're not keeping up.

If you find yourself feeling pressured to spend beyond your means due to social influences, try taking a step back and reassessing your priorities. Unfollow accounts that make you feel like you're not measuring up, and seek out content that inspires you to live your best life within your means. Surround yourself with friends who support your financial goals and share your values, rather than those who constantly encourage you to spend, spend, spend.

Remember: true happiness and fulfillment come from living a life that's authentic to you, not from keeping up with someone else's highlight reel. So stay true to yourself, spend wisely, and don't let social pressure derail your financial journey.

Breaking the habit

So, how can we combat these psychological triggers and take control of our spending habits? The first step is simply being aware of them. When you find yourself feeling the urge to make an impulsive purchase, take a moment to pause and ask yourself what's really driving that desire. Are you buying something because you really need it, or because you're trying to fill an emotional void or keep up with someone else's lifestyle?

Another helpful strategy is to create a personal reward system that encourage saving over spending. For example, let's say you have a goal to save $500 over the next few months. Every time you resist the urge to make an unnecessary purchase and instead put that money towards your savings goal, give yourself a small reward, like watching an episode of your favorite show or treating yourself to a homemade dessert. Over time, these small rewards can help reinforce positive spending habits and make saving money feel more enjoyable and satisfying.

Evaluating Needs vs. Wants

In the grand scheme of personal finance, there's a vital skill that every savvy spender must master: the art of distinguishing between essential needs and discretionary wants. It's a battle as old as time itself – or at least as old as the first caveman who had to choose between a new club for hunting and a fancy painting for his cave wall.

In today's world, we're constantly bombarded with advertisements and messages telling us that we absolutely must have the latest and greatest products. From smartphones that can do everything but wash dishes to designer clothes that cost more than a month's rent, it's easy to get caught up in the whirlwind of consumerism.

But here's the thing: *learning to separate what we truly need from what we simply want in the moment is crucial for maintaining financial stability.*

When you're faced with a purchasing decision, take a step back and ask yourself: is this something I genuinely need, or is it just a fleeting desire? Will this purchase contribute to my long-term goals, or is it just a temporary rush of retail therapy?

Now, this doesn't mean you have to live like a monk and deny yourself all of life's little pleasures. Treating yourself occasionally is perfectly fine – after all, what's the point of working hard if you can't enjoy the fruits of your labor? The key is finding a balance between necessary expenses and the occasional indulgence.

Think Longer Term

So, how can we get better at evaluating needs vs. wants? One helpful strategy is to consider the difference between immediate gratification and long-term satisfaction. That new video game or trendy outfit might give you a quick rush of excitement, but will it still bring you joy and fulfillment a month or a year from now?

On the flip side, spending money on things like education, experiences with loved ones, or investments in your future can lead to a deeper sense of satisfaction and well-being over time.

The 24 Hour Rule

Imagine that you're scrolling through your favorite online store when, suddenly, a shiny new gadget catches your eye. Your finger hovers mere millimeters over the "add to cart" button, ready to seal the deal...

But wait! Before you take the plunge, consider trying the 24 hour rule. This simple strategy involves giving yourself a full day to think over any non-essential purchases before pulling the trigger.

During this time, ask yourself:

Do I really need this item, or is it just a passing fancy?

How will this purchase fit into my overall financial goals?

Is there a more cost-effective alternative?

Often, you'll find that the initial excitement fades away over the course of a day, and you'll be able to make a more clear-headed decision about whether the purchase is truly worth it.

Mind Over Matter

Ultimately, the key to mastering needs vs. wants is to cultivate a mindset of mindful consumption. This means being intentional and thoughtful about the purchases you make and focusing on items that add real value and meaning to your life. It's not about depriving yourself of all pleasure or indulgence but rather being selective and deliberate about where you choose to spend your hard-earned money.

For example, let's say you're a passionate musician and you've been eyeing a new guitar for months. While a new instrument might seem like a "want" at first glance, if playing music is a core value and source of joy for you, investing in a quality guitar that will last for years could be seen as a worthwhile "need." On the other hand, if you're simply feeling the urge to buy the latest fashion trend or tech gadget because everyone else has it, that's likely a "want" that you can easily do without.

As you practice evaluating needs vs. wants, keep in mind that everyone's priorities and values are different. What might be an essential need for one person could be a frivolous want for another, and that's okay. The key is to get clear on what matters most to you and to use that as a guidepost for your spending decisions.

Cost-Benefit Analysis of Purchases

This might sound like a fancy business term, but really, it's just a way of weighing the pros and cons of a potential purchase to determine if it's truly worth it.

One key aspect of cost-benefit analysis is assessing value beyond just the price tag. It's easy to get caught up in looking for the cheapest option or the biggest discount, but sometimes, a higher-priced item can actually be a better value in the long run.

Real-world examples

For example, let's say you're in the market for a new backpack for school. You find one option that's really cheap, but it's made with flimsy materials and doesn't have a lot of storage space. On the other hand, you find a higher-quality backpack that costs more upfront, but it's made with durable materials, has plenty of pockets and compartments, and comes with a lifetime warranty. While the second option might be more expensive in the short term, it could end up being a better value over time because it will last longer and serve your needs better.

Here's a more complex example...

Let's say you're in the market for a new laptop. One option is a budget-friendly model with basic specs and minimal features. The other option is a more expensive, high-performance laptop from a reputable brand known for its durability, speed, and advanced features.

At first glance, the cheaper laptop might seem like the more attractive choice. However, when you consider factors like processing power, storage capacity, battery life, and overall build quality, the pricier option starts to look more appealing.

While the high-performance laptop comes with a higher upfront cost, its superior specs and features can provide significant benefits in the long run. Faster processing speeds and more RAM can save you time and frustration when running multiple programs or working on resource-intensive tasks. A larger, high-quality display can reduce eye strain and enhance your overall user experience. A more durable build can mean fewer repairs and a longer lifespan for your device.

Moreover, the more expensive laptop can open up more opportunities to earn money through online gigs and freelance work. With a reliable, high-performance device, you can take on remote jobs such as video editing, graphic design, or computer-aided drafting (CAD). The extra income earned through these activities can help offset the initial cost of the laptop and even provide a valuable return on your investment.

When you factor in these potential financial benefits alongside the laptop's superior performance and longevity, the cost-benefit analysis starts to favor the more expensive, high-quality option. While it may require a larger upfront investment, the long-term value provided by a top-tier laptop can make it the smarter choice for your needs and goals.

Lifetime Cost

Another important factor to consider in cost-benefit analysis is the lifetime cost of a purchase. This includes not just the upfront purchase price, but also any ongoing costs associated with owning and maintaining the item over time.

Here's an example of the lifetime costs involved in, not an item, but an animal — a cute little puppy. Even if you were to adopt this puppy for free from an animal shelter, there are still a boatload of lifetime costs to consider, such as:

- Basic necessities (food, toys, bedding, grooming supplies)
- Home repairs (from when Scruffy was "teething")
- Routine veterinary care (annual check-ups, vaccinations, preventive medications)
- Unexpected medical expenses (injuries, illnesses)
- Training and pet-sitting services (obedience classes, doggy daycare, boarding)
- Pet rent, deposits, and potential liability insurance
- Time investment for daily care and attention

That adorable, fluffy face might be hard to resist, but remember: those big, soulful eyes are silently pleading, "*Adopt me, and I promise to love you unconditionally... and also drain your wallet for the next 15 years or so*".

Opportunity Cost

Every dollar you have represents an opportunity. When you spend money on one thing, *you're also choosing not to spend it on something else*. It's important to weigh these trade-offs carefully and make sure you're allocating your money in a way that aligns with your priorities and goals.

The key is to weigh not only what you're gaining from buying something, but also consider what you could be missing out on by losing the purchasing power of those dollars.

For example, consider the decision to buy a brand new gaming console that costs $500. While the console promises many hours of entertainment, it's important to consider the opportunity costs associated with both the financial investment and the time spent playing. That $500 could instead be used to enroll in several high-quality courses that you could invest your time into for a permanent boost in your skillset and marketability.

Evaluating these alternatives helps ensure that your spending and time allocation align with long-term personal and professional growth goals. By understanding the opportunity cost, you can make more intentional and beneficial decisions.

Stretching Your Dollar Further

Level up your spending game and make your hard-earned cash go the extra mile. With a few smart shopping strategies up your sleeve, you'll be able to score the best deals, save some serious dough, and still get your hands on the stuff you need (*and maybe even a few things you want*). So, let's dive in and explore some tips and tricks for making your dollars go further.

Compare Prices Like a Pro

Never settle for the first price tag you see. With a little bit of sleuthing, you can often find the same item for a lower price elsewhere. Before you pull the trigger on a purchase, take a few minutes to shop around and compare prices from different retailers, both online and in-store. Don't forget to factor in any shipping costs or membership fees that might apply.

Pro Tip: Use price comparison websites or apps to make the process even easier. These handy tools do the legwork for you, scouring the internet for the best deals on the products you're looking for. Some popular options include Google Shopping, PriceGrabber, and ShopSavvy.

Coupon Clipping 2.0

Forget about scissors and the Sunday paper—couponing has gone digital! These days, you can find coupons and discount codes for just about anything with a quick online search. Before you make a purchase, always do a quick Google search for the retailer's name plus "*coupon code*" or "*promo code*." More often than not, you'll uncover a treasure trove of deals just waiting to be applied to your order.

Another great way to snag coupons is by signing up for your favorite retailers' email newsletters or following them on social media. Many brands will send exclusive discounts and promotions directly to their subscribers or followers.

<u>Pro Tip</u>: Use a separate email address for these subscriptions to avoid cluttering up your primary inbox.

Sale Season Savvy

Timing is everything when it comes to scoring the best deals. Most retailers follow a fairly predictable sale schedule throughout the year, so it pays to be strategic about when you shop. For example, end-of-season sales are a great time to stock up on clothing and accessories for the following year. Holiday weekends like Memorial Day, Labor Day, and Black Friday/Cyber Monday are also known for their deep discounts across a wide range of products.

Of course, it's not always possible (or practical) to put off purchases until the next big sale comes around. In those cases, keep an eye out for flash sales, daily deals, or clearance events that pop up throughout the year. Sign up for email alerts from your favorite retailers or follow deal-sharing websites like Slickdeals or Wirecutter to stay in the loop.

Second-Hand Steals

Who says you have to buy everything brand new? Shopping second-hand is a smart way to save big on everything from clothing and accessories to electronics and home goods. Check out local thrift stores, consignment shops, or online marketplaces like eBay, Poshmark, or Facebook Marketplace for gently used items at a fraction of their original price.

Not only is buying second-hand easier on your wallet, but it's also better for the environment. By giving pre-loved items a new home, you're helping to reduce waste and keep perfectly good products out of landfills. Talk about a win-win!

The Art of Negotiation

Believe it or not, prices aren't always set in stone. In some cases, you may be able to negotiate a lower price or score additional perks just by asking. This is especially true when shopping for big-ticket items like electronics, furniture, or appliances. If you're buying in-store, don't be afraid to ask the salesperson if they can offer any discounts or throw in free delivery or installation.

When shopping online, try reaching out to the retailer's customer service team via live chat or email to inquire about any current promotions or discounts that might not be advertised on their website. The worst they can say is no, but you might be surprised at how often a little friendly haggling can pay off.

The Bottom Line

At the end of the day, smart shopping is all about being a savvy consumer and making informed decisions with your money. By taking the time to compare prices, seek out deals and discounts, and think outside the (*brand new*) box, you can stretch your budget further and get more bang for your buck.

Just remember: at the end of the day, the best deal isn't always the cheapest one. It's important to balance price with factors like quality, durability, and overall value. That almost-free, well-worn, thrift store t-shirt might seem like a steal in the moment, but unless you're going for that "*post-apocalyptic*" look, it might be worth investing a little extra in a t-shirt that won't disintegrate at the mere sight of a washing machine. Trust me, your wallet (*and your dignity*) will thank you in the long run.

So, go forth and shop smart, my frugal friend! With these strategies in your arsenal, you'll be well on your way to becoming a master of the bargain hunt.

Activity: Spending Diary

Now that we've covered all these key concepts of smart spending, it's time to put them into practice! One of the best ways to get a handle on your spending habits is to keep a spending diary. This means writing down every single purchase you make, no matter how small or seemingly insignificant.

1. **Choose Your Tool**: Decide whether you'll use a physical notebook, a digital spreadsheet, or a budgeting app to record your expenses.
2. **Record Daily**: Every day for the next month, write down every purchase you make. Include the date, what you bought, how much it cost, and optionally, how the purchase made you feel or why you decided to buy it.
3. **Review Monthly**: At the end of the month, review your entries. Look for patterns or trends in your spending. Identify any emotional triggers or frequent impulse buys.
4. **Analyze and Plan**: Use your findings to pinpoint areas for improvement. Set specific, achievable goals for the next month, such as limiting dining out expenses or setting aside a fixed amount for savings.
5. **Stay Consistent**: Keep the diary going and adjust your goals as needed, using it as a tool to guide and improve your spending habits.

At the end of the month, take some time to review your spending diary and reflect on your habits. Look for patterns and trends—are there certain triggers or emotions that tend to drive your spending? Are there any areas where you're consistently overspending or making impulse purchases?

Use this information to identify opportunities for improvement and set some clear goals for yourself moving forward. Maybe you want to challenge yourself to stick to a certain budget for eating out next month, or to put a certain amount of money towards your savings goals each week. Whatever your goals are, use your spending diary as a tool to help you stay accountable and on track.

Chapter 6
Credit and Debt: A Double-Edged Sword

Too many people spend money they haven't earned, to buy things they don't want, to impress people they don't like. —Will Rogers

Credit is like a double-edged sword. When used wisely, it can help you achieve your goals and build a strong financial foundation. But when mismanaged, it can lead to a crushing burden of debt that can take years to overcome. That's why it's so important to gain an understanding of credit and debt as early as possible so that you can learn to wield its mighty power responsibly.

Understanding Credit

Before we get into the nitty-gritty of using credit, let's take a step back and understand how it works.

When you use credit, you're essentially borrowing money from a lender (like a bank or credit card company) with the promise to pay it back over time, usually with interest. The lender is taking a risk by trusting you to repay the money, so they charge interest as a way to compensate for that risk and make a profit.

It's like they're saying, "*Sure, we'll lend you the money, but we're not running a charity here. We expect to get paid for our troubles and then some!*" The interest is the price you pay for the convenience of using someone else's money.

Credit can be a useful tool when used responsibly, but it's important to understand that *it's not free money*. It's essentially a loan with strings attached, and those strings can quickly turn into a tangled web of debt if you're not careful.

So, when you're swiping that credit card, just remember that every purchase is like a little "IOU" note that you're signing.

Types Of Credit

There are a few different types of credit you might encounter as a teenager or young adult:

- **Credit cards:** These are probably the most common form of credit. With a credit card, you're given a credit limit (the maximum amount you can borrow) and you can use the card to make purchases or withdraw cash. You'll need to make at least the minimum payment each month, and if you don't pay off your balance in full, you'll be charged interest on the remaining amount.
- **Student loans:** If you're planning to go to college, you might need to take out student loans to cover the cost of tuition, books, and living expenses. These loans can come from the government or private lenders, and they usually have lower interest rates than other types of credit. However, they also come with a lot of responsibility – you'll need to start paying them back after you graduate, even if you're not making a lot of money yet.
- **Personal loans:** A personal loan is a lump sum of money that you borrow from a bank or credit union and pay back over a set period of time, usually with fixed monthly payments. These loans can be used for a variety of purposes, like consolidating debt, paying for a big purchase, or covering an emergency expense.
- **Mortgages:** Okay, so you're probably not in the market for a house just yet, but it's still good to know what a mortgage is since they're a big part of most people's financial lives. A mortgage is a loan used to buy a home, and it's usually paid back over 15-30 years. The house itself serves as collateral for the loan, which means if you don't make your payments, the lender can take possession of the house.

Key Credit Terms

No matter what type of credit you're using, there are a few key terms you should know:

- **Credit limit:** The maximum amount you can borrow on a credit card or line of credit.
- **Interest rate:** The percentage in interest that you'll be charged each month if you don't pay off your balance in full.

- **Minimum payment:** The smallest amount you're required to pay each month to keep your account in good standing.
- **Credit score:** A number that represents your creditworthiness and helps lenders decide whether to approve you for credit and at what interest rate.

We'll talk more about credit scores later in this chapter, but for now, just know that your credit score is like a grade for how well you manage credit. The higher your score, the better!

The Pros and Cons of Using Credit

On the positive side, credit can be a valuable financial tool that offers flexibility and opportunity. It allows individuals to make purchases or investments that might otherwise be out of reach. When used responsibly, credit can help build a strong credit history and score. A good credit standing can open doors to better financial products, terms, and even certain career or housing prospects.

However, credit also comes with significant risks and potential drawbacks. Overreliance on credit can lead to unmanageable debt, especially if spending habits are not kept in check or if unexpected financial challenges arise. It's almost like the credit card companies are saying, *"Hey, want to buy something you can't afford? No problem! Just use this little magic, plastic rectangle, and worry about the consequences later!"* Before you know it, you're sitting in your apartment, surrounded by things you bought on credit, wondering where all your money went. The worst part? Not only are you broke, but you also owe someone else money.

It's a balancing act. You want to enjoy the benefits of credit without falling into the trap of debt.

The Pros Of Using Credit:

- **Build your credit score:** By making on-time payments and keeping your balances low, you can demonstrate to lenders that you're a responsible borrower and improve your credit score over time.
- **Make large purchases:** Sometimes, you might need to make a big purchase that you can't afford to pay for all at once (like a car or a computer for school). Using credit can allow you to spread out the cost over time, making it more manageable.
- **Cover emergency expenses:** Life happens, and sometimes unexpected expenses pop up (like a car repair or a medical bill). Having a credit card

or personal loan can give you a safety net to fall back on in these situations.

- **Earn rewards:** Some credit cards offer rewards programs where you can earn points, miles, or cash back on your purchases. If you use your card regularly and pay off your balance in full each month, these rewards can add up to significant savings over time.

The Cons Of Using Credit:

- **Debt:** If you don't stay on top of your payments or you borrow more than you can afford to pay back, you can quickly find yourself in debt. And the longer you carry a balance, the more interest you'll accrue, making it harder to get out of debt. Remember when we talked about *compound interest*? Well, carrying high-interest debt is the polar-opposite of it. It's like being stuck in quicksand—the more you struggle, the deeper you sink. Before you know it, you're up to your eyeballs in interest charges, and your minimum payments are barely making a dent.
- **Temptation to overspend:** When you have a credit card or line of credit, it can be tempting to spend more than you normally would. After all, you're not seeing the money come directly out of your bank account. But remember – just because you can borrow the money doesn't mean you should. It's important to stick to your budget and only spend what you can afford to pay back.
- **Fees:** Many credit cards come with annual fees, balance transfer fees, cash advance fees, and other hidden costs. If you're not careful, these fees can add up quickly and make your debt even harder to pay off.
- **Impact on your credit score:** If you miss payments, max out your credit cards, or default on your loans, it can have a serious negative impact on your credit score. This can make it harder to get approved for credit in the future, and you may end up paying higher interest rates as a result.

Credit is like a powerful tool in your financial toolbox—it can help you build a strong credit score, make important purchases, and navigate life's unexpected challenges. But like any tool, it's important to learn how to use it properly to avoid hurting yourself in the process.

The key is to educate yourself on responsible credit use, including paying your bills on time, keeping your balances low, and avoiding the temptation to overspend just because you have a shiny new credit card burning a hole in your pocket.

Building and Maintaining a Good Credit Score

Now that we've covered the basics of credit and debt, let's talk about the importance of building and maintaining a good credit score.

Your credit score is your financial report card – it reflects how well you manage credit and how risky you are as a borrower. Lenders use your credit score to decide whether to approve you for credit, and at what interest rate. Landlords, employers, and even cell phone companies may also use your credit score to make decisions about you.

So, how is your credit score calculated? There are a few key factors that go into it:

- **Payment history:** This is the most important factor in your credit score. It looks at whether you've made your payments on time, and if you have any late payments, collections, or defaults on your record.
- **Credit utilization:** This is how much of your available credit you're using at any given time. It's generally recommended to keep your credit utilization below 30% (so if you have a $1,000 credit limit, try to keep your balance below $300).
- **Length of credit history:** The longer you've been using credit, the better. This shows lenders that you have experience managing credit responsibly.
- **Types of credit:** Having a mix of different types of credit (like credit cards, student loans, and a car loan) can also help your score.
- **New credit inquiries:** Every time you apply for new credit, it results in a hard inquiry on your credit report. Too many hard inquiries in a short period of time can be a red flag to lenders.

So, how can you build and maintain a good credit score as a teenager or young adult? Here are a few tips:

1. **Start with a secured credit card or credit-builder loan:** If you're new to credit, you might have a hard time getting approved for a regular credit card. A secured credit card or credit-builder loan can help you build credit without taking on too much risk. With a secured card, you put down a cash deposit that serves as collateral for your credit limit. With a credit-builder loan, you borrow a small amount of money and make monthly payments, which are reported to the credit bureaus. It's an easy way to get the ball rolling.

2. **Use credit responsibly:** Once you have a credit card or loan, it's important to use it responsibly. Make your payments on time every month, and try to pay off your balance in full if possible. If you can't pay in full, at least make the minimum payment and work on paying down your balance over time.
3. **Monitor your credit report:** You're entitled to a free credit report from each of the three major credit bureaus (Equifax, Experian, and TransUnion) once a year. Take advantage of this and review your credit report regularly for errors or signs of fraud. If you see anything suspicious, dispute it right away.
4. **Don't apply for too much credit at once:** Remember, every time you apply for credit, it results in a hard inquiry on your credit report. Too many of these can ding your score, so only apply for credit when you really need it.
5. **Be patient:** Building a good credit score takes time. It's not something that happens overnight, but with consistent, responsible credit use, you can gradually improve your score over time.

By following these tips and using credit responsibly, you'll be well on your way to building a strong credit foundation that will serve you well throughout your adult life.

The Dangers of Debt

While using credit responsibly can be a good thing, it's important to be aware of the dangers of debt. When you borrow money, you're committing to paying it back – with interest. And if you're not careful, that debt can quickly spiral out of control.

Here are a few common debt traps to watch out for:

- **High-interest credit cards:** Credit cards can be a convenient way to make purchases, but they often come with high interest rates (especially for people with lower credit scores). If you only make the minimum payment each month, you could end up paying a lot more in interest over time.
- **Payday loans:** These are short-term loans that are designed to be paid back on your next payday. They often come with extremely high interest rates and fees, which can make them very difficult to pay off. It's best to avoid payday loans altogether if possible.
- **Rent-to-own programs:** These programs allow you to rent items (like furniture or electronics) with the option to buy them at the end of the

rental period. However, the total cost of the item usually ends up being much higher than if you had bought it outright, and you may end up paying a lot in fees and interest.

- **Overusing student loans:** While student loans can be a helpful way to pay for college, it's important to borrow only what you need. Taking out more loans than necessary can leave you with a lot of debt to pay back after graduation, which can be a big financial burden.

Avoiding The Debt-Trap

It's all too easy to fall into the trap of spending more than you can afford, only to find yourself drowning in a sea of minimum payments and interest charges. Before you know it, you're playing a game of financial whack-a-mole, trying to keep up with your bills while your credit score sinks faster than a submarine with screen doors.

So, how do you avoid this financial faux pas?

- **Live within your means:** Avoid spending more than you earn, and stick to a budget that allows you to save money each month.
- **Save up for big purchases:** Instead of relying on credit to make big purchases, try to save up the money in advance. This can help you avoid taking on debt and paying interest.
- **Use credit responsibly:** Only charge what you can afford to pay back, and make your payments on time each month.
- **Have an emergency fund:** Try to save up a small emergency fund (even just a few hundred dollars) that you can use to cover unexpected expenses. This can help you avoid turning to credit or loans in a pinch.
- **Seek help if you need it:** If you find yourself struggling with debt, don't be afraid to seek help. Talk to a financial advisor or credit counselor who can help you create a plan to pay off your debt and get back on track.

Remember, debt isn't always avoidable, nor should it be avoided outright. By being proactive and making smart financial choices, you can minimize your risk, keep your debt under control, and learn to wield credit like the helpful financial tool it's meant to be and avoid treating it like a bottomless piggybank.

ACTIVITY: Credit & Debt Quiz

Test your knowledge concerning the important topic of "Credit & Debt" by taking a quick, 8-question quiz:

PERSONAL FINANCE FOR TEENAGERS

1. What is credit? a) Money you have in your bank account b) The ability to borrow money with the promise to pay it back later, often with interest c) A gift card for your favorite store d) A type of currency used in foreign countries
2. Which of the following is NOT a type of credit? a) Credit cards b) Student loans c) Amazon Gift Cards d) Payday loans
3. What does a credit score represent? a) The amount of money you have in your savings account b) Your creditworthiness and how risky you are as a borrower c) The number of credit cards you own d) Your monthly income
4. Which factor is most important in determining your credit score? a) Payment history b) Length of credit history c) Types of credit d) New credit inquiries
5. What is the recommended credit utilization percentage to maintain a good credit score? a) 50% b) 75% c) 30% d) 90%
6. How often are you entitled to a free credit report from each of the three major credit bureaus? a) Once a month b) Once a year c) Every two years d) Never
7. Which of the following is NOT a good tip for avoiding debt? a) Living within your means b) Saving up for big purchases c) Using credit responsibly d) Taking out the largest loans possible.
8. If you're struggling with debt, what should you do? a) Ignore the problem and hope it goes away b) Take out more loans to pay off your existing debt c) Seek help from a financial advisor or credit counselor d) Cut up all your credit cards and never use them again

Answer Key: 1b, 2c, 3b, 4a, 5c, 6b, 7d, 8c

Chapter 7
Investing 101

Know what you own, and know why you own it.
—Peter Lynch

Investing is one of the most powerful tools you have for building long-term wealth and creating the life you want. Also, anyone can start investing, no matter how much cash you have or how little you know about the stock market!

Most people think that the #1 goal of investing is to *"get rich"*, but that's entirely wrong. *What it's really about is giving yourself options and freedom.* It's about being able to afford the things that matter to you—whether that's traveling the world, starting your own business, or being able to help out your family. And the earlier you start investing, the more time you have for your money to grow.

Buying Assets

First things first, let's break down what investing actually means. Basically, investing is all about putting your money into an asset (like stocks, bonds, real estate, gold, etc.) with the expectation of that asset increasing in value over time. In other words, instead of just letting your cash sit around doing nothing, you're putting it to work so it can grow.

When you invest, you're basically becoming the owner or part-owner of whatever you're investing in. So, if you buy a stock, congrats—you own a tiny piece of that company! And if that company makes money and grows, the value of your stock goes up, too. Sometimes, the company might even send you a slice of their profits just for being an owner—that's called a dividend.

But here's the thing—investing is not a get-rich-quick scheme. It's a long-term game that requires patience and discipline. There will be times when your investments go up in value and times when they go down. That's just part of the ride. The key is to stay focused on your big-picture goals and not get too caught up in the day-to-day ups and downs.

Ways To invest

Picture yourself strolling down the aisles of a financial supermarket, where the shelves are lined with a dizzying array of investment products. Each one promises to be the key to unlocking your financial dreams, like a shiny new toy begging to be taken home. But before you start tossing random investments into your cart like a kid in a candy store, it's important to take a step back and consider your options.

The point is—there's no one-size-fits-all approach to investing. What works for your neighbor or your second cousin twice removed might not be the right fit for you. It's all about figuring out your own financial recipe based on your goals, risk tolerance, and personal taste.

Here's an overview of the basic investment types:

Stocks

You've probably seen it in the movies—the intense stock trader, eyes glued to a wall of computer screens filled with charts and numbers, frantically making deals and watching their fortune grow (or disappear) with each passing second. While the reality of stock trading may not be quite as dramatic, it's true that investing in stocks can be an exciting and potentially lucrative way to grow your wealth over time.

When you buy a stock, you're buying a piece of ownership in a company. It's like becoming a mini-mogul, without the private jet and the corner office. Plus, some companies even pay dividends to their shareholders, which is like getting a little bonus check just for being an owner.

One thing to keep in mind about stocks is that they can be quite unpredictable. They have their moments of exhilarating growth, but they can also take sudden dives that might leave you feeling uneasy. Much like navigating a stormy sea, the key is to remain steady and not let your emotions steer the ship. If you can maintain your composure through these ups and downs, stocks can be a potent tool for building wealth over time.

Bonds

When you buy a bond, you're basically lending money to a company or government. It's like being a bank but without the stuffy suits and the free lollipops. The borrower promises to pay you back the original amount (called the principal) plus interest over a set period of time, usually several years. It's like you lend someone some money, and they give you back an IOU, but with a little extra *somethin' somethin'* on top.

Bonds are generally less risky than stocks because you know exactly how much you'll get back and when. They're like the slow and steady tortoise to the stock market's manic hare. But that doesn't mean they're completely risk-free. If the borrower defaults on their payments, you could be left holding the bag (a bag that used to contain money *but no longer does*). This doesn't happen often, but it's a possibility. Still, for investors who want a little more stability in their portfolio, bonds can be a solid choice.

Mutual Funds and ETFs

These are like baskets of investments that can include stocks, bonds, and other assets all mixed together. It's like going to an all-you-can-eat buffet and getting a big plate with a little bit of everything piled on it. When you invest in a fund, you're pooling your money with other investors to buy a mix of different investments, which can help spread out your risk.

The beauty of mutual funds and ETFs (Exchange-Traded Funds) is that you don't have to be a financial whiz to invest in them. You don't have to spend hours pouring over stock charts or analyzing bond yields—the fund managers do all the heavy lifting for you. It's like having a personal chef for your investments, minus the fancy hat and the French accent. Of course, you'll pay a fee for their services, but for many investors, it's worth it for the convenience and peace of mind.

Index Funds

Imagine you're at a gigantic farmers market. Instead of spending hours examining every apple, carrot, and head of lettuce, you simply buy a small piece of every single stand. That's essentially what an index fund does in the world of investing.

Index funds are the cool, laid-back cousin of mutual funds and ETFs. They're like the reliable family car of the investment world—not flashy, but dependable and gets you where you need to go without emptying your wallet. It's as if someone took a snapshot of the entire market (or a big chunk of it) and turned it into one easy-to-buy package.

Consider Vanguard to be your go-to company for investing in index funds. Vanguard is like the pioneer of index funds. They've been doing this longer than anyone else and they're known for keeping costs super low, which means more money stays in your pocket.

So, why are investors head over heels for index funds?

- **They're cheap to own:** Index funds typically have lower fees than actively managed funds. They don't need a team of suit-wearing analysts trying to outsmart the market.
- **They play the field:** By tracking an entire index, you're instantly diversified across hundreds or even thousands of companies. It's like going to a buffet and tasting a little bit of everything.
- **They're low maintenance:** You don't need to pick individual stocks or time the market. Just buy the index and hold on for the long term. It's perfect for those who'd rather spend their time binge-watching their favorite shows than poring over financial statements.
- **They've got street cred:** Over long periods, index funds have often outperformed actively managed funds, especially after accounting for fees. It's like they've cracked the code of the investing universe.

For many investors, especially beginners, index funds offer an easy, low-cost way to get started with investing. They're like the "set it and forget it" option of the investment world. So, if you're looking for a simple, cost-effective way to dip your toes into the investing pool, index funds might just be your new best friend.

Real Estate

Buying real estate directly is like playing a high-stakes game of Monopoly, except with real cash and actual buildings. It's not for the faint of heart, but if you've got the guts and the capital, it can be a rewarding way to invest. Just be prepared to deal with the occasional leaky roof, problem tenant, and 2 a.m. phone call about a clogged toilet. It's all part of the charm of owning real estate.

If you're not quite ready to go all-in on the property ownership game, a real estate Investment Trust (REIT) can be a more accessible way to dip your toes into the real estate pool. REITs are like the mutual funds of the real estate world. They own and manage a portfolio of properties, and you can buy shares in the trust just like you would with a stock. They come in all shapes and sizes, from residential to commercial, and offer a way to invest in real estate without the massive capital outlay and hands-on management that comes with buying property directly. Plus, they typically offer higher returns than many other types of investments.

Cryptocurrencies

Cryptocurrencies like Bitcoin and Ethereum have been stealing the spotlight lately. Known for their roller coaster-like volatility, these digital currencies can make your financial portfolio feel a bit like a daring adventure at an amusement park.

When considering whether to invite Bitcoin or Ethereum to your investment party, it's wise to start with a solid foundation of traditional investments tailored to your financial goals and risk appetite. Think of it as enjoying a sturdy, balanced meal before indulging in dessert. This mix might include stocks, bonds, mutual funds, and perhaps some real estate—a bit less exciting but reliably nourishing over the long term.

As your confidence and knowledge expand, feel free to spice up your portfolio with a sprinkle of cryptocurrencies. Just remember that while they can add a dash of excitement and the potential for big returns, they can be quite risky.

Risk vs. Reward

One of the core concepts to understand about investing is the relationship between risk and reward. In general, investments that have the potential to earn more money also come with a higher degree of risk, AKA: *losing money*. On the flip side, investments that are less risky usually have lower potential returns. They might not make you rich quickly, but they can provide steadier and more predictable yields.

Weighing Risk

So, how much risk should you take? That depends on your goals and timeline. If you have the time, money, and stomach to ride out the ups and downs of the market, you might be comfortable taking on more risk for the potential of higher returns. But if you're saving up for a short-term goal (like buying a car or paying for college), you might want to play it a bit safer.

One way to think about risk is to imagine a spectrum, with low-risk investments (like bonds) on one end and high-risk investments (like some stocks or cryptocurrencies) on the other end. Most people's portfolios will fall somewhere in the middle, with a mix of different types of investments.

Protect the eggs

Another way to manage risk is through diversification—affectionately known in financial circles as *not putting all your eggs in one basket.*

Imagine you're a farmer with a thriving egg business. You've got a flock of hens that lay delicious, fresh eggs every day, and you rely on those eggs for your livelihood. Now, picture yourself collecting all those eggs and carefully stacking them up into a single basket.

Risky move, isn't it? All it takes is one little stumble and you've got the makings of the world's largest omelet.

When you concentrate all your resources into a single venture, you leave yourself vulnerable to potential catastrophes. If that one investment fails, your entire financial future could be jeopardized.

The solution? *Diversification.*

Just as a wise farmer would distribute their eggs across multiple baskets to mitigate risk, a savvy investor will spread their money across various assets. This way, if one investment underperforms or faces a setback, the overall impact on your portfolio is minimized. Your other investments can help cushion the blow and keep you on track toward your financial goals.

Of course, diversification isn't a magic bullet. It can't entirely eliminate risk, and it's still possible to experience losses even in a well-diversified portfolio. However, by embracing the principle of not putting all your eggs in one basket, you can significantly reduce your exposure to potential disasters and increase your chances of weathering any financial storms that come your way.

Building Your Portfolio

Okay, so you know the basics of investing and the different types of investments out there. But how do you actually put it all together into a portfolio that works for you? That's where asset allocation comes in.

Asset allocation is just a fancy way of saying, "*deciding how much of your money to put into different types of investments.*"

A common approach is to decide on a mix of stocks, bonds, and other assets based on your age, goals, and risk tolerance.

For example, let's say you're 16 years old and you're investing for the long haul (like retirement). You might start with a portfolio that looks something like this:

- 70% stocks (for long-term growth potential)

- 25% bonds (for stability and income)
- 5% cash/short-term investments (for short-term goals)

As you get older and closer to needing your money, you might start shifting more of your portfolio into bonds and cash to reduce your risk. So, by the time you're in your 60s, your portfolio might look more like this:

- 50% stocks
- 40% bonds
- 10% cash/short-term investments

Of course, these are just examples—your actual asset allocation will depend on your specific goals and circumstances. As you learn more about investing, you might decide to add other types of investments to your portfolio, like real estate or crypto.

Putting Your Investing Plan into Action

Now that you've got a solid understanding of the different types of investments and how to craft a portfolio that aligns with your financial goals and risk tolerance, you might be itching to dive right in and start putting your money to work. But hold up! If you're not quite 18 yet, you'll need to get a parent or guardian involved to officially start investing. Think of it like getting your learner's permit before you can officially hit the road solo.

Here's a step-by-step guide to getting started:

1. **Set your goals:** Before you start investing, it's important to know what you're investing for. Are you saving up for a big purchase (like a car or a house down payment)? Investing for retirement? Building an emergency fund? Write down your goals and how much money you'll need to reach them.
2. **Open an account:** If you're under 18, you'll need a parent or guardian to open an account on your behalf. You'll be looking for a "Custodial Account" or a "Joint Brokerage Account". Once you are 18, you can have your own account. Look for an account with low fees and a good selection of investment options.
3. **Decide on your asset allocation:** Based on your goals and risk tolerance, decide how you want to split your money between stocks, bonds, and other investments.

4. **Choose your investments:** Once you've decided on your asset allocation, it's time to pick your specific investments. Look for low-cost index funds or ETFs that give you broad exposure to different parts of the stock and bond markets. As you learn more, you can start adding individual stocks or other types of investments to your portfolio.

5. **Set up automatic contributions:** To make investing a habit, set up automatic transfers from your bank account into your investment account. Start with whatever amount you can afford (even $10 or $20 a week can really add up over time!), and increase your contributions as your income grows.

6. **Monitor and rebalance:** As your investments grow (or shrink) over time, your asset allocation might start to drift away from your target. For example, if your stocks do really well, they might start to take up a bigger chunk of your portfolio than you originally planned. To keep things on track, check in on your portfolio a few times a year and rebalance as needed.

Teen Investors Who Are Crushing It

Still not convinced that investing is for you? Check out these real-life stories of teens who are making big things happen:

- **Saahil, 19:** Saahil started investing when he was just 16 years old, using money he earned from tutoring and freelance web design. He started with a mix of index funds and individual stocks, and has already grown his portfolio to over $7,000. "*Investing has taught me so much about how the world works*," Saahil says. "*It's not just about making money—it's about understanding business and even the global economy.*"

- **Maya, 16:** Maya got interested in investing after taking a personal finance class at her high school. She started by investing $50 a month from her part-time job, and has slowly built up a diversified portfolio of stocks and bonds. "*I love watching my investments grow,*" Maya says. "*It's like planting a seed and watching it turn into a huge tree.*"

- **Jamal, 15:** With the aid of his Grandpa, Jamal went an entirely different route. Instead of buying stocks, he buys rare gold and silver coins. He started off by purchasing an American Gold Eagle coin with the money he saved from birthdays and allowance—and a little help from his Grandpa. While the value of gold can fluctuate in the short term, Jamal understands that precious metals have historically been a reliable store of value over long periods. He plans to gradually expand his collection, focusing on high-quality, rare coins that have the potential to grow in value due to their scarcity and historical significance.

Investing Myths: Busted!

I know we've talked about a lot in this chapter, so before we wrap it up, let's bust some common myths about investing that might be holding you back:

- **Myth #1:** You need a lot of money to start investing. Not true! You can start investing with just $5 a week — or even less! The amount isn't nearly as important as starting early and being consistent.
- **Myth #2:** Investing is too risky. While all investments come with some level of risk, there are ways to manage that risk through diversification and asset allocation. Historically, the stock market has actually been one of the best ways to grow your wealth over the long term.
- **Myth #3:** Investing is only for old people. No way! In fact, the earlier you start investing, the more time you have to let your money grow and compound over time. So don't wait—start investing as young as possible!

ACTIVITY: Practice Trading Account

Ready to put your investing knowledge into action? Let's set up a practice investment account and get some hands-on experience with the market. This is an excellent way to get very real experience, but without risking any real money.

Setting Up Your Practice Account

1. **Choose a stock market simulator:** There are lots of free options out there, like Investopedia's Stock Simulator, Wall Street Survivor, or HowTheMarketWorks. These simulators let you practice investing with virtual money, so you can learn the ropes without risking any real cash.
2. **Create an account:** Once you've picked a simulator, sign up for an account. You'll usually need to provide some basic info like your name and email address, and also create a username and password. It's best to have a parent help with this.
3. **Explore the platform:** Take some time to familiarize yourself with the simulator's interface. Look for things like your account balance, the stock search function, and any educational resources or tutorials.
4. **Fund your account:** Most simulators will give you a set amount of virtual cash to start with (like $100,000). This is your risk-free "play money" to invest in the stock market.

Building Your Practice Portfolio

1. **Set some goals:** Before you start investing, take a minute to think about what you want to achieve. Are you trying to grow your money as much as possible? Learn about a specific industry or type of investment? Manage risk? Write down your goals so you can refer back to them as you build your portfolio.
2. **Do your research:** Use the simulator's stock search function to look up companies you're interested in. Read through their financial statements, news articles, and analyst reports to get a sense of their business and growth prospects.
3. **Make your first trades:** When you're ready, place your first virtual trades! Most simulators will let you buy and sell stocks, bonds, ETFs, and other investments just like you would with a real brokerage account.
4. **Monitor your progress:** Keep an eye on how your investments are doing over time. Most simulators will give you real-time stock quotes and portfolio performance data. Use this info to track your returns, spot trends, and make adjustments as needed.

Learning from Your Practice Trades

- **Reflect on your strategy:** As you build your practice portfolio, take some time to reflect on your investment strategy. What's working well? What could you improve? Are you taking on too much (or too little) risk?
- **Learn from your mistakes:** Everyone makes mistakes when they're learning to invest—that's part of the process! If a trade doesn't go your way, don't beat yourself up. Instead, try to learn from the experience and use that knowledge to make better decisions next time.
- **Keep learning:** The stock market is always changing, so it's important to keep learning and staying up-to-date. Read investing books and articles, follow financial news, and talk to other investors to keep expanding your knowledge.
- **Have fun:** Investing can be serious business—but it can also be a lot of fun! Enjoy the thrill of watching your virtual portfolio grow, and don't be afraid to take some calculated risks. Remember, this is all practice—so have fun and keep learning!

Chapter 8
Protecting Your Money

If you don't protect your money, you will have no means to protect anything else in your life.
—Tony Robbins

So far, you've learned about the importance of budgeting, saving, making smart spending decisions, and even ways of investing your hard-earned cash. But there's one more crucial aspect of financial literacy that we need to discuss: *protecting your money.*

In today's digital age, financial security is more important than ever. From identity theft to online scams, there are countless threats out there that can put your financial well-being at risk.

But don't worry—by arming yourself with the right knowledge and tools, you can keep your money safe and secure. In this chapter, we'll dive into the basics of financial security, including how to protect yourself from identity theft, stay safe while banking online, and safeguard your digital footprint.

Basics of Financial Security

First things first, let's talk about the fundamentals of financial security. It's about being proactive in managing your finances and taking steps to ensure that your money is always safe and secure.

Financial Audit

One of the most important aspects of financial security is regularly conducting audits. This means taking the time to review your personal financial statements and accounts, looking for any unauthorized transactions or discrepancies. It might sound tedious, but trust me—it's worth it. By catching any suspicious activity early on, you can prevent small issues from turning into very big problems down the line.

To conduct a financial audit, start by gathering all of your financial statements, including bank statements, credit card bills, and investment account statements. Review each transaction carefully, looking for any charges or withdrawals that you don't recognize. If you spot anything suspicious, contact your financial institution immediately to report the issue and take steps to resolve it.

Here are some specific steps you can take to conduct a thorough financial audit:

1. Make a list of all your financial accounts, including bank accounts, credit cards, investment accounts, and any other accounts that hold your money.
2. Gather all relevant statements and documents for each account, going back at least a few months.
3. Review each transaction on your statements, checking for any unfamiliar or unauthorized charges.
4. Pay particular attention to small, recurring charges that you might have forgotten about, such as subscriptions or membership fees.
5. If you find any suspicious activity, contact the relevant financial institution immediately to report the issue and start the process of recovering any lost funds.
6. Consider using budgeting apps or software to help you keep track of your spending and spot any unusual activity more easily.

Document Storage

Another key aspect of financial security is secure document storage. This means keeping all of your important financial documents, such as bank statements, tax returns, and investment account statements, in a safe and secure location. Ideally, you should store physical documents in a fireproof safe or lockbox, and keep digital copies in an encrypted storage solution, such as a password-protected cloud storage account.

Back It Up

Picture this: you've been diligently tracking your budget, saving for your future, and maybe even planning a side hustle to boost your income. All your important financial documents are neatly organized on your computer. But what happens if your trusty laptop decides to take an early retirement, gets stolen, or simply crashes without warning? All of your hard work could disappear in an instant.

That's where the smart habit of regularly backing up your crucial financial files comes in handy. By copying your documents to an external hard drive or a secure cloud storage service, you're essentially creating a safety net for your financial records.

Imagine the relief you'll feel when you can quickly access your backup files and carry on with your financial plans without missing a beat. After all, it's better to be safe than sorry—especially when "sorry" involves trying to recreate lost financial documents while sobbing over a tear-soaked keyboard.

Scams

It's also crucial to stay alert and informed about common financial scams and frauds to avoid falling victim to them. Scammers are like modern-day pirates, always on the lookout for their next unsuspecting victim.

Staying one step ahead means questioning anything that sounds too good to be true, guarding your personal information like it's the secret formula for Coca-Cola, and remembering that even the most convincing con artists can't guarantee you a quick fortune.

Being informed and skeptical is your best defense—because when it comes to your finances, it's always better to trust your gut than let an unsolicited scam email convince you of being the rightful heir to the vast fortune of a recently departed Arabian Prince.

Speaking of scams, here are some different types:

- **Phishing scams:** These are fake emails or messages that appear to be from legitimate companies or institutions, often asking you to click on a link or provide personal information. Be very cautious about unsolicited messages, and always verify the sender before taking any action.
- **Romance scams:** These often start on dating apps or social media, with scammers building a fake relationship with their target before asking for money to help with an emergency or to come visit. Be wary of anyone you meet online who asks for money, no matter how convincing their story may seem.
- **Employment scams:** These often involve fake job postings, or unsolicited job offers that require you to pay for training or supplies upfront. Legitimate employers will never ask you to pay to start a job.

- **Cryptocurrency scams:** With the rise of cryptocurrencies like Bitcoin, there has also been an increase in related scams, such as fake investment opportunities or "pump and dump" schemes. Be very cautious about any crypto-related investments and always do your own research before putting any money in.

By being aware of these common scams and taking steps to protect your financial information, you can greatly reduce your risk of falling victim to financial fraud. Remember, if something seems too good to be true, it probably is!

Identity Theft Protection

One of the biggest threats to financial security in today's digital age is identity theft. Identity theft occurs when someone steals your personal information, such as your Social Security number or credit card details, and uses it to open fraudulent accounts or make unauthorized purchases in your name. It can be a nightmare to deal with, often taking months or even years to recover from fully.

The good news is that there are steps you can take to protect yourself from identity theft. One of the most important things you can do is regularly monitor your credit reports from the three major credit bureaus: Equifax, Experian, and TransUnion. Your credit report contains a detailed history of your credit accounts and payment history and is often the first place where signs of identity theft will appear.

Credit Report Check

By law, you are entitled to one free credit report from each bureau every year. You can request your reports online at AnnualCreditReport.com, or by calling 1-877-322-8228. Review your reports carefully, looking for any accounts or inquiries that you don't recognize. If you spot anything suspicious, contact the credit bureau immediately to dispute the information and place a fraud alert on your account.

Freeze!

Another way to protect yourself is by placing a credit freeze on your accounts. A credit freeze restricts access to your credit report, making it much harder for identity thieves to open new accounts in your name. To place a freeze, you'll need to contact each credit bureau individually and provide proof of your identity. You can lift the freeze at any time if you need to apply for new credit, but it provides an extra layer of security when you don't.

Keep it Personal

Ben Clardy

Another important aspect of identity theft protection is securing your personal information. This means being cautious about sharing sensitive details, such as your Social Security number or bank account information, especially online or over the phone. It also means taking steps to physically secure your personal documents, such as shredding sensitive papers before throwing them away and using complex passwords for all of your online accounts.

High Security

I'm ashamed to admit it, but once upon a time I actually used the password "*PASSWORD*", for my email account. Not the smartest decision concerning my personal security, but I've learned a lot since then.

Now my password is:

NvrGnnaGvUup_NvrGnnaLtUdown_1987!

(Not really, but that's a pretty good one, right?)

When creating passwords, it's important to use a combination of upper and lowercase letters, numbers, and special characters. Avoid using easily guessable information like your birthdate or pet's name, and never use the same password for multiple accounts. Consider using a password manager to help you generate and store strong, unique passwords for all of your accounts.

Damage Control

If you do suspect that your identity has been stolen, it's important to act quickly to minimize the damage. Here are some steps to take:

1. Contact the credit bureaus to place a fraud alert on your account. This will make it harder for anyone to open new accounts in your name.
2. Report the theft to the Federal Trade Commission (FTC) at IdentityTheft.gov. The FTC can help you create a recovery plan and provide additional resources and support.
3. Contact any creditors or financial institutions where you believe fraudulent activity has occurred. Close any compromised accounts and request new account numbers and passwords.
4. Consider placing a credit freeze on your accounts, which will prevent anyone from opening new accounts in your name without your explicit permission.
5. File a report with your local police department, especially if you have evidence of the theft or know the identity of the thief.

6. Keep detailed records of all correspondence related to the theft, including dates, names, and contact information. This will be important if you need to dispute any fraudulent activity or take legal action.

Remember, recovering from identity theft can be a long and difficult process, but staying vigilant and taking quick action can help minimize the damage and get you back on track.

Online Banking Safety

In today's digital age, online banking has become a convenient and essential tool for managing our finances. But with the convenience of online banking also comes the risk of cyber threats and scams. To keep your money safe while banking online, it's important to follow some key best practices.

Two Factor Authentification

One of the most important things you can do to secure your online banking accounts is to enable two-factor authentication (2FA). 2FA adds an extra layer of security beyond just a password, typically by requiring you to enter a one-time code sent to your phone or email whenever you log in to your account. This makes it much harder for hackers to gain unauthorized access to your accounts, even if they manage to steal your password.

Most major banks and financial institutions offer 2FA as an optional security feature, so be sure to enable it on all of your accounts. It may take a few extra seconds to log in each time, but the added security is well worth the minor inconvenience.

When setting up 2FA, be sure to use a phone number or email address that only you have access to. Avoid using shared or public accounts, as this could compromise the security of your 2FA codes.

In addition to enabling 2FA, it's also important to use strong, unique passwords for all of your online banking accounts. Avoid using easily guessable information like your birthdate or address, and never use the same password for multiple accounts. Consider using a password manager to help you generate and store complex passwords securely.

Public Wi-Fi

It's also important to be cautious about conducting financial transactions over unsecured or public Wi-Fi networks. These networks are often unencrypted, meaning that anyone nearby can potentially intercept your data and steal your sensitive information. Whenever possible, conduct online banking and other financial transactions over a secure, private network, such as your home Wi-Fi or a virtual private network (VPN).

If you do need to access your online banking accounts while on the go, be sure to use your cellular data connection instead of public Wi-Fi. You can also use a VPN app to encrypt your data and protect your privacy, even on public networks.

By following these best practices and staying vigilant about potential threats, you can enjoy the convenience of online banking while keeping your money safe and secure.

Protecting Your Digital Footprint

In addition to securing your online banking accounts, it's important to protect your overall digital footprint to maintain your financial security. Your digital footprint includes all of the information about you that exists online, from your social media profiles to your search history and online purchases. If this information falls into the wrong hands, it can be used to steal your identity, access your financial accounts, or worse.

One of the best ways to protect your digital footprint is to be mindful of your privacy settings and permissions on social media and other online accounts. Take the time to review your settings regularly, and make sure that you're only sharing information with trusted friends and contacts. Be especially cautious about sharing financial information online, such as your income, bank account details, or credit score.

Here are some specific steps you can take to protect your privacy on social media:

- Review your privacy settings and adjust them to limit who can see your posts and personal information. Consider making your accounts private so that only approved followers can see your content.
- Be cautious about accepting friend requests or follows from people you don't know in real life. Scammers often use fake profiles to try to gain access to personal information
- Avoid sharing sensitive personal information, such as your full birthdate, address, or phone number, on your public profiles.
- Be mindful of the photos and videos you share, and avoid posting anything that could reveal sensitive information, such as your location or financial status.

- Use strong, unique passwords for all of your social media accounts, and enable two-factor authentication whenever possible.

It's also important to be cautious about the information you share on other online platforms, such as online forums, comment sections, or personal websites. Avoid sharing sensitive personal or financial information in public spaces, and be mindful of the digital trail you leave behind.

Device Security

It's also important to secure your mobile devices, such as your smartphone or tablet, with strong passwords, fingerprint recognition, or facial recognition. These devices often contain a wealth of sensitive information, including financial data and login credentials, making them a prime target for thieves and hackers. By securing your devices with strong authentication measures, you can help prevent unauthorized access to your information.

Here are some additional tips for securing your mobile devices:

- Enable automatic software updates to ensure that your device is always running the latest security patches and features.
- Download apps only from trusted sources, such as the official app store for your device. Avoid downloading apps from third-party sites or links, as these may contain malware or other security threats.
- Be cautious about granting apps access to your location, contacts, or other sensitive information. Only allow access to apps that you trust and that have a legitimate need for the information.
- Use a secure password manager to help you generate and store strong, unique passwords for all of your accounts, including those accessed on your mobile device.
- Enable remote wiping capabilities on your device, so that you can erase all of your personal information if your device is ever lost or stolen.

Defunct Device Disposal

Picture this: you're about to bid farewell to your trusty old laptop, the one that's been with you through thick and thin. It's served you well, but now it's time for an upgrade. So, you wipe a nostalgic tear from your eye, and prepare to send your digital companion off to greener pastures.

But wait! Before you hand over your beloved device to a stranger or toss it in the trash, there's something crucial you must do:

Ensure that all your personal information is securely erased from its memory banks.

Now, you might be tempted to simply drag all your files to the trash and call it a day. But hold on there, buckaroo! Just because you can't see those files anymore doesn't mean they're gone for good. With the right tools and a little bit of technical wizardry, a determined snoop could resurrect your deleted data faster than you can say "identity theft."

To truly protect your digital footprint, you'll need to take a more thorough approach. Enter data eraser tools. These powerful programs will scour every nook and cranny of your device, completely obliterating your personal information. Sounds extreme, but that's exactly what we want in this case.

But if you really want to satisfy your insatiable appetite for information destruction, you can take things a step further...

Imagine yourself in a dimly lit room, hunched over your old hard drive, cackling maniacally—power drill in hand. With a few well-placed holes through the platters, you'll render that drive more unreadable than a doctor's handwriting. It's the ultimate form of data destruction.

So, as you say goodbye to your old digital devices, remember: your personal information is a precious commodity. With a little bit of effort and the right tools, you can ensure that your digital footprint stays safe, secure, and out of the wrong hands.

ACTIVITY: Financial Security Checklist

Utilize this checklist to evaluate and enhance your financial security measures, ensuring the protection of your finances.

1. Conduct a Financial Audit:

- Review your bank, credit card, and investment statements for unauthorized transactions.
- Use budgeting apps to monitor spending and identify anomalies.
- Report any suspicious activities to your financial institutions immediately.

2. Secure Your Documents:

- Store physical financial documents in a fireproof safe.

- Maintain digital copies in encrypted storage like password-protected cloud services.
- Shred sensitive documents before disposal.
- Regularly back up important digital documents.

3. Protect Your Identity:

- Obtain and review your free credit reports annually.
- Enable two-factor authentication for online accounts.
- Use strong and unique passwords.

4. Stay Safe Online:

- Be wary of unsolicited requests for personal information.
- Verify sources before clicking links or downloading attachments.
- Conduct financial transactions over secure, private networks.
- Limit personal information shared on social media and online.

5. Secure Your Devices:

- Set strong passwords on all devices.
- Regularly update devices and apps with security patches.
- Install reputable antivirus software.
- Enable device location and remote wiping features for lost or stolen devices.
- Be selective about app permissions.

6. Dispose of Old Devices Securely:

- Use certified data eraser tools to wipe old devices.
- Physically destroy old storage devices to prevent data recovery. *Power drill, sledgehammer... I won't judge.*

Reminder: Financial security is an ongoing effort. Regularly update your security practices to address new threats. Stay proactive and vigilant to safeguard your financial future.

Chapter 9
Planning For Major Life Expenses

Savings only have meaning when you have a purpose for them. Plan for what's important.
—Robert Kiyosaki

As you navigate through life, you'll encounter a variety of significant financial milestones. These larger expenses can be daunting, especially if you're not prepared. But here's the good news: by anticipating them early on, you can set yourself up for success and achieve your goals without breaking the bank.

Saving for a First Car, College and Travel

One of the most important things you can do as a young person is to start saving and planning for the big expenses that come with adulthood. Whether it's buying your first car, paying for college, or taking that dream vacation, taking a smart financial approach can make all the difference.

Your First Car

When it comes to making your first car purchase as a teenager, it's essential to approach the decision with a mix of excitement and practicality. While it might be tempting to go for that shiny new sports car that's been catching your eye, a more prudent choice would be to opt for a reliable used vehicle.

Not only can a pre-owned car save you a considerable amount of money upfront, but it can also help you sidestep the rapid depreciation that new cars experience in their first few years. Think of it as letting someone else take the financial hit while you reap the benefits of a well-maintained, wallet-friendly ride.

Of course, before you start your car-buying adventure, it's crucial to consider the total cost of ownership beyond the sticker price. Insurance, maintenance, and fuel costs can pile up faster than your growing pile of laundry, so be sure to factor these expenses into your budget.

To get the best deal possible, put on your detective hat and do some thorough research. Compare prices from multiple dealerships and sellers, and don't be afraid to channel your inner negotiator. Remember, a little haggling can go a long way in saving you some hard-earned cash.

By making a smart, informed decision when buying your first car, you'll be setting yourself up for a smoother financial journey down the road. And who knows? You might even impress your friends with your savvy car-buying skills while they're still trying to figure out how to parallel park.

College-Bound

Another major expense you might encounter as a young adult is paying for higher education. Whether you're planning to attend a four-year university, community college, or vocational school, the cost of tuition, books, and living expenses can quickly add up. That's why it's important to start planning and saving for college as early as possible.

One popular option for college savings is a 529 plan. These tax-advantaged investment accounts allow you to save money specifically for education expenses, and many states offer additional tax benefits for contributions. Another option is a Coverdell Education Savings Account (ESA), which functions similarly to a 529 plan but with lower contribution limits and more flexibility in how the funds can be used.

When planning for college, it's also important to consider the impact of in-state versus out-of-state tuition. Attending a public university in your home state can often be significantly cheaper than going out of state or to a private school. However, if you have your heart set on a particular program or school, it may be worth the extra cost. The key is to weigh your options carefully and make an informed decision based on your goals and financial situation.

Travel

Finally, let's talk about travel. While it may not be as essential as transportation or education, exploring new places and cultures can be a truly life-enriching and perspective-enhancing experience. However, travel can also be expensive, especially if you're planning international trips or luxury getaways. That's why it's important to start saving for travel early and to be strategic about how you allocate your funds.

One effective strategy is to set specific travel goals and create a dedicated savings fund for each one. For example, if you're dreaming of backpacking through Europe after graduation, start setting aside a portion of your income each month into a separate account earmarked for that trip. You can also look for ways to save on travel expenses, such as booking flights and accommodations well in advance, traveling during off-peak seasons, and taking advantage of student discounts and loyalty programs.

By prioritizing your travel goals and being proactive about saving, you can turn your dream adventures abroad into a reality without breaking the bank.

Wedding Budgeting

For many young couples, diving into wedding planning can be their first plunge into deep financial waters together. Given that the average wedding in the United States can cost about as much as a brand-new car, it's no surprise that sticker shock can turn what should be a joyous occasion into a nail-biting budgetary circus. Trying to juggle the costs of venues, catering, and all those flowers *(why are there always so many flowers?)* can make even the calmest couples consider eloping.

Get Real

The first step to tackling the financial beast that is a wedding is to have a real heart-to-heart talk with your fiancé. Start by laying all your financial cards on the table — *and no bluffing!* This is where you figure out if your wedding budget is more about champagne and caviar or beer and pretzels.

Determine how much you can truly afford to save for the wedding without banking on winning the lottery in the meantime, and then allocate your funds with that number in mind. This approach helps ensure that your wedding plans are built on a foundation of financial sanity rather than whimsical thinking.

Focus Where It Matters Most

It's easy to fall into the trap of blowing half your budget on things like a designer dress that costs more than a downpayment on a house or floral arrangements that rival a botanical garden. Remember, while these things might make for stunning photos, they don't actually do much to enhance the overall enjoyment of your guests.

Instead, focus your financial firepower on the aspects of the wedding that genuinely matter and improve the experience—like ensuring the food is delicious, the band can actually play, and the photographer won't just take blurry selfies. These are the elements you'll actually remember—not the 500 custom, hand-embossed place cards.

Keep It Simple

Simplicity isn't just a style, it's a budgetary strategy. Think about hosting a smaller, more intimate gathering rather than a blockbuster wedding that might rival an awards show in logistics and cost. Perhaps choose a venue that's naturally beautiful, like a public park or a family backyard, where Mother Nature does most of the decorating for free.

Investing in some tasteful lighting and elegant decor can turn a simple space into a fairy-tale setting. This way, you can save on venue costs and splurge on things that enhance the ambiance without draining your bank account.

Avoid Financing

When it comes to paying for your wedding, it's important to approach the process with a clear head and a realistic budget. While it may be tempting to splash out on your big day, taking on significant debt to finance your nuptials can put a lasting strain on your new marriage and your long-term financial health.

Instead of relying on loans or credit cards to cover the cost of your wedding, consider saving up and paying for as much as possible out of pocket. This may mean making some tough choices and sacrifices in the short term, but it will pay off in the long run by allowing you to start your married life on a solid financial footing.

If you do receive contributions from family members, be sure to have an open and honest conversation about any expectations or strings attached to the money. It's important to make sure everyone is on the same page and that you're not feeling pressured to spend more than you're comfortable with.

Ultimately, the key to a successful and stress-free wedding is to focus on what really matters: celebrating your love and commitment to each other. By prioritizing your values and being mindful of your spending, you can create a meaningful and memorable day without breaking the bank or taking on unnecessary debt.

Homeownership Basics

For many people, buying a home is the biggest financial decision they'll ever make. It's a major milestone that can provide a sense of stability, security, and pride—but it's also a significant investment that requires careful planning and consideration.

Consider The "Hidden" Costs

We've talked about this before, but one of the first things to understand about homeownership is that it comes with a huge variety of costs beyond just the mortgage payment.

- **Utilities**: As a homeowner, you'll be responsible for paying all utility bills, including electricity, gas, water, sewer, and trash collection. These costs can vary greatly depending on the size of your home and your usage habits.
- **Property taxes**: You'll be responsible for paying annual property taxes based on the assessed value of your home. These taxes can vary widely depending on your location and are often used to fund local services like schools, libraries, and public safety.
- **Insurance**: Homeowners insurance is essential to protect your investment and provide financial security against unexpected events like property damage, theft, personal liability, and even natural events like flooding, tornados, and hurricanes.
- **HOA fees**: If you purchase a home within a community governed by a Homeowners' Association (HOA), you'll likely have to pay monthly or annual dues. These fees often cover the maintenance of common areas, amenities, and sometimes even exterior upkeep of your home.
- **Landscaping and yard maintenance**: Keeping your lawn and garden in tip-top shape can be costly, especially if you need to hire professionals for tasks like mowing, trimming, and fertilizing.
- **Pest control**: Depending on where you live, you may need to budget for regular pest control services to keep critters like termites, ants, or rodents at bay.
- **Renovations and upgrades**: As a homeowner, you might want (or need) to update things like flooring, appliances, or fixtures over time. Even minor renovations can be expensive, so it's wise to set aside funds for these projects.
- **Furniture and decor**: Unless you're downsizing, you'll likely need to purchase additional furniture and decor to fill your new home. This can

be a significant expense, especially if you have a larger space to furnish.

- **Emergency repairs**: Unfortunately, unexpected repairs like a leaky roof, burst pipe, or broken HVAC system can happen at any time. Having an emergency fund specifically for your home can help soften the blow of these surprise expenses.

By considering all of these potential costs, you'll be better equipped to create a comprehensive budget for homeownership. Remember, being prepared for these expenses can make the difference between a stressful and a successful homeowning experience!

Down Payment

Another key factor to consider is the down payment. In general, the larger your down payment, the lower your monthly mortgage payments will be. A larger down payment can also help you qualify for a better interest rate and avoid the need for private mortgage insurance (PMI). However, saving up for a substantial down payment can take time and discipline, especially if you're also juggling other financial priorities.

So, how much should you aim to save for a down payment? A good rule of thumb is to put down at least 20% of the purchase price. For example, if you're eyeing a home that costs $200,000, you'll want to have around $40,000 saved up. Now, I know what you might be thinking: *"I'll be as old as my grandparents by the time I save that much!"* But fear not, my friend. There are plenty of strategies you can use to speed up your savings, like automating your contributions, cutting back on unnecessary expenses, and exploring down payment assistance programs.

Of course, if you're struggling to come up with a 20% down payment, don't despair. You can still purchase a home with a smaller down payment, but be prepared to pay for Primary Mortgage Insurance (PMI), which is essentially an extra fee tacked onto your monthly mortgage payment to protect the lender in case you default.

At the end of the day, saving for a down payment takes patience, persistence, and a little bit of creativity. But trust me, when you're finally able to turn the key and step into your very own home, all that hard work will be worth it.

Mortgages

When it comes to choosing a mortgage, there are a few different options to consider. Fixed-rate mortgages offer predictable monthly payments over the life of the loan, while adjustable-rate mortgages (ARMs) may start with a lower interest rate but can fluctuate over time based on market conditions. There are also government-backed loan programs, such as FHA and VA loans, which can offer more flexible qualification requirements and lower down payment options for certain borrowers.

Ultimately, the type of mortgage that's right for you will depend on your individual financial situation and goals. It's important to do your research, compare rates and terms from multiple lenders, and choose a loan that aligns with your long-term financial plan.

Think Big Picture

When you're gearing up to shop for a home, it's crucial to keep your financial feet on the ground. Just because a bank might be willing to throw a mountain of money your way doesn't mean you should use it all to buy your dream castle. Remember, *the bank wants to load you up with debt for as long as possible—* because that means more money for them.

Sure, the idea of living in a home fit for royalty sounds great until you remember that castles come with royal upkeep costs too! Instead, take a good look at your income, debts, and how much you want to save for things like future vacations. Pick a home that fits your budget comfortably. Your bank account will thank you, and you'll still be able to afford your Netflix subscription.

Remember Maintenance

Ah, the delicate dance of budgeting for home maintenance—a tango where every move must be precise, every task foreseen, lest your hot water heater decides it's time for a spontaneous lunar vacation, oblivious to the roof in its path.

Let's say you have a humble abode valued at $100,000. Following the sage advice of financial gurus, you might want to earmark around 1% to 3% of that value annually for maintenance. That translates to roughly $83 to $250 a month, give or take, depending on the quirks and whims of your particular homestead.

Now, don't go digging behind the couch cushions for exact change just yet. Remember, this figure isn't set in stone; it's more like a compass pointing you in the general direction of financial preparedness. Some months, you might breeze through needing to replace only a lightbulb, while others might demand a bit more coin for unexpected surprises.

The key is to start with a solid estimate, stay nimble, and always keep a little extra in your back pocket for those inevitable "*home, sweet home*" moments.

Retirement Savings for Young Adults

When you're young and just starting out in your career, retirement can feel like a distant and abstract concept. After all, you have decades ahead of you to worry about saving for the future, right?

Well, not exactly. You've heard it before... *the earlier you start saving, the more time your money has to grow and compound over time*. In fact, thanks to the power of compound interest, even small contributions, especially early on, can have a significant impact on your retirement nest egg way down the line.

410K

So, how can you get started with retirement savings as a teen or young adult? One of the best options is to take advantage of employer-sponsored retirement plans, such as 401(k)s or pension plans. Many employers offer matching contributions, which means they'll match a certain percentage of the money you contribute to your retirement account. This is essentially free money that can help supercharge your savings over time.

If your employer doesn't offer a retirement plan or you're self-employed, you can also open an individual retirement account (IRA) on your own. There are two main types of IRAs: traditional and Roth. With a traditional IRA, you pay taxes when you retire. With a Roth IRA, you pay taxes before the money goes into the account.

I know that's getting into blah territory, so just remember this—when dealing with the whole "traditional" vs. "Roth" IRA thing, it really just depends on when you want to deal with taxes—now or later. For now, just remember that the most important thing is to start saving as early as possible so your money has plenty of time to grow!

Thinking Way (WAY) Ahead

The retirement conundrum—a perplexing puzzle where dreams of jet-setting clash with the allure of lazy afternoons with a good book. Do you envision sipping Mai Tais on a beach in Bora Bora, or do you imagine yourself being more of a *"binge-watch TV in your pajamas"* kind of retiree?

Whether you're plotting a lavish lifestyle filled with yachts and caviar or dreaming of cozy nights by the fireplace with loved ones and a faithful four-legged friend, your retirement savings plan needs to be as unique as you are. After all, there's no one-size-fits-all approach to funding your golden years. It's all about finding that perfect balance between living your best life and not having to shake your piggy bank upside down to make ends meet.

The 80% Rule

One helpful rule of thumb is the "80% rule," which suggests that you'll need to replace about 80% of your pre-retirement income to maintain your standard of living in retirement. So, if you're currently earning $50,000 per year, you'll need to have enough savings to generate about $40,000 per year in retirement.

Of course, this is just a rough estimate, and your actual retirement needs may vary based on a variety of factors, such as your health, life expectancy, and inflation rates. That's why it's important to work with a financial advisor or use online retirement calculators to create a personalized savings plan that takes into account your unique circumstances and goals.

The key is to start saving as early and as consistently as possible, even if you can only afford to contribute a small amount each month. Over time, those small contributions can add up to a significant nest egg that will provide you with financial security and freedom in your golden years.

Wrap-Up

At your age, it's easy to feel like the future is a distant, abstract concept and that you have all the time in the world to worry about things like buying a car, paying for college, planning a wedding, buying a home, and saving for retirement. However, the truth is that these significant financial milestones are headed your way a whole lot faster than you realize.

By taking the time to educate yourself about these upcoming expenses and the strategies you can use to manage them, you'll be able to navigate them predictably when it's time. With a little bit of foresight, planning, and discipline, you can manage these major financial milestones with confidence and set yourself up for a bright and secure future.

Activity: Life Expense Project

If you're ready to start planning for a major life expense, like buying a home, planning a wedding, or saving for retirement, this step-by-step activity will help you create a detailed and actionable plan. Let's get started!

Step 1—Choose your goal: Pick a major life expense that you want to start saving for. It could be something in the near future, like buying a car or paying for college, or a longer-term goal, like a down payment on a house or a dream vacation. Write down your chosen expense and make it specific.

Step 2—Research the costs: Once you have your goal in mind, it's time to do some research. Use online resources, such as real estate listings, wedding planning websites, or college cost calculators, to get a realistic estimate of how much money you'll need to save. Don't forget to factor in related expenses, like closing costs when buying a home or textbooks and supplies for college.

Step 3—Set a timeline: Now that you have a savings target in mind, break it down into smaller, more manageable milestones. Set realistic deadlines for each milestone based on your income, expenses, and other financial commitments. For example, if you're saving for a down payment on a house, you might aim to save $5,000 in the first year, $10,000 in the second year, and so on until you reach your goal.

Step 4—Identify potential obstacles: Life has a way of throwing curveballs when we least expect it. Take some time to brainstorm potential roadblocks or challenges that could impact your ability to save, such as unexpected expenses, changes in income, or competing financial priorities. Come up with strategies for overcoming these obstacles and staying on track with your savings plan.

Step 5—Create a budget: To turn your plan into action, you'll need a detailed budget that accounts for your income, expenses, and savings goals. Look for areas where you can cut back on discretionary spending, like dining out or subscription services, and redirect that money toward your savings. Consider boosting your income through side hustles, freelance work, or selling unwanted items. To make saving easier, set up automatic transfers from your checking account to a dedicated savings account each month.

Step 6—Track your progress: Staying motivated is key to achieving any long-term goal. Create a visual representation of your savings plan, such as a chart or graph, and update it regularly to track your progress. Celebrate each milestone along the way and use any setbacks as an opportunity to reassess and adjust your plan as needed.

By following these steps and staying committed to your goal, you'll have a huge head-start on planning for your major life expenses. Remember, the earlier you start saving and planning, the more time you'll have to reach your target and the less stress you'll feel along the way.

Chapter 10

Philanthropy and Financial Sharing

No one is useless in this world who lightens the burdens of another. —Charles Dickens

Philanthropy involves donating money, resources, or time to help make life better for other people. This practice isn't just about the impact you can make on the world—significant as that is—it also enriches your own life.

When you give your time, skills, or money to a cause you care about, you're not just helping others—you're also gaining a sense of purpose, connection, and fulfillment that can't be measured in dollars and cents.

The Importance of Giving Back

It's easy to get caught up in our own lives and struggles, especially when we're young and still figuring things out. But the truth is, we're all part of something much bigger than ourselves—a community, a society, a world that needs our help.

When we give back, we're not just making a difference in the lives of others—we're also strengthening the very fabric of our communities. Think about it: every time you volunteer at a local food bank, donate to a school fundraiser, or support a charity that provides clean water to families in need, you're helping to create a more compassionate and sustainable world for everyone.

Tithing

One approach to giving back is to commit to donating a percentage of your income, such as 10%, to causes you care about. This practice, known as tithing, has roots in various religious traditions but has been adopted by many as a way to make giving a regular habit.

By setting aside a portion of your income for tithing, you ensure that giving back remains a priority even as your financial situation changes. You can choose to donate your 10% to a single cause or spread it out among multiple organizations that align with your values.

Perspective Shift

The benefits of giving back go beyond just the tangible impact on others. Studies have shown that engaging in philanthropy and volunteering can actually boost our own well-being and happiness. When we focus on helping others, we shift our attention away from our own problems and gain a sense of perspective and gratitude. We also build connections with like-minded people and develop new skills and knowledge that can serve us well in other areas of our lives.

In fact, some experts believe that cultivating a habit of generosity and giving back can be one of the most powerful things we can do for our mental and emotional health. It's a way of tapping into our innate desire to be part of something larger than ourselves and to use our unique gifts and talents to make a difference in the world.

The Ripple Effect

Of course, giving back doesn't have to mean donating large sums of money or dedicating all your free time to volunteering. Even small acts of kindness and generosity can have a ripple effect, inspiring others to pay it forward and creating a culture of compassion and mutual support.

Imagine if everyone in your community committed to doing one small act of kindness or generosity each day. Whether it's helping a neighbor with their groceries, donating a few dollars to a local charity, or simply offering a smile and a kind word to someone who looks like they could use it. Over time, those small actions would add up to a tidal wave of positive change, transforming your community from the inside out.

So, as you navigate your own financial journey, don't forget to make room for giving back. Whether it's through volunteering your time, donating your money, or simply spreading kindness and compassion wherever you go, every act of generosity matters—and it all starts with you.

Finding Causes You Care About

Now that we've established why giving back is so important, let's talk about how to get started. One of the biggest challenges many people face when it comes to philanthropy is figuring out where to direct their time, energy, and resources. With so many worthy causes and organizations out there, it can be overwhelming to know where to begin.

The Big Questions

That's why the first step in any philanthropic journey is to identify the causes and issues that truly resonate with you.

- What are the problems in the world that keep you up at night?
- What are the injustices that make your blood boil?
- What are the dreams and aspirations you have for your community, your country, or the planet as a whole?

These are the questions that can help guide you toward the causes and organizations that align with your deepest values and passions. Because when you're working on something that truly matters to you, it doesn't feel like work at all. It feels like a calling, a purpose, a way of making your mark on the world.

What's Important To You - and Why?

One way to start identifying your philanthropic priorities is to take some time for self-reflection and exploration. Write down a list of the issues and causes that you care about most, and think about why they matter to you.

- Maybe you're passionate about protecting the environment because you grew up near a beautiful natural area that's now under threat from development.
- Maybe you're committed to fighting poverty because you've seen firsthand how lack of access to education and opportunity can hold people back.
- Maybe you're dedicated to supporting the arts because you believe in the power of creativity and self-expression to transform lives and communities.

Whatever your reasons, take the time to really understand what drives you and what you want to achieve through your philanthropic efforts. This will help you narrow down your focus and find organizations and initiatives that align with your goals and values.

Once you have a sense of what matters most to you, it's time to start researching potential charities and non-profit organizations to support. This is where due diligence comes in—because not all charitable organizations are created equal, and it's important to make sure your hard-earned money and time are going to reputable, effective, and transparent groups.

Navigating Charities

One excellent resource for researching charities is Charity Navigator, a website that provides detailed ratings and information on thousands of non-profit organizations. You can search for charities by cause, location, or rating, and get a clear picture of their financial health, accountability, and transparency.

Other helpful resources include GuideStar, which provides in-depth financial and programmatic data on non-profits, and the Better Business Bureau's Wise Giving Alliance, which sets standards for charitable accountability and evaluates organizations based on those criteria.

When researching potential charities to support, it's important to look beyond just the surface-level marketing and branding. Take the time to read through their mission statements, annual reports, and financial statements to get a sense of how they operate and what kind of impact they're having.

Look for organizations with a clear track record of success, a commitment to transparency and accountability, and a focus on long-term, sustainable change rather than short-term band-aid solutions.

Local, National, or Global

It's also worth considering whether you want to focus your philanthropic efforts on local, national, or global causes. Each level of impact has its own unique challenges and opportunities, and there's no one-size-fits-all answer.

Some people prefer to support local organizations that are making a difference in their own backyard. In contrast, others are drawn to global initiatives that address systemic issues on a broader scale. Ultimately, the key is to find a balance that feels right for you and aligns with your personal values and priorities.

Remember, finding causes you care about is an ongoing process. Your priorities and interests may shift over time as you learn and grow. But by starting with a clear sense of what matters most to you and doing your due diligence to find reputable organizations to support, you'll be well on your way to making a meaningful impact through your philanthropic efforts.

CAUTION: Not All Causes Are Noble

In today's world of social media and instant information, it's easy to get caught up in the hype surrounding various causes and movements. However, not all causes are created equal, and some even have hidden agendas and misinformation at their core.

These shameful causes heavily rely on people being uninformed and fueled by strong emotions, such as anger, fear, or a sense of injustice. They may use inflammatory language or sensationalized stories to provoke an emotional response rather than presenting a balanced and factual perspective. By preying on people's emotions and lack of knowledge, these causes can quickly gain traction and support, even if their underlying goals or methods are twisted and harmful.

One of the first steps in educating yourself on the true purpose of the cause, charity, or movement is to look beyond the surface-level messaging and dig deeper into the facts and data behind the scenes. Be wary of sources that seem to push a particular agenda or that rely heavily on anecdotal evidence rather than hard facts.

Ask yourself:

- Who stands to benefit from this cause?
- Is this cause built on a foundation of love or hate?
- Is it's purpose to tear people down or build them up?
- Are there any hidden political or financial interests at play?
- Are the leaders transparent about their goals?

By critically examining the underlying factors behind a cause, you can better assess whether it aligns with your own values and priorities.

Another key aspect of educating yourself is to seek out diverse perspectives and engage in open-minded dialogue with others. Don't just surround yourself with people who already agree with you. Actively seek out differing viewpoints and be willing to listen and learn from those who may challenge your assumptions. This can help you gain a more nuanced and well-rounded understanding of complex issues, and can also help you identify potential red flags or areas of concern.

Ultimately, the key to avoiding false causes is to approach philanthropy and activism with a critical and discerning eye. Don't just follow the crowd or jump on the latest bandwagon. Take the time to educate yourself, ask tough questions, and make informed decisions based on facts and evidence. By doing so, you can ensure that your efforts to make a difference in the world are truly meaningful, effective, and positive.

Volunteering Your Time

While donating money to charitable causes is undoubtedly important, it's not the only way to make a difference in the world. In fact, one of the most potent forms of philanthropy is volunteering your time and skills to support the causes you care about.

Volunteering offers a unique opportunity to get hands-on with the issues and organizations you're passionate about and to see the impact of your efforts firsthand. Whether you're tutoring kids at a local school, helping out at a community garden, or using your professional skills to support a non-profit's mission, volunteering allows you to be an active participant in creating positive change.

Skill-Based Volunteering

One particularly impactful way to volunteer is through skills-based volunteering, where you use your unique expertise and experience to support a charitable organization's work.

For example, if you're a graphic designer, you could volunteer to create marketing materials for a local non-profit. If you're a web developer, you could help build a website for a grassroots advocacy group. If you're a writer, you could contribute content to a charity's blog or newsletter.

Skills-based volunteering not only allows you to make a tangible difference in the work of a charitable organization, but it also offers a chance to build your skills and experience in a meaningful way. It's a win-win situation. You get to give back to a cause you care about while also sharpening your own skillset along the way.

Making Connections

Another benefit of volunteering is the opportunity to build connections with like-minded individuals and organizations. When you volunteer, you're joining a community of people who share your passion for making a difference in the world. You'll meet new friends, learn from experienced activists and leaders, and become part of a network of changemakers who support and inspire each other.

These connections can be particularly valuable for young people who are just starting out in their careers or exploring their personal and professional interests. Volunteering can open doors to new opportunities, mentorship relationships, and even job prospects down the line. It's a way of building social capital and expanding your horizons in a way that feels authentic and aligned with your values.

The Role of Youth in Philanthropy

When it comes to philanthropy and financial sharing, young people have a particularly unique and powerful role to play. As the leaders of tomorrow, you have the energy, creativity, and vision to drive social change and build a better world for everyone.

Fresh Perspectives

One of the key ways that young people can make a difference through philanthropy is by bringing fresh perspectives and new ideas to the table. Because youth are often less constrained by traditional ways of thinking and doing things, they're able to approach problems with a sense of curiosity, experimentation, and innovation. They're not afraid to challenge the status quo or to imagine bold new solutions to complex challenges.

This kind of outside-the-box thinking is precisely what's needed to tackle some of the most significant issues facing our world today. From environmental issues to social inequality to healthcare access to educational disparities. By bringing your unique perspective and skills to bear on these challenges, you have the potential to create real, lasting change.

Advocating For Change

Another way that youth can make a difference through philanthropy is by serving as powerful advocates and change agents within their communities. Because young people are often deeply connected to the issues and challenges facing their peers and neighbors, they're uniquely positioned to raise awareness, mobilize support, and drive grassroots action.

For example, imagine a group of high school students who are passionate about reducing food waste and hunger in their community. They could start by organizing a food drive at their school, collecting surplus food from local businesses and farms, and distributing it to families in need. They could also advocate for policy changes at the local level, such as incentives for businesses to donate excess food or funding for school meal programs.

By taking action and speaking out on the issues that matter most to them, young people can inspire others to get involved and create a ripple effect of positive change. They can also build valuable leadership skills and gain a sense of empowerment and agency in shaping the world around them.

Barriers For Participation

Of course, getting involved in philanthropy and financial sharing as a young person isn't always easy. Many youth face barriers to participation, such as lack of access to resources, limited time and energy, or skepticism from adults who may not take their ideas and contributions seriously.

That's why it's so important for adults—whether they're parents, teachers, mentors, or community leaders—to support and empower young people in their philanthropic efforts. This can mean providing resources and guidance, connecting youth with like-minded organizations and individuals, or simply listening to their ideas and taking them seriously.

It's also important for young people themselves to seek out opportunities for education and leadership development in the philanthropic space. This can include attending workshops and conferences, joining youth-led organizations and networks, or seeking out mentorship from experienced activists and changemakers.

Connected Community

By investing in their own learning and growth, young people can build the skills, knowledge, and confidence they need to be effective advocates and leaders in the philanthropic world. They can also connect with a community of peers who share their passion for making a difference and who can offer support, inspiration, and accountability along the way.

Ultimately, the role of youth in philanthropy is about recognizing the incredible potential and power that young people have to create positive change in the world. By empowering and supporting youth to get involved in charitable giving and volunteering, we're not only making a difference in the lives of others—we're also investing in the future leaders and changemakers who will shape our world for generations to come.

Activity: Charity Research Project

Enhance your understanding of philanthropy and discover how you can contribute to causes you care about.

Step 1: Identify Your Interests

Write down three issues or causes that you are passionate about. These could range from environmental conservation to supporting education for underprivileged children.

Step 2: Research

Choose one cause from your list. Use the internet to find three charities that work in this area. Look for information on their missions, the work they do, and their impact.

Step 3: Evaluate Credibility

For each charity, check their transparency and credibility. Use resources like Charity Navigator, GuideStar, or the Better Business Bureau to see ratings and reviews.

Step 4: Interview or Visit

If possible, arrange a visit or a virtual meeting with a representative from one of the charities. Prepare at least five questions about how they use donations, their significant projects, and how volunteers can get involved.

Step 5: Reflect

Write a one-page reflection on what you learned. Include:

- Why the cause is important to you?
- Which charity did you feel most aligned with and why?
- How can you see yourself contributing to the cause in the future, either through donations, volunteering, or raising awareness?

By completing this project, you will gain a better understanding of how charitable organizations operate and the significant impact your contributions can make. You'll also develop skills in research, critical thinking, and effective communication.

Chapter 11

Conclusion

First off, a **_HUGE congratulations_** to you!

You've made it to the end of our journey together through the world of personal finance. You've learned practical tips and strategies for managing your money, as well as the mindset and habits that can set you up for long-term financial success.

But more than that, **_you've taken a measurable step towards financial literacy and empowerment_**. By dedicating your time and attention to this book, you've shown a commitment to understanding and taking control of your future.

Thank you for choosing to invest in yourself and your financial future.

Thank you for giving me the opportunity to share my knowledge and insights with you.

Thank you for being a part of a growing movement of young people who are taking control of their financial lives and blazing a trail toward a brighter tomorrow.

Keep learning, keep growing, and most of all, keep believing in yourself and your limitless potential.

With gratitude and admiration,

Ben Clardy

Growth Mindset for Teens

Build Confidence, Boost Resilience, and Unlock Your Full Potential in School and Beyond

GROWTH
M I N D S E T
FOR TEENS

Build Self-Confidence, Boost Resilience, and Unlock Your Full Potential in School and Beyond

DARE TO
CREATE YOUR
BEST LIFE

BEN CLARDY

Chapter 1
Changing Your Mindset

"You grow through what you go through."
— Tyrese Gibson

The sound of sneakers squeaking against polished hardwood fills the gym as you stand there, heart racing. It's time for basketball tryouts. You've been counting down the days, visualizing this moment for weeks. But now that you're here, your mind betrays you with snapshots from last summer. All those missed shots in your backyard, the ball clanking off the rim again and again.

The thought creeps in before you can stop it:

"Maybe I'm just not cut out for this."

That right there? That's what psychologists call a *fixed mindset* — the silent voice whispering that your abilities are carved in stone and that past failures predict future ones. It's like wearing invisible chains that hold you back from reaching your full potential.

But here's the thing about those invisible, mental chains:

Once you learn to recognize them, *you can break them.*

Fixed Mindset vs. Growth Mindset

Picture two students both getting C's on their math tests. The first student slumps in their chair, thinking, *"This proves it — I'm just bad at math."* The second thinks, *"Okay, I guess I need to study more."*

Same class. Same grade. Two completely different takeaways.

That first student? They're stuck in a fixed mindset, believing their abilities are like concrete — once set, they never change. It's comfortable in a way because if you can't change then why even try?

The trouble with a fixed mindset is that it's a trap. It keeps you locked inside a box that you built without even knowing it. You're trapped by your own expectations, leaving little room for improvement, resilience, or discovery.

The second student? They're practicing a growth mindset. They see that C not as a reflection of their worth but as feedback — *valuable feedback* — that can be applied to get a better result next time. This mindset can transform a setback into a comeback. Maybe they'll try new study techniques, ask for help after class, or break down complex problems into smaller pieces.

For the second student, it's not just about the grade anymore; it's about the journey of becoming better. And here's the real magic: that second student isn't just learning math — they're building a toolkit of resilience and adaptability that will serve them far beyond any single test or classroom.

Mindsets Aren't Permanent

It's not as simple as being either "*Team Fixed*" or "*Team Growth.*" Instead, imagine a slider that moves back and forth depending on the situation. Maybe you have a growth mindset about sports but get stuck in fixed thinking when it comes to public speaking.

The goal isn't to flip some magical switch to *"GROWTH-MODE ACTIVATED!* Instead, the goal is to learn how to catch yourself when you're in that fixed space and gently shift your thinking into a more growth-oriented mindset.

Take Marcus, for example. Now, a seasoned chef who can coax magic out of the simplest ingredients. Ten years ago, you wouldn't have found him within ten feet of a kitchen. "*I burn water,*" he used to joke, but beneath the self-deprecating humor lay a genuine belief: cooking was something other people could do. People with natural talent. People who grew up learning family recipes. Not him. Every attempt at making dinner ended with takeout and a sink full of ruined pots.

But something shifted when his grandmother got sick. She'd always been the one to make his favorite dish – a delicious curry that filled the house with warmth and memories. Watching her health decline, Marcus faced a choice: let the recipe die with her, or push through his fear of failure.

He started small, just chopping vegetables at her kitchen table while she directed from her chair. Each weekend, he'd try one component of the dish. The onions burned the first five times. The spices were never quite right. But instead of seeing each mistake as proof that he *"just wasn't a cook,"* he started viewing them as steps toward mastery.

That curry became his gateway to a whole new relationship with cooking. Once he proved to himself that he could learn one dish, the fixed mindset began to crack — *the chains began to fall away*. He started watching cooking shows not with envy but with curiosity. Each failed recipe became a new puzzle to solve. A new challenge that brought him closer to his goal.

Today, Marcus teaches cooking classes, and he starts each session by sharing stories of his *"burning-water days."* He now recognizes, clear as day, that same old fixed mindset in his students' eyes — the belief that they're just "*not good at cooking.*" But he knows better. He's learned that culinary skill isn't some fixed trait you're born with, but a skill you gradually master, one burnt entrée at a time.

What changed for Marcus?

He shifted the way he viewed setbacks and challenges. Rather than seeing them as reasons to quit, he began using them as opportunities for improvement.

The Science Behind the Mindset

Each time you learn something new, your brain physically changes. It's what scientists call *neuroplasticity*. It creates new connections between neurons, strengthening pathways like well-worn trails in a forest. When you embrace a growth mindset, you're not just thinking differently — you're literally rewiring your brain for resilience and learning!

Dr. Carol Dweck, the researcher who first identified these mindset patterns, found something fascinating in her studies. When students learned about how their brains could grow and change, their motivation and grades improved. The simple act of understanding that improvement is possible actually makes it more likely to happen. Simply knowing that you *can* change makes it more likely that you *will* change.

If there is just one thing that you take away from this entire book, remember this:

The moment you truly understand that your abilities can grow — *that your intelligence, your talents, your capabilities aren't fixed* — you've already won! **This single realization is the key that unlocks everything else.**

Highlight it, circle it, tear this page out and pin it on your wall... whatever it takes to remember that this is the spark that lights the fire. The first domino that sets all others in motion.

Keep this in mind as we go forward.

One Word That Changes Everything

We all have that inner critic. That little, annoying voice that loves to remind us of every mistake, every awkward moment, every failure.

But what if we could teach that voice a new language?

Great news... *you can* — and it all starts with one little word:

YET.

Next time you catch yourself thinking, *"I can't,"* just add that one word to the end.

Here's how drastically it changes things...

*"I can't solve these equations... **yet**."*

*"I'm not good at public speaking... **yet**."*

That single word transforms dead ends into doorways.

When you say, *"I can't do this **yet**,"* you're telling your brain there's hope — that with effort, with time, with practice, you can and will improve.

But this isn't just feel-good philosophy. Science backs it up.

Research shows that people with growth mindsets:

- Bounce back faster from setbacks
- Take on more difficult challenges
- Learn from criticism instead of avoiding it
- Achieve more of their goals

It's like they've unlocked a cheat code for life. Not because things are easier for them, but because they see challenges from a vastly different perspective than most people. You can do the same.

"Shy Kai" and the Ripple Effect

Think of your mindset like a small stone dropped into a still pond. The ripples slowly spread outward, touching areas of your life you might not expect.

To illustrate this, let me share a story about Kai, a quiet kid who sat in the very back of his English class.

Kai started the year believing he was *"just shy."* But when we talked about a growth mindset, something clicked. He began seeing his social skills as something he could develop, rather than being a fixed trait.

The first small step forward was simple. He challenged himself to say "*hey*" to one new person each day. That's it. Just a simple "*hey.*" The first few times, his voice shook, and he quickly looked away. But each small success built on the last.

After a week, he started adding "*How was your weekend?*" to his *"heys."* When group work came around, instead of silently nodding along, he pushed himself to ask one question about the assignment. Some days were more challenging than others — there were still moments when his heart raced before speaking up. But rather than seeing these moments as proof that he was "*too shy,*" he began viewing them as practice rounds.

Each interaction, whether smooth or awkward, was another rep in building his social confidence. By the end of the first month, something remarkable happened: during a class discussion about *The Great Gatsby*, Kai raised his hand. Not just to answer a question, but to challenge another student's interpretation!

His voice was steady, his points clear. The same kid who once hid in the back row was now sparking deep classroom debates and connecting with classmates in ways he never thought possible. Not because he magically became a different person, but because he gave himself permission to grow.

Here's where Kai's story gets even more interesting:

His confidence rippled outwards.

His grades improved, not because he suddenly got smarter, but because he started asking questions when he was confused instead of hiding his uncertainty. Where once he nodded silently through confusion, he began raising his hand: "*Could you explain that another way, please?*" Each question felt like revealing a secret at first, but as classmates chimed in with, "*I was wondering that too,*" Kai realized questions weren't exposing weakness — they were building strength.

When the school newspaper put out a call for new writers, something unexpected happened. Instead of immediately thinking, *"I could never,"* Kai heard a tiny voice asking, "*Why not?*" He started with small assignments — covering school assemblies and interviewing teachers he knew. By spring, he was pitching his ideas and working on feature stories. Each new challenge still brought butterflies to Kai's stomach, but he noticed something interesting... *they felt more like excitement rather than fear.*

That's the thing about mindset work. It's never just about improving one area. The improvements tend to overflow and seep into other areas. It's contagious in the best possible way!

The confidence Kai built in English class spilled into Spanish, where he stopped worrying about perfect pronunciation and started actually conversing. The shy kid from the back of English class didn't disappear — he evolved into a fuller version of himself, one who understood that discomfort wasn't a wall to hide behind, but a door to walk through.

Growth is a Lifelong Journey

A growth mindset isn't something you achieve once and check off your list. It's a practice you return to again and again. Think of it like tending a garden. You don't plant seeds once and expect them to bloom forever. You water, you weed, you adapt to the seasons. Sometimes, storms will come and damage what you've grown. But instead of seeing destruction, you start to see opportunities – chances to rebuild stronger, to try new techniques, to grow something even more beautiful than before. Every setback becomes soil for future growth.

This journey you've embarked on isn't about erasing doubt or fear. Those are innate parts of being human. Instead, it's about building a deeper trust in your ability to learn, to adapt, to rise again. Each time you choose to see a challenge as an invitation rather than a barrier, you're strengthening this trust. Each time you replace "*I can't*" with "*I can't **yet**,*" you're planting a seed for future breakthroughs.

The beauty is that it starts exactly where you are, with the very next choice you make. Maybe that's taking on a project that scares you, or returning to something you've always thought you couldn't do. Perhaps it's simply catching yourself in a moment of fixed thinking and asking, "*What if I looked at this differently?*"

These small shifts, these tiny moments of choosing growth over fear – *they add up.* Day by day, choice by choice, they build into something extraordinary: a life where challenges don't diminish you, but reveal what you're capable of becoming.

TRY IT: Create your first YET statement

Take a few minutes to catch your fixed mindset in action:

1. Think of a time that you wanted to do something, but you told yourself, *"I'm not good at that."* Write it here: _____
2. Now add *"yet"* to the end of that statement and write it again: _____ **...yet.**
3. What's one small step you could take this week toward changing this belief? Write it here: _____

This simple shift in language can begin to change how you think about your abilities. Post your *"yet statement"* somewhere you'll see it daily as a reminder that you're always capable of growth.

Chapter 2
Embracing Challenges

"All things are difficult before they are easy."
–Thomas Fuller

The assembly hall pulses with nervous energy. Conversations bounce off the walls, mixing with the whir and hum of dozens of science fair projects coming to life.

A robot arm extends with mechanical precision. Chemical reactions bloom in vibrant colors. And here you stand, next to your carefully crafted solar system model, wondering if you've made a terrible mistake.

Why didn't I choose something more impressive?

The judging begins in ten minutes. Your heart quickens as you imagine the questions coming your way. Every rotation of your model's planets feels slower and more clunky than before. As you make final adjustments to Saturn's rings, you notice some uncomfortable feelings within you.

That unsteady tremble in your hands?

That flutter in the pit of your stomach?

That electric tension buzzing in your mind?

Here's what most people miss in moments like these:

Despite the discomfort of these feelings, <u>they're not warning signs.</u>

Instead, these uncomfortable impulses are your brain's way of letting you know that you're in the zone where growth is actively happening.

The invisible zone we're talking about here *is just beyond your comfort zone,* and there are endless situations in life that will push you there, such as:

- Intimidating science fair presentations
- Math problems that seem utterly impossible
- Asking your crush to go to the movies
- Raising your hand in class when you're not 100% confident
- Sitting with a new group at lunch
- Auditioning for the school musical or play
- Starting a conversation with someone you want to be friends with
- The sports tryout that tests your limits
- Speaking up when you see someone being treated unfairly
- Sharing your art or writing with others
- Standing up to peer pressure

The potential situations are endless, but the interesting thing about it is that each time you're presented with a new challenge, you essentially only have two options for how to react:

Option #1: Retreat back into your comfort zone and stay the same

Option #2: Push beyond your comfort zone **and grow**

Why Challenges are Essential for Growth

Life has a way of continuously presenting us with obstacles. While it's natural to wish for an easier path, these challenges aren't accidents or unfortunate detours — *they're the very foundation of our personal development*!

Every time you step outside your comfort zone, you expand your understanding of what's possible.

Is it uncomfortable? *Yep!*

Will you sometimes fail? *Yep!*

When you're beyond the bounds of your comfort zone, your mind resists, and your confidence wavers. But with each unsteady step forward, you map new terrain in your capabilities.

Consider Sarah, a freshman who joined her school's debate team despite being absolutely terrified of public speaking.

Her first attempt was exactly what she feared. Her voice shook, she lost her train of thought, and she sat down feeling utterly defeated.

But she came back the following week.

And the week after that.

Each debate taught her something new. She learned to channel her nervous energy into preparation. She discovered that stumbling over words wasn't fatal — *it was just feedback about where to focus her practice*. Most importantly, she learned that confidence isn't something you wait to feel before taking action — *it's something you build through facing challenges*.

This is how *real growth* happens. Not through comfortable repetition of what you already know, but through the willingness to attempt what lies just beyond your current abilities and comfort.

Musicians don't become great by playing only the pieces they've mastered. Artists don't evolve by staying within familiar techniques. Scientists don't make breakthroughs by exploring only what's already known.

They grow by embracing *the edge of possibility*.

It's this mental shift that transforms every challenge from a threat into an opportunity for growth.

Learning to Embrace the Process

Real growth happens when we engage with challenges fully, not just endure them. Anyone can grit their teeth and push through difficulty, but the magic happens when we fully embrace these challenging moments and accept them as the opportunities that they are.

This shift in perspective changes everything.

Think about your most recent challenge. Maybe you bombed a presentation. Froze during a game. Stared at a blank page, unable to write that first sentence. That flutter in your stomach, that anxious tension in your mind? Most people interpret those feelings as warning signs. They pull back. Play it safe. Stay comfortable.

But what if these feelings weren't warnings at all?

What if they were signals pointing you toward growth?

Learn to welcome that spark of nervous energy. Chase that feeling of being right on the edge of your capabilities. The most significant moments of growth happen when you're slightly uncomfortable, when the challenge feels just beyond your current reach.

The key lies in asking different questions.

Not *"Why am I so bad at this?"* but *"What could make this better?"*

Not *"When will this get easier?"* but *"What am I learning from this difficulty?"*

Not *"How can I avoid this feeling?"* but *"What opportunities does this tension reveal?"*

These questions transform challenges from threats into experiments. They convert anxiety into curiosity. They turn setbacks into data points. Most importantly, they shift your focus from judgment to growth. This isn't just positive thinking — *it's about **intentional** thinking* — the kind that produces lasting, positive growth.

Of course, the resulting transformation isn't immediate or constant. Some days, old doubts creep back in. Nervousness still appears before important moments. But now you understand these feelings differently. They're not warning signs — they're growth signals. They're not telling you to stop — they're showing you where to push forward.

Those butterflies in your stomach before a performance? *Welcome them.*

That tension before a big game? *Embrace it.*

The nervous energy before a presentation? *Let it fuel you.*

These feelings aren't your enemy. They're signals that you're alive, growing, pushing into new territory. They're the feeling of potential becoming reality.

This is where real growth lives — not in the comfortable spaces, but right at the edge of your current abilities. Learn to love that edge. Seek it out. Because that's where challenges meet opportunity, where potential meets growth, where you discover what you're truly capable of becoming.

The Power of Strategic Feedback

Every success and failure contains hidden lessons. Most people miss them entirely, seeing only the outcome.

Consider how a skilled athlete prepares for competition. They don't just practice;

- They film their performance
- They study their movements
- They analyze their decisions under pressure

Each review reveals subtle patterns: a slight hesitation before crucial plays, a tendency to rush when tired, and moments of perfect form that can be replicated. This detailed analysis transforms vague impressions into precise insights.

We all have blind spots — patterns we can't see because we're too close to them. External feedback fills these gaps in our perception. A teacher might notice that you grasp concepts intuitively but skip crucial steps in showing your work. A coach might spot tension in your form that you've never noticed. A peer might point out that your ideas are brilliant, but your explanations jump too quickly between points.

This feedback isn't criticism. It's a spotlight illuminating your path to improvement. When a music teacher points out that you speed up during complex passages, they're literally handing you the key to better performance. When a debate coach notes that your voice drops at the end of important points, they're giving you precise data that you can use to do better next time.

The most successful people in any field master this art of gathering and using feedback. This approach transforms random outcomes into reliable progress. Each piece of feedback adds another layer of understanding. What seemed like luck — *good or bad* — becomes a clear pattern you can adjust and improve. The more you understand these patterns, the more control you gain over your growth.

Sustaining Growth Through Challenges

Progress isn't a steady climb upward. Some days you surge ahead, mastering new skills and breaking through barriers. Other days you seem to slide backward, struggling with things that felt easy just yesterday. This inconsistency trips up many people who expect constant forward momentum.

Do not be confused or discouraged by this!

Think about learning a new song on guitar. One day, your fingers flow smoothly across the strings, hitting every note perfectly. The next day, you can barely remember where to place your hands. This isn't failure — it's your brain and body integrating new skills. Those apparent steps backward often precede significant breakthroughs.

The same pattern appears in every aspect of learning. Some days feel effortless and productive. Others feel like you're starting over from scratch. Understanding this pattern changes everything. Instead of getting discouraged by temporary setbacks, you begin to see them as natural rhythms in your growth. Those "*off days*" aren't failures — they're often signs that you're pushing your boundaries in precisely the right ways.

The key isn't to avoid these fluctuations but to work with them. Create systems that keep you moving forward even when motivation dips. Set aside specific times for practice. Prepare your environment to make showing up easier. Build in recovery periods — not as breaks from growth, but as essential parts of the process.

Most importantly, learn to measure progress over time rather than day to day. Look for trends across weeks and months rather than hours and days. Notice how setbacks often precede breakthroughs. Pay attention to how periods of apparent stagnation frequently lead to sudden improvements.

Remember: Growth isn't about perfection — *it's about persistence*. It's about getting back up after each setback, adjusting your approach when needed, and keeping your long-term direction even when the short-term path gets messy.

The Power of Shared Challenges

Growth might feel like a solitary journey, but the most significant breakthroughs often come through facing challenges together.

When we tackle complex tasks alone, it's easy to become overwhelmed or discouraged. With the right partners, those same challenges become opportunities for accelerated growth.

Our brains are wired for social learning. A challenging workout becomes more manageable with a training partner. An intricate piece of music feels more approachable when practiced with others. Complex problems become clearer when discussed with peers. This isn't coincidence — *it's human nature at work*.

The most effective growth partnerships balance challenge and support. They push us beyond our comfort zones while providing the encouragement needed to persist. Think of two students tackling advanced math problems together. They're sharing strategies, catching each other's mistakes, celebrating breakthroughs, and maintaining momentum when the problems get tough.

However, not all partnerships enhance growth. The key lies in finding people who share both your commitment to improvement and your willingness to embrace challenges.

Look for partners who:

- Welcome difficult tasks as learning opportunities
- Support you through struggles while maintaining high standards
- Offer honest feedback with genuine encouragement
- Help analyze setbacks rather than avoid them
- Celebrate effort as much as success

The right partnership transforms how you approach challenges. Complex tasks become interesting puzzles to solve together. Setbacks become shared learning experiences. Progress accelerates as you benefit from each other's insights and experiences.

Understanding the Bigger Picture

Every significant challenge you face reshapes your capabilities in ways that extend far beyond the immediate task. Each new challenge you embrace adds capabilities that serve you in unexpected ways.

Consider these real-world examples:

A student who persistently tackles complex subjects isn't just *"book smart."* They're developing:

- The ability to break overwhelming challenges into manageable pieces
- Comfort with uncertainty and complex problems
- Resilience through repeated effort and adjustment
- Systematic approaches to learning and growth

These same capabilities later help them excel ***in any challenging endeavor***, from starting a business to managing complex projects.

An athlete facing increasingly difficult training isn't just building physical skills. They're developing:

- The ability to push through discomfort productively
- Systematic approaches to improvement
- Recovery and adaptation strategies
- Mental toughness under pressure

Every challenge you face today prepares you for opportunities you can't yet imagine.

Think about that for a minute…

Those moments that push your limits, test your courage, and make your heart race — they're not just temporary obstacles…

<u>They're the building blocks of your future self.</u>

The courage you build facing one challenge becomes strength for more significant moments ahead. The resilience you develop through each setback transforms into an unshakeable core of confidence. The persistence you practice today becomes the power to pursue dreams you haven't even dreamed of yet!

Your future self will look back at these moments — not seeing the struggles, but recognizing them as the turning points where you began becoming who you were meant to be. What feels like a challenge today is actually the foundation of something extraordinary tomorrow.

TRY IT: Choose Discomfort

I'm going to make a wild guess that you're going to feel tempted to skip this activity. That *"I'd rather not"* feeling, is your limited mindset that's actively working to keep you comfortable, unchanged, and safe within your familiar *(but limiting)* patterns.

Can you feel yourself resisting?

If you can… *GOOD!*

This is an opportunity to take a step towards growth.

<u>Choose a current challenge in your life</u> — something that pushes you out of your comfort zone. It could be academic, athletic, social, or personal.

<u>WRITE IT DOWN</u>:

1. The challenge you want to tackle

2. One small step you'll take this week to face it

3. Someone who can support you along the way

Remember: The goal isn't perfection – *it's progress.*

By pushing past that initial resistance and writing it down, you've proven something critical to yourself:

You can choose growth over comfort!

Put this note somewhere you'll see it daily. Let it remind you that challenges aren't obstacles — ***they're opportunities.***

Chapter 3
Learning From Criticism

"Criticism is something we can avoid easily by saying nothing, doing nothing, and being nothing." – Aristotle

You're standing at the front of the classroom, your presentation notes clutched in sweating hands. Your heart is racing. In a few moments, you'll have to present your project to your entire class.

The worst part, is that this isn't just a regular presentation. It's *a peer feedback session* where the other students get to weigh in and critique both your project and your presentation skills.

Your mind is spinning with panicked thoughts:

What if they don't understand my topic?

What if I stumble over my words?

What if they think my project is stupid?

Listening to criticism isn't easy, especially when you've poured hours of work into something that feels deeply personal. The thought of your classmates picking apart your presentation makes your stomach twist into knots.

But here's the truth: feedback isn't about tearing you down. It's about helping you grow stronger, more confident, and more skilled. Every comment - even the ones that sting a little - is an opportunity to see your work through fresh eyes.

Imagine if you could transform that wave of anxiety into excitement about improving. What if, instead of dreading criticism, you started seeing it as a secret weapon for becoming better?

When you learn to look past the initial discomfort and focus on the core message, feedback becomes less about highlighting flaws and more about encouraging progress. It's like having a mirror held up that shows you exactly where you can shine even brighter.

Types of Criticism: Constructive vs. Destructive

Picture this:

You've just finished a presentation in class. Your heart's still racing when your friend leans over and whispers, *"Hey, you had great ideas, but you were speaking so fast I missed some of them. Try slowing down next time?"*

That's **constructive criticism**.

Then there's the kid in the back who snickers, *"Wow, that was painful to watch."*

That's **destructive criticism**.

See the difference?

One points toward improvement. The other just points and laughs. One offers a specific observation and a path forward; the other is just empty, meaningless words.

Constructive criticism is like having a trusted advisor in your corner. When another classmate mentions, *"The research was solid, but maybe add some visuals next time to help us follow along,"* they're not just pointing out what could be better — they're showing you how to make it better. They're giving you specific tools to level up your presentation game.

Destructive criticism? It's more like having a heckler in the crowd. *"You suck"* or *"I was bored"* offers no guidance, no purpose, no value. It's just words meant to shake your confidence. These comments might sting, but they're empty.

When you know what real feedback looks like, you can filter out the noise and focus on what helps you grow. That comment about speaking too fast? It's a gift — specific, actionable information you can use next time. The snicker from the back of the room? That's just static on the radio — tune it out.

This skill becomes your secret weapon in all presentations moving forward. When your teacher suggests breaking up long sections with discussion questions, that's gold — try it next time. When they recommend practicing in front of a mirror to work on eye contact, that's another tool for your toolkit. When someone just says "*boring,*" well, that tells you more about their small-minded limitations than anything that concerns you.

But here's where it gets interesting:

Learning to recognize good feedback doesn't just help you receive criticism better — it makes you better at giving it, too. Instead of telling a classmate, *"That was bad,"* you learn to say, "*The opening really grabbed my attention, but I lost track of the main points in the middle. Maybe try using transitions to connect your ideas?*" You become the kind of person who builds others up instead of tearing them down.

Think of it as developing your personal feedback filter. Every piece of criticism that comes your way goes through this filter. "*Try speaking slower*" — that's useful. "*Your voice sounds weird*" – that's meaningless noise that provides no value whatsoever.

This isn't just about surviving criticism — it's about using it as fuel for growth. Every piece of constructive feedback is a stepping stone toward becoming a more confident, skilled presenter. Every bit of destructive criticism becomes an opportunity to demonstrate resilience.

The real power comes when you start seeking out feedback instead of avoiding it. You begin to recognize that those moments of constructive criticism, though sometimes uncomfortable, are actually gold mines of opportunity.

Words have power. Constructive criticism harnesses that power for growth. Destructive criticism tries to use it for harm. Learning to tell the difference? That's real growth that you can use you're entire life.

The Power of Self-Reflection

Ever catch yourself replaying a moment in your mind? Maybe it's something someone said about your work, your ideas, your choices. The words echo, and suddenly, you're feeling all those emotions again.

This is where self-reflection begins.

Most people let these moments slip by, carrying the weight of criticism without examining what it means. Those who master self-reflection transform these echoes into insights.

Think about your last reaction to criticism. Really think about it.

Did you feel your defenses rise?

Did your mind start crafting comebacks before the person even finished speaking?

Or did you actually hear what they were saying?

Honest self-examination feels like cleaning out a closet – pulling everything into the light, examining each piece, and deciding what serves you.

Uncomfortable? *Yes.*

Transformative? *Absolutely.*

Try this: Next time you receive feedback, pause before reacting. Notice your immediate emotional response. Is your heart racing? Are your thoughts scattered? Are you already dismissing what you're hearing? These natural physical and emotional reactions reveal your deeper patterns.

Reflection Journaling

A reflection journal can be an invaluable tool to learn more about how you react to feedback. You can use an actual journal, a notebook, or even a note on your phone. Take note of both the feedback you receive and how you respond.

Look for patterns:

Do you reject criticism about specific topics?

Accept it more easily from some people than others?

React differently when you're stressed versus when you're calm?

Each journal entry adds another piece to your personal puzzle, revealing where you're growing and where you're stuck. Maybe you notice you instantly shut down when someone critiques your writing, but you're open to feedback about your athletic performance.

Why the difference?

What can one situation teach you about the other?

Self-reflection turns every piece of feedback into a mirror, revealing both others' perceptions and your own self-image. Catch those automatic, unhelpful thoughts:

- *"They just don't understand,"*
- *"I'll never be good enough,"*
- *"Why even try?"*

Challenge these thoughts. Question them. Control them.

Set aside dedicated time for this practice. Maybe Sunday evenings, or quiet moments before bed. Review recent feedback you've received, examining your responses:

- What was your first reaction?
- What did that reaction reveal?
- How might you respond differently now?

Over time, something remarkable happens. Your initial reactions to criticism begin to shift. That defensive wall lowers sooner. Your mind opens faster. You spot opportunities in critiques before feeling threatened.

Through self-reflection, each piece of feedback becomes a doorway to deeper understanding, transforming how you grow and learn.

Strategies to Handle and Absorb Criticism

Criticism can feel overwhelming, especially when emotions run high. Here are some ways to most effectively receive criticism:

- **Active listening is key**. When someone offers feedback, your first reaction might be to defend yourself. Instead, try focusing on understanding what's being said. One way to do this is by paraphrasing — or repeating back what you've heard in your own words. This approach shows that you're really trying to grasp the critique rather than just reacting negatively to it. For example, if your teacher says, "*Your report could use more detail,*" you might respond with, *"Are you saying I should add more specifics to make my point clearer?"* This simple technique clarifies the feedback and also opens up a conversation about how you can improve.
- **Emotional processing** is another essential part of managing criticism. You're not the only one who reacts emotionally to feedback. However, recognizing those emotional responses is crucial for self-awareness. You can always write down your feelings after receiving criticism. This will give you insight into why certain comments trigger specific emotions. I also find that taking a deep breath to calm my nerves works well. This reduces immediate emotional reaction. So, when you feel criticism is overwhelming you, close your eyes and take slow, deep breaths. This

small practice can shift your mood, allowing you to approach feedback more rationally.

- **Seek clarification** when feedback seems unclear or confusing. Questions are powerful tools for transforming vague critiques into actionable advice. If you receive criticism like, *"You need to learn to work better in a team,"* ask specific questions to get clarity. You might say, *"Can you give me an example of what I do that indicates I don't work well in teams?"* This not only helps you understand the issue but also provides clear steps on how to improve. Seeking clarity reduces misunderstandings and demonstrates a genuine interest in using criticism constructively.
- **Reframing critiques** is another strategy that can change how you perceive negative feedback. Looking at criticism from a different perspective can turn potentially demoralizing remarks into opportunities for growth. For instance, if a teacher says, *"Your presentation was too short,"* instead of thinking, *I failed,* try reframing it to, *"I have room to expand and include more information next time."* This shift in thinking helps transform negative feedback into a constructive tool, encouraging personal development rather than stifling your progress.

Putting It All Together

Like learning any new skill, it takes practice to get comfortable with criticism. The more you use these tools, the more natural they become.

Think about a musician learning a complex piece of music. They don't tackle the entire song at once — they break it down into manageable sections. Similarly, you don't have to become a feedback master overnight. Start with one piece of criticism. Apply your filter. Practice your active listening. Try your reframing techniques.

Each time you face feedback, you have a choice:

- *A) Fall back into old patterns*
- *B) Try a new approach*

Every small success builds confidence. Every challenge becomes an opportunity to refine your skills.

Remember that presentation example from earlier? The next time you're in a similar situation, you'll be ready. You'll have your feedback filter in place. You'll know how to separate valuable insights from empty criticism. Most importantly, you'll understand that each piece of constructive feedback is another step toward your goals.

Ready to put these ideas into practice?

Let's start with a simple exercise...

TRY IT: The Feedback Filter

Take the next 10 minutes to test your new feedback filter. Think of the last time someone gave you feedback – good or bad, big or small. Maybe it was about a presentation, an assignment, or even your gaming skills. Got it in mind? Good.

1. First, write down exactly what they said. Don't soften it or make it nicer — put down their exact words.
2. Now comes the interesting part. Let's sort this feedback using your new filter. What part of their comment was actually valuable — something specific you could act on? Write that down.
3. What part was just noise, vague criticism, or unhelpful comments?
4. Finally, take the valuable part and turn it into one specific action you could take to improve. Make it something concrete you could start doing this week.

That's it! You've just practiced one of life's most valuable skills — filtering feedback to find the gold and let the gravel fall away.

Chapter 4
Building Resilience

*Hardships often prepare ordinary people for
an extraordinary destiny.* –C.S. Lewis

Imagine this: Everything you prepared for, everything you worked toward, just fell apart in spectacular fashion. Your face burns with embarrassment. Your confidence is shattered. And right now, you have to make a choice:

Let this moment break you, or find a way to come back stronger.

This is where resilience begins.

Not the fluffy, motivational-poster kind of resilience that tells you to "*keep smiling*" or "*everything happens for a reason.*" We're talking about real resilience — the kind that turns crushing defeats into comeback fuel. The kind that doesn't just help you survive tough moments, but teaches you how to rise from them stronger than before.

Every person you admire has stood precisely where you're standing. They've felt that same burning embarrassment, that same shattered confidence, that same urge to disappear. What sets them apart isn't that they never failed — *it's what they chose to do next.*

Real Stories Of Resilience

Resilience doesn't just help you survive trying moments — it transforms them into stepping stones for growth. History is packed with people who faced enormous, seemingly unbeatable odds and came out stronger. Their stories are proof that resilience isn't just a nice idea. It's profoundly transformative.

Consider the story of Nelson Mandela. Picture a young man in South Africa, standing up to apartheid; a brutal system that treated Black citizens as less than human. Mandela believed in equality so fiercely that he spent 27 years in prison for it. Imagine losing nearly three decades of your life, locked away, with no guarantee that freedom would ever come. Even against terrible odds, Mandela didn't let prison break him. Instead, he used it as a classroom. He read, strategized, and prepared for the moment he could lead others. When he finally walked free, Mandela became South Africa's first Black president, using his position to unite a divided nation and steer it toward equality. His resilience didn't just free him — it helped free a country.

Or take Anne Frank. She wasn't a world leader; she was a teenager, just like you. During World War II, Anne and her family hid in a cramped attic for over two years, trying to avoid Nazi persecution. Imagine never being able to go outside, living in constant fear, with every sound potentially giving you away. But Anne didn't let fear consume her. Instead, she wrote. In her diary, she poured out her hopes, her frustrations, and her belief that people were still good at heart. Her resilience turned her private thoughts into one of the most powerful testaments to human courage the world has ever known through *"The Diary Of Anne Frank."*

And then there's Malala Yousafzai. Growing up in Pakistan, she loved school, but extremists in her town didn't think girls should be educated. Malala refused to stay silent. She spoke out, knowing it made her a target. When she was just 15, an attacker tried to silence her permanently. But Malala's story didn't end there. She survived, and she didn't just recover — she came back louder, stronger, and more determined than ever. By the age of 17, she had become the youngest person to win the Nobel Peace Prize, inspiring millions to fight for education and equality.

Here's the thing about these stories: they're not just about surviving — they're about choosing growth. Mandela didn't just endure prison; he transformed it into a foundation for leadership. Anne didn't let her confinement crush her spirit; she turned it into a legacy of hope. Malala didn't let violence stop her; she turned it into fuel for change.

This is what resilience looks like. It's not an absence of fear or struggle, but a refusal to let those things define you. And it's not reserved for world leaders, activists, or historical icons. It's in the everyday moments, too.

Maybe for you, it's raising your hand in class when you're not 100% sure of the answer. Or trying out for the team after last year's rejection. Or reaching out to someone new, knowing they might say no. Or standing up for what you know is right, even in the face of difficult circumstances. These moments matter because this is how resilience is built. One small act of courage at a time.

Building Your Resilience Muscles

Think of resilience like a muscle. You wouldn't walk into a gym and try to lift the heaviest weights on day one. Instead, you build strength gradually, consistently, one rep at a time.

The same goes for resilience. It's built through daily habits, small choices, and regular practice. Each time you face a challenge, push through discomfort or bounce back from a setback, you're building that strength.

The Power of Routine

Chaos hits differently when you've got a solid foundation. That's what routine gives you. Not the boring, repetitive kind, but a rhythm that keeps you steady when everything else feels shaky.

When your world turns upside down, having certain anchors — maybe your morning playlist, your evening run, or even just your specific way of organizing your backpack — these become your secret weapons against uncertainty. It's like having a personal force field that helps you stay focused when everything around you goes crazy.

Start small. Maybe it's setting your alarm 15 minutes earlier to have some quiet time. Or creating a study ritual that feels more like self-care than a chore. Build your morning routine one piece at a time. Add an evening wind-down that helps you reflect and recharge. To establish a supportive routine, the key isn't perfection. It's consistency.

These routines become your foundation. When tough times hit, they're the steady ground you stand on. They remind you that even when some things are out of control, you still have power over how you approach each day.

The Challenge Game

Real growth happens just outside your comfort zone. That space where your heart beats a little faster, your palms get a bit sweaty, but something inside you whispers, "*let's give it a try.*"

We're not talking about massive, terrifying leaps. Think small steps that make your heart beat just a little faster. Raising your hand in class when you're not 100%

sure. Starting a conversation with someone new. Trying that sport you've always watched from the sidelines. Sharing your art even though it's not *"perfect."*

Each small challenge you take on is like a rep for your resilience muscles. Every time you push past that initial *"nope, can't do it"* feeling, you're getting stronger. The key is to start small and build up. Maybe today it's answering one question in class. Next week, it's volunteering for a presentation. The month after? Leading a group project.

The Reflection Revolution

Your mind is constantly telling you stories about yourself. But are you listening? Really listening?

We've talked about journaling a bit already — not the *"dear diary"* kind, but the kind that helps you understand your own story better. Write about your challenges, your victories, even your face-plants.

What worked?

What didn't?

What would you try differently next time?

These aren't just words on a page. They're the blueprint of your growth that helps you gradually build up your personal resilience over time.

Flipping the Failure Script

That test you bombed? That tryout that went sideways? That social situation that still makes you cringe? They're not endpoints — they're data points. Each one tells you something useful about what to try next.

Stop seeing failure as a wall. Start seeing it as feedback. Every *"mistake"* is actually information about what to adjust, what to rethink, and what to try differently next time. It's like having a GPS for growth. When you take a wrong turn, it doesn't yell at you; it just recalculates and shows you a new route.

This isn't about positive thinking or pretending setbacks don't hurt. It's about training yourself to ask better questions:

"What can I learn from this?" instead of *"Why did this happen to me?"*

"How can I adjust?" instead of *"What's wrong with me?"*

Think about any skill you've mastered. Maybe it's a video game, a sport, or an instrument. You didn't get good by getting everything right the first time, did you?

You got good by trying, failing, adjusting, and trying again. Each failure taught you something new about how to succeed.

Remember, every resilient person you admire started precisely where you are — building their resilience one small habit at a time. They felt the same fears, faced the same doubts, and made the same mistakes. What set them apart wasn't natural talent or luck. It was their willingness to keep going, keep learning, and keep growing.

Building Your Support System

Think of the last time everything felt too heavy to handle alone. That moment when your confidence cracked, when the challenge seemed too big, when giving up felt like the only option.

Now, imagine having a team in your corner. Not just cheerleaders, but people who genuinely get it. People who know how to help you turn setbacks into comebacks.

This is where your support network comes in.

Your Resilience Team

A strong support system isn't just about having people around – it's about having *the right people* around. The ones who:

- See your struggle, but believe in your strength
- Listen without judgment but push you toward growth
- Share their own battle stories and how they made it through
- Remind you of your progress when you can only see how far you have to go

These aren't just friends — they're your resilience builders. When your confidence wavers, they hold that belief for you until you can reclaim it.

Finding Your People

Building this network takes intention. It's about recognizing who makes you stronger and who drains your resilience reserves.

Look for people who've faced similar challenges and come out stronger. Their experience isn't just inspiring, it's also a roadmap you can learn from.

Mentors who push you beyond your comfort zone while showing you how to handle the discomfort. Maybe it's that coach who knows exactly when to push and when to support. Or that teacher who sees potential in you that you haven't discovered yet. Friends who make space for both your struggles and your triumphs. The ones who let you vent, but don't let you stay stuck. The ones who celebrate your wins without competing. The ones who remind you of your strength when you forget.

Being a Resilience Builder

Here's something powerful:

While you're building your support network, you're also learning to be that support for others. When you share your struggles and victories, you're showing others what resilience looks like in action.

This isn't about having all the answers. It's about being present, being honest, and being willing to grow together. When you help someone else push through a challenging moment, you're actually strengthening your own resilience muscles, too.

Remember, no one builds resilience alone. Even the strongest people you know have a support system. They've learned that true strength isn't about handling everything solo. It's about knowing when to lean on others and how to help them lean on you.

Your resilience journey is unique to you, but you don't have to walk it alone. Start building your team today. Look around.

- Who makes you feel stronger?
- Who helps you bounce back?
- Who shows you what's possible?

Those are your people. That's your team. And together, you're all becoming more resilient, one challenge at a time.

The Long-Term Benefits of Support Network

Studies show that people with strong social connections have better mental health, lower stress levels, and even longer lifespans. A good support network reminds you that you're not alone, no matter how tough life gets.

On the flip side, isolation can make challenges feel insurmountable. Without people to rely on, stress and uncertainty can become overwhelming, leading to feelings of helplessness.

Resilience doesn't mean handling everything on your own — it means knowing when to ask for help and who to ask. By investing in your support network, you're not just preparing for the hard times; you're also building a foundation for success, joy, and growth.

TRY IT: Strengthen Your Resilience

Resilience isn't just about tackling challenges head-on — it's also about knowing when to lean on others and offering support in return. Take these three steps to build and strengthen your support network while practicing resilience:

Step 1: Identify Your Support Circle

Grab a notebook or open a notes app and create a simple list of the people in your life who uplift and inspire you.

Think of:

- Friends who make you feel heard and valued
- Teachers, mentors, or coaches who push you to grow
- Family members who support you unconditionally

Once your list is ready, reflect on how each person has helped you in the past. Do they give great advice? Are they good at listening? Acknowledging their strengths will remind you of the connections you already have and the resilience they've helped you build.

Step 2: Strengthen One Connection

Choose one person from your list and make an effort to deepen your bond. This could mean:

- Inviting a friend to hang out face-to-face (grab a coffee, go for a walk, or just chill together).
- Writing a heartfelt thank-you note to someone who's been there for you during tough times.
- Opening up about a current challenge and asking for advice or support.

Building stronger relationships doesn't have to be complicated—it's about showing others you value them and are willing to invest in your connection.

Step 3: Be a Resilience Builder for Someone Else

Now, flip the script. Think of someone who might need *your* support this week. Maybe it's a friend struggling with school, a sibling feeling overwhelmed, or even a classmate who seems a little down.

Do one small thing to show them you care:

- Offer to help with a problem they're facing.
- Check-in with a quick text or phone call. (Something simple, like *"Hey, how are you holding up?"*)
- Celebrate something they've accomplished recently.

Being there for others strengthens your resilience by reinforcing empathy, problem-solving, and connection.

Chapter 5

Self-Reflection and Goal Setting

"If you don't know yourself, you don't know anything."
– Socrates

Imagine this:

You're standing at a crossroads of potential. On one side, a path of familiar comfort. On the other, a trail of unknown challenges and untapped possibilities. Your heart races with a mix of excitement and uncertainty.

Maybe it's a dream you've been hesitating to pursue. A skill you've always wanted to master. A goal that feels just beyond your reach. The potential is there, humming with energy, but something keeps holding you back. A whisper of doubt. A fear of failure. The uncomfortable feeling of stepping outside your comfort zone.

We've all been there. Staring at that invisible barrier between where we are and where we want to be. Close enough to see the possibility, but somehow unable to take that first step.

You might tell yourself;

"This would be so much easier, IF ONLY..."

It's a natural human trait to wish for more ideal circumstances. We spend our lives wanting the world to change. Wanting easier challenges, better situations, different rules, or an advantage. We tend to blame our struggles on everything around us. Bad luck. Unfair teachers. Impossible situations.

The simple fact of the matter is that there's only one thing that you can control...

Yourself.

This is where self-reflection begins. Not the vague *"think about your feelings"* kind of reflection. We're talking about the powerful practice of truly understanding yourself, your reactions, your patterns, and your unique way of seeing the world. It's about learning to read your own story just as carefully as you'd read someone else's.

Every incredible journey starts with self-understanding. Whether you're trying to write a story, choose a career path, or figure out why certain situations always seem to trip you up. The ability to look inward with honesty and curiosity is one of the most powerful skills you can master. While others are fruitlessly demanding the world adapt to them, you'll be building the self-awareness that lets you adapt, grow, and ultimately reshape the world around you.

The first step is _self-reflection_. It's about pausing to examine your thoughts, actions, and motivations — uncovering the patterns that guide your decisions.

The second step is _goal-setting_. Attaining the ability to craft a set of intentional, meaningful, attainable goals that transform your insights into action — and your action into results.

By combining self-reflection with goal-setting, you create a powerful loop of growth. Reflection helps you understand where you are, and goal-setting shows you where to go. Together, they provide the tools to navigate life's crossroads, making each decision purposeful and aligned with the future you want to build.

The Power of Self-Reflection

Self-reflection is like holding up a mirror. Not to judge yourself, but to truly see yourself. It's an active practice of understanding why you think, feel, and act the way you do. Without it, you're like a traveler without a map, wandering aimlessly through life's choices and challenges. With it, you become a navigator of your journey, equipped to chart a path that's both purposeful and fulfilling.

Think about it: every decision you make and every interaction you have stems from how you see yourself and the world around you. If you don't take the time to reflect, those choices can feel random or disconnected. But when you pause to look inward, you gain clarity. You start to see patterns — how you react to stress, what motivates you, and where you tend to get stuck. These insights become the foundation for growth.

Why Self-Reflection Matters

Your "*why*" is the core purpose that drives everything you do. It's deeper than just goals or achievements — it's the fundamental reason behind your actions, the values that light you up inside, and the impact you want to make in the world.

Think of your "*why*" as your internal compass. It's the answer to the most critical question you can ask yourself:

"Why do I do what I do?"

For some people, their "*why*" might be about making a difference in their community. For others, it could be about personal growth, creativity, or supporting their family.

Let's break it down with an example. Say you're passionate about environmental protection. Your surface-level goal might be to recycle or join an environmental club. But your deeper "*why*" could be about preserving the planet for future generations, or feeling a connection to the natural world, or believing that every individual can create meaningful change.

When you're clear about your "*why,*" decisions become easier. Challenges become more manageable. Setbacks don't derail you because you understand the larger purpose driving your actions. It's like having an internal navigation system that keeps you focused and motivated, even when the path gets tough.

Without a clear "*why,*" you might find yourself:

- Feeling constantly scattered
- Pursuing goals that don't truly excite you
- Losing motivation quickly
- Struggling to make meaningful choices

But when you connect with your "*why,*" everything changes. Your actions become more intentional. Your energy becomes more focused. Your life starts to feel more meaningful and aligned.

Self-reflection is the key to uncovering this powerful purpose. It's about digging beneath the surface, asking yourself the tough questions, and discovering what truly matters to you.

The Three Pillars of Reflection

To start reflecting effectively, focus on three key areas:

1) Your Patterns

Take a look at the habits and behaviors that define your daily life.

Do you procrastinate when faced with enormous tasks?

Do you recognize any bad habits that you'd be better off without?

Do you thrive under pressure or crumble under stress?

Identifying these patterns helps you understand what's working and what's holding you back.

2) Your Triggers

Everyone has emotional triggers — situations or comments that spark strong reactions. Maybe you feel defensive when someone critiques your work, or you get overwhelmed when plans change suddenly. Reflection helps you pinpoint these triggers and uncover the beliefs behind them, giving you the power to respond thoughtfully instead of reacting impulsively.

3) Your Values

What truly matters to you? What motivates you to keep going, even when things get tough? Reflecting on your values helps you align your decisions with what's most important, creating a sense of purpose that guides your actions.

How to Start Reflecting

Self-reflection doesn't require hours of meditation or deep philosophical musings. It starts with simple questions, asked with curiosity rather than judgment:

- What's been working well lately, and why?
- What challenges did I face, and how did I handle them?
- What did I learn about myself from this experience?

Even five minutes a day spent journaling or thinking about these questions can lead to powerful insights. Over time, you'll start to notice themes — things that consistently energize or drain you, strategies that help you succeed, and habits that hold you back.

Turning Reflection into Action

Reflection isn't just about understanding yourself. You have to use that understanding to make better choices. Once you've identified a pattern or learned something new about yourself, ask:

- How can I use this insight to improve?
- What's one small change I can make today?

For example, if you realize that you're most productive in the morning, you might start scheduling your most demanding tasks for that time. If you notice that negative self-talk often creeps in before significant challenges, you could practice reframing those thoughts with affirmations like, *"I've prepared for this, and I can handle it."*

Reflection gives you the tools to take ownership of your growth. Instead of feeling stuck or overwhelmed, you start to see each moment as an opportunity to learn and adapt.

Setting Life-Changing Goals

Understanding challenges is essential. But creating meaningful change requires something more:

Structured , intentional, methodical **action**.

This is where S.M.A.R.T. goal-setting becomes invaluable. It's an acronym that stands for **S**pecific, **M**easurable, **A**chievable, **R**elevant, **T**ime-Bound.

Think of it not as a rigid formula, but as a framework for turning aspirations into tangible achievements.

Let's say you want to learn how to drive a car. Here is an example of how you can create this goal using the S.M.A.R.T. framework:

Specific: *"I want to learn how to drive"* sounds straightforward until you actually sit behind the wheel. What exactly do you need to learn? A **specific** goal breaks this down into clear skills:

"I want to master the essential driving skills for my license test – smooth acceleration and braking, precise steering, parallel parking, highway merging, and navigating intersections safely."

Now, THAT's a specific goal. You're not just *"learning to drive"* – you're developing specific abilities that add up to you becoming a competent driver. This clarity helps you focus your practice time effectively instead of wondering what to work on next.

Measurable: Just counting hours behind the wheel doesn't tell you if you're improving. You need concrete ways to track progress. For parallel parking, count how many attempts you need to park correctly. For highway driving, track how smoothly you maintain your speed and position in your lane. For general skills, note how often your parent or instructor needs to give corrections during each practice session.

These *measurements* transform vague progress into clear data. Instead of wondering if you're getting better, you'll know exactly where you've improved and what still needs work.

Achievable: While you might dream of driving like an expert immediately, rushing into advanced skills is a recipe for frustration. Start with mastering the basics in empty parking lots. Smooth starts and stops, turning with precision, backing straight. Once these feel natural, move to quiet residential streets. Build up to busier roads only when you're consistently handling quieter ones well.

This gradual progression keeps you challenged without becoming overwhelmed, which helps the task remain *achievable*. Each small success builds confidence for the next step, creating momentum rather than anxiety.

Relevant: Connect your driving goals to what matters in your life. Maybe you want to help with family errands, drive yourself to school or work, or gain more independence. Think about specific, *relevant* trips you'd like to make or responsibilities you'd like to take on.

These personal connections provide motivation during challenging moments. When you're struggling to master a particular skill, remembering why it matters to you personally helps maintain your determination.

Time-bound: Without deadlines, practice can drift aimlessly. Create a realistic timeline that drives steady progress: First two weeks for parking lot basics. Next three weeks for residential streets. Following four weeks for busier roads and highway practice. Final three weeks for perfecting all skills before your test.

These deadlines create urgency while remaining realistic. They help you pace your learning and ensure you're making consistent progress toward your goal.

Putting It All Together

Initial goal: *"Learn how to drive."*

S.M.A.R.T. Version:

"Complete 40 hours of supervised driving practice over the next three months. Master basic car control in empty lots during weeks 1–2, residential driving in weeks 3–5, busy streets in weeks 6–9, and highway driving in weeks 10–12.

Practice parallel parking for 15 minutes each session until I can park successfully 8 out of 10 times. Complete practice driving test with instructor by week 11, focusing week 12 on any weak areas. Pass official driving test by end of month three."

This structured approach transforms an intimidating goal into clear, actionable steps. Each element of SMART works together, creating a realistic path from complete beginner to licensed driver.

In the end, it's about progress. By breaking down your biggest goals into clear, measurable steps, you create a map for success. Each small achievement builds confidence. Each setback provides valuable feedback. Step by step, what once seemed impossible becomes inevitable.

Reflection Journaling

Think of every experience as a story waiting to be understood. That impressive presentation you nailed. That test that totally went sideways. That moment when everything clicked in practice. Each one holds clues about how you learn, grow, and perform at your best.

Don't get hung up on the format. Whether it's a leather-bound notebook, a notes app on your phone, or a document in the cloud – what matters is that you can capture insights when they're fresh and review them when you need guidance.

The Art of Capturing Moments

Imagine you just finished a major presentation. Instead of just feeling relieved it's over, take a moment to record what happened:

"History presentation today. Started shaky – hands trembling during first slide. But found my rhythm after the introduction. Audience seemed really engaged during the personal story section. Lost my place once but recovered by asking the class a question while I gathered my thoughts."

That's a nice start, but break it down even further:

- What worked? *The personal story grabbed attention*
- What challenged you? *The opening moments, losing your place*
- How did you adapt? *Turning a stumble into audience engagement*
- What would you do differently? *Maybe start with the story next time*

The big difference here is that you're not just remembering what happened – *you're actively learning from it*. Maybe you discover that starting with your strongest material helps you find confidence faster. Or that connecting with your audience makes you less focused on your nervousness.

Expanding Your Awareness

Over time, expand on your entries and go even deeper by creating different sections in your journal:

Performance Patterns: Notice how different approaches affect your results. Maybe you discover you understand math concepts better when you draw them out visually. Or that you retain information longer when you explain it to someone else. These aren't just random observations – they're clues about how your mind works best.

Energy Patterns: Track when you feel most alert, creative, or focused. You might find you solve problems better in the morning, or that your creativity peaks late at night. This isn't just interesting – it's valuable data about when to tackle different types of challenges.

Environmental Factors: Note which conditions help or hinder your performance. Background music might help you focus on some tasks but distract you during others. Certain study spots might energize you, while others make you sleepy.

Using Your Insights

Here's where most people stop. They collect observations but never use them. Your journal should be more than just a record to look back on – it should be a tool for active improvement.

When you notice a pattern, design an experiment:

- If background music helps you focus, create specific playlists for different types of work
- If you understand concepts better by teaching them, start a study group
- If you perform better after one particular warm-up routine, make it a non-negotiable part of your preparation

This is taking what you learned about yourself and then setting yourself up for even greater levels of success by controlling as many elements as possible. It's putting the knowledge that you're learning about yourself to use as best as possible to maximize your results.

Making It a Habit

Set specific times for journaling:

- Quick notes right after important events
- Weekly review to spot patterns
- Monthly reflection to plan adjustments

Create prompts that help you dig deeper:

- What surprised me this week?
- What patterns am I noticing?
- What experiments should I try next?
- What's working that I should do more of?

The Bigger Picture

Over time, this practice transforms growth from random improvement into strategic development. Each experience becomes more than just a moment – it becomes a lesson, a stepping stone, a piece of the puzzle that is you.

Your journal will become your personal manual for success, written one insight at a time. It really is a lot like creating an instruction manual for yourself — the trick is that you have to figure out how you work in order to write it.

Your journal reveals not just what you're capable of, but also how to access your best performance consistently. It shows you not just where you want to go, but also the specific steps that will take to get you there.

This isn't just about getting better – it's about understanding the unique way you get better. It's about turning your growth from guesswork into science, from hope into strategy, from random progress into deliberate development.

TRY IT: Your First Self-Discovery Page

Think about something that happened this week that triggered a strong reaction in you – *good or bad*. Maybe you crushed a presentation. Perhaps you backed away from a challenge. Maybe something small bothered you more than it should have.

Write down:

1. What exactly happened: _____
2. How you reacted (thoughts, feelings, actions): _____
3. One pattern this might reveal about you: _____

That's it! You've just written your first growth journal entry. Place it somewhere you'll see it every day.

Remember: Understanding yourself isn't something that spontaneously occurs — it happens one intentional moment of awareness at a time.

Chapter 6
Building Unshakeable Self-Belief

"Whether you think you can, or you think you can't – you're right."
– Henry Ford

Imagine this:

You're scrolling through social media late at night. Each swipe reveals another perfectly curated moment from someone else's life. A friend crushing their dance recital. Your classmate celebrating another academic award. That girl from math class living what looks like a dream life.

And there you are, in your quiet room, feeling somehow... less.

Why can't I be more like them?

This thought – this exact moment of comparison and self-doubt – is where most people get stuck. They let these feelings of *"not enough"* define them, limit them, and hold them back.

Most people don't understand that self-belief isn't some magical confidence that certain people are born with. Believing in yourself is not about never feeling scared or uncertain — and it's definitely not about being perfect.

Self-belief is about understanding a simple but powerful truth:

You don't have to be perfect to be worthy. You don't have to have it all figured out to take the next step. You don't have to feel ready to begin.

Look at anyone who's achieved something remarkable – in sports, academics, business, art, or anything. What separates them from those who gave up?

It's the simple choice to keep going when others would quit.

There's a word for someone who refuses to give up — *unstoppable.*

Who can defeat someone who, despite doubts and setbacks, always finds a way to take one more step forward?

This unstoppable quality doesn't come from being fearless – it comes from having unshakeable belief in yourself and your ability to find a way through.

The biggest obstacle you'll ever face isn't the challenge in front of you. *It's the doubt inside you.*

Master that, and you become *unstoppable.*

The Power of Affirmations

Your inner voice is the most consistent narrator in your life. It comments on your choices, judges your performance, and all too often, questions your worth. Left unchecked, it tends to echo the same doubts and fears on repeat:

I'll never get this right.

I'm not good enough.

That kind of recurring negative thinking is what tends to bury people in a hole that they dug for themselves without even knowing it, BUT... there's good news...

That little voice can be reprogrammed to be positive!

It can be reshaped. It can become your greatest coach and your most loyal cheerleader. To reshape and reprogram that little voice in your head, we use a simple, but effective tool called *affirmations.*

What Exactly Are Affirmations?

Affirmations are positive statements you choose to repeat to yourself. They're designed to challenge negative beliefs and build mental resilience. They help you focus on your strengths, your potential, and the steps you can take to improve.

Think of affirmations as a steering wheel for your thoughts. Without them, your mind can easily veer into negative territory, reinforcing limiting beliefs like *"I can't do this."* But with affirmations, you consciously steer your thinking toward growth and possibility.

Affirmations work because your brain is constantly creating and reinforcing neural pathways. When you repeatedly think, *"I'm not capable,"* your brain strengthens that pathway, making it easier to think that same thought again and again. Affirmations interrupt this process. They carve out new pathways — ones rooted in self-belief, confidence, and resilience. Over time, these new pathways become the default.

What Makes a Great Affirmation?

Not all affirmations are effective. The most powerful ones meet you where you are but point toward where you want to go. They should feel believable, even if they stretch your comfort zone a little. If an affirmation feels like a lie, your brain will reject it, and it won't stick.

Here's the difference:

- Ineffective: *"I'm amazing at everything!"*
- Effective: *"I'm improving a little more every day."*

Good affirmations acknowledge the journey while reinforcing your ability to grow. Some good examples:

- *"Every challenge I face helps me grow stronger."*
- *"I am capable of figuring things out."*
- *"I'm learning and improving through every experience."*
- *"I face tough situations with courage and determination."*

These statements don't demand perfection. Instead, they encourage progress and resilience.

Overcoming Negative Self-Talk

We all have moments when our inner voice turns critical.

- *"I'm so bad at this."*
- *"I always mess up."*
- *"Why do I even try?"*

These thoughts can feel automatic and overwhelming, but they're not as immovable as they seem.

When a negative thought surfaces, don't try to shove it away. That often makes it stronger. Instead, approach it with curiosity.

Ask yourself:

- *Where did this thought come from?*
- *Is it really true?*
- *What evidence do I have for or against it?*

Once you've examined the thought, reframe it in a way that focuses on growth. For example:

- Negative: *"I always fail at presentations."*
- Reframed: *"I'm learning to become a stronger presenter every time I try."*

It's all about changing the way you look at struggles and negativity and then reframing them so that they can be used as fuel for growth and improvement. The thing is, these thoughts are going to be used for something either way... *either tearing you down or building you up...* so you might as well **_choose_** to have them working for you rather than against you.

Integrating Affirmations into Your Life

Affirmations only work if they're practiced consistently. Think of them as mental workouts. Just like physical exercise builds muscle, repeating affirmations builds stronger, more resilient thought patterns.

1) Start Your Day with Intention: Begin each morning by saying two or three affirmations that resonate with you. Take a moment to breathe deeply and focus on the meaning behind the words.

For example:

- *"I am capable of handling today's challenges."*
- *"I am growing stronger and wiser every day."*

2) Use Affirmations as Reset Buttons: When you're about to face a challenge — like a test, a presentation, or a difficult conversation — hit the reset button. Take a deep breath and repeat your affirmations. This will help you center and find your focus so that you can proceed onwards with the confidence of knowing that no matter the outcome of the challenge at hand, it's going to benefit you.

3) Reflect at the End of the Day: Before bed, revisit your affirmations and think about how they shaped your actions.

Ask yourself:

- *How did I embody these beliefs today?*
- *What can I do tomorrow to live them more fully?*

4) Anchor Them in Your Environment: Write your affirmations where you'll see them often: on sticky notes, in your planner, or as a phone background. Let them become part of your everyday surroundings.

Pairing Affirmations with Action

Affirmations are not magic. They don't work <u>unless you do</u>. Their real power comes when you pair them with effort.

You can say, *"I'm going to have 6-pack abs"* a million times, but unless you pair it with putting in the work, nothing is going to happen.

If you tell yourself, *"I'm prepared for this exam,"* back it up by studying diligently.

If you affirm, *"I can handle difficult conversations,"* take the time to plan what you'll say and practice staying calm.

When you combine affirmations with action, you create a powerful, positive feedback loop. The more you act on your affirmations, the more believable they become. And the more you believe them, the more motivated you are to take action. The more action you take, the closer you get to your goals. You see how it works.

Why Affirmations Are Worth It

At first, affirmations might feel awkward or forced, especially if your inner critic has been running the show for a long time. But stick with it. Over time, they'll feel less like something you're trying and more like something you are.

Imagine replacing *"I'm not good enough"* with *"I'm figuring this out."* Surely you see how that shift could change the way you approach challenges, setbacks, and even everyday moments?

Affirmations don't erase struggles — they help you navigate them with strength and clarity. They transform your inner voice from a source of doubt into a source of encouragement. Every time you choose an affirmation that reinforces your potential, you're taking a small but powerful step toward becoming the person you're meant to be.

Visualization: Training Your Mind

Tomorrow's presentation has been looming over you for weeks. But instead of letting anxiety take over, you're about to learn a powerful tool that champions use to perform at their best.

Close your eyes.

Take a slow breath.

Now play the scene vividly in your mind:

You're walking confidently to the front of the room, each step purposeful and strong. Your classmates' eyes are on you, and instead of that familiar knot of fear, you feel something electric coursing through you – a mixture of excitement, purpose, and readiness. Your shoulders are back, head high, a slight smile playing at your lips because you know something they don't: **You've got this.**

You've prepared for this moment. Every word, every gesture, every slide is locked into your mind. As you turn to face the class, you feel centered, grounded, and entirely in control. Your opening line flows out precisely as you practiced. Your voice is strong and clear, carrying naturally to the back of the room. You see heads nodding, faces lighting up with interest. Some students even lean forward in their seats, drawn in by your energy and confidence.

Time seems to slow down as you hit your stride. Each point lands perfectly. Your gestures feel natural, emphasizing key ideas exactly when they should. When you pause for effect, the silence holds perfect tension. You're not just giving a presentation – you're commanding the room, sharing something valuable — making a powerful, positive impact.

This isn't just daydreaming. This is mental rehearsal. Olympic athletes use this exact technique before competing, musicians before performances, and surgeons before complex procedures. You're not just imagining success; you're actively programming your brain for it.

When you visualize an action with enough detail and emotion, your brain creates neural pathways similar to those formed during actual practice. Think about that for a minute: You're essentially giving yourself extra rehearsal time, building muscle memory without moving a muscle. Elite performers in every field use this exact technique *because it works.*

But here's the key: Visualization isn't about pretending everything will be perfect. It's about preparing yourself to handle whatever comes your way. In your mental rehearsal, include how you'll handle challenges:

- A little stumble as you walk to the front
- A question you weren't expecting
- A moment where you lose your place
- A distraction in the room

See yourself handling each situation with calm confidence. Because when these moments come in real life *(and they will)*, your brain will recognize them and know what to do.

Making It Real: A Step Beyond Imagining

Champions don't just visualize occasionally. They make it a systematic practice. Think of it like building mental muscle. Just as athletes follow a training schedule, you need a visualization routine that works for you:

Find your time: Maybe it's right before bed, when your mind is quiet. Or during your morning shower, when ideas flow freely. Or on the bus to school, with your headphones creating a bubble of focus. Pick a consistent time when you can immerse yourself undisturbed.

Make it vivid: Engage all your senses. What do you see? The faces in the crowd, the setup of the room, the slides on the screen. What do you hear? The sound of your voice, the rustle of movement, the silence of attention. What do you feel? The temperature of the room, your feet planted firmly, your breathing steady and controlled. The more detail you include, the more powerful the practice becomes.

Feel it: Don't just see yourself succeeding — *feel* the emotions. The confidence flows through you when you nail your opening. The satisfaction of fielding a tricky question smoothly. The pride of finishing strong and knowing you gave it your all.

Capturing the Vision

This is where journaling, again, is incredibly powerful. After each visualization session, write down what you saw, felt, and learned. This is an essential step because it's reinforcing the neural pathways you're building.

Create specific journal entries:

- What scenarios did you visualize?
- Which parts felt most real?

- What strategies did you imagine using?
- How did you handle challenges in your mental rehearsal?
- What emotions came up during the practice?

Over time, these journal entries become a personal playbook for success. You'll start noticing patterns: which visualization techniques work best for you, which challenges you've prepared for, and which areas need more mental practice.

The Compound Effect

Think of each visualization session, each journal entry, and each small win as a deposit in your confidence bank. Over time, these deposits compound. Your mental rehearsals become more detailed and effective. Your ability to handle challenges improves. Your belief in yourself grows stronger.

This is how real, lasting confidence is built. Not through empty affirmations or wishful thinking, but through systematic mental preparation and recognition of your progress.

When the big moment comes — whether it's a presentation, performance, or competition — you're not just walking in with hope. You're walking in with *evidence-based confidence*. You've already succeeded dozens of times in your mind. You've documented your capabilities. You've proven to yourself that you can handle challenges.

This is how champions are made. Not in the moment of performance, but in the countless moments of preparation that came before. Mental preparation is just as important as physical practice. Sometimes, it's even more important.

Every time you practice visualization, you're not just preparing for one moment — you're building a skill that will serve you in every challenge you face. You're developing the ability to see success, plan for obstacles, and perform under pressure.

Whether you're preparing for a presentation, a game, a performance, or any other challenge, this combination of visualization, journaling, and celebrating progress creates an upward spiral of improvement. Each element reinforces the others, building a foundation of confidence that grows stronger with every practice session.

TRY IT: Create Your Own Vision Board

Dedicating some time and energy to this exercise can provide a massive boost to your motivation and confidence.

Here's how to get started:

1) Choose Your Space: Decide on a location where you'll display your vision board. Perhaps your desk, bedroom wall, or even the inside of your locker. This should be a place where you'll see it regularly.

2) Gather Your Supplies: You'll need a physical board or surface to work with, along with magazines, printouts, stickers, markers, and any other visual materials that speak to your goals and dreams.

3) Reflect on Your Aspirations: Take some time to get clear on what you want to achieve — both in the short-term and long-term. Consider areas like academics, extracurriculars, relationships, personal growth, and your vision for the future.

4) Create Your Board: Arrange your chosen images, words, and symbols on the board in a way that feels inspiring and meaningful to you. Don't overthink the layout. Let your intuition guide you.

5) Display Your Vision Board: Once you've created your masterpiece, hang it up in your designated space. Make sure it's somewhere you'll see it often so it can work its magic on your subconscious mind.

6) Maintain and Update: Your vision board isn't a one-and-done project. Revisit it regularly, adding new elements or rearranging things as your goals and priorities evolve.

As you create and interact with your vision board, pay attention to how it makes you feel. Visualize yourself achieving the things represented on the board. Let it fill you with excitement, determination, and a deep sense of purpose.

Remember, a vision board is a powerful tool, but it only works when combined with consistent effort and action. Use it to keep your focus sharp and your motivation high as you work towards turning your dreams into reality.

Chapter 7

Cultivating Curiosity and Lifelong Learning

The biggest risk is not taking any risk.
–Mark Zuckerberg

The Curious Case of Two Teenagers

It was a crisp autumn afternoon when the school bell rang, signaling the end of another day. As students flooded the bustling hallways, two teenagers, Nora and Lucas, made their way towards the exit, their paths destined to diverge in the years ahead.

On the surface, Nora and Lucas appeared quite similar. Both were bright, capable students navigating the vibrant chaos of high school. But scratch beneath the surface, and you'd uncover a striking contrast between them.

Nora was a perpetual questioner, her mind alive with curiosity. While her classmates were content to simply recite facts and formulas, Nora yearned to understand the "*why*" and "*how*" behind everything.

Rather than seeing school as a chore, Nora viewed it as a thrilling expedition, each subject a portal into uncharted realms waiting to be explored. On weekends, you'd find her tinkering with code, experimenting in the kitchen, or losing herself in thick volumes about the farthest reaches of the universe. For Nora, learning wasn't a means to an end - *it was a passion*.

Lucas, on the other hand, was the quintessential "*good student*". He dutifully completed his assignments, studied for tests, and checked all the boxes. But his approach lacked the spark that animated Nora's every step. Where she saw possibility, he saw only obligation. Where she had unquenchable curiosity, his motivation was simply to *"get good grades."* As the years passed, Nora and Lucas's paths couldn't have been more different.

Lucas stuck to his original plan. Good grades in college. A safe job. No risks. No unexpected turns. He thought having a steady plan meant success.

Nora's curiosity took her somewhere else entirely.

During a college internship, she discovered a community in rural Guatemala struggling with unreliable electricity. Instead of just feeling bad, she asked questions. How could solar technology help? What obstacles were preventing access? Her curiosity wasn't just academic — it was practical.

By graduation, Nora had partnered with local engineers to design a low-cost solar panel specifically for rural communities. Her "*what if*" approach had turned a classroom idea into a real solution that could change lives.

When Lucas heard about her project, he was stunned. How did she go from a random college internship to creating actual technology? The answer was simple: she never stopped asking questions. Never stopped wondering. Never accepted "*that's just how things are*" as a final answer.

While Lucas was working a predictable marketing job, Nora was traveling, speaking at conferences, and continuing to solve real-world problems. Her curiosity hadn't just opened doors — it had created entirely new pathways.

Nora saw the world as a series of fascinating puzzles waiting to be solved. Lucas saw the world as a set of instructions to follow.

What made the difference for Nora?

Curiosity

Your Secret Weapon for Growth

Curiosity isn't just a natural instinct; it's your innate superpower that unlocks endless opportunities for personal growth and self-discovery. As a teen, embracing curiosity is like having a magic key that opens doors to new ideas, experiences, and possibilities.

Why Curiosity Matters

Imagine navigating life with a magnifying glass, always ready to examine the world more closely. That's the essence of curiosity – a powerful force that pushes you to explore the unknown, challenge assumptions, and see things from fresh perspectives.

The Benefits of Being Curious

By asking questions, exploring new ideas, and challenging assumptions, you open yourself up to a world of growth and discovery. Curiosity fuels resilience, empowers you to adapt to life's challenges, and ignites personal evolution. Let's dive into some of the key benefits of cultivating a curious mindset.

Explore New Ideas: Asking "*why*" is the first step to mind-expanding discoveries. Curiosity compels you to dig beneath the surface, unraveling the fascinating reasons behind everything from historical events to cutting-edge scientific breakthroughs. It's like being an intrepid explorer, venturing into uncharted intellectual territory.

Challenge Assumptions: Curiosity is the antidote to accepting things at face value. It encourages you to question the status quo, consider alternative viewpoints, and arrive at well-reasoned conclusions. When you're curious, you're not afraid to ask probing questions and challenge conventional wisdom.

Adapt and Overcome: Life is full of ups and downs, but curiosity is your secret weapon for resilience. By seeking out new approaches and innovative solutions, you develop the adaptability to bounce back from setbacks and navigate challenges with confidence.

Fuel Personal Growth: Curiosity is the spark that ignites personal evolution. As you explore subjects in depth, you expand your horizons, broaden your perspective, and transform the way you engage with the world around you. It's not just about acquiring knowledge; it's about becoming a more well-rounded, open-minded version of yourself.

Make Informed Choices: Curiosity is the foundation of critical thinking. By seeking out diverse perspectives, analyzing data, and reasoning through complex issues, you develop the skills to make decisions based on sound judgment rather than blindly following the crowd.

Transform Your Social Life: Curiosity is the ultimate social lubricant. When you show genuine interest in others' stories and experiences, you forge more profound, more meaningful connections. Your openness and willingness to learn from diverse perspectives will draw people to you like a magnet.

The Magic of Conversation: Curious people make the best conversationalists. By actively listening and engaging in thought-provoking discussions, you create a space for ideas to flourish and relationships to thrive. You'll be amazed at the insights and shared interests that emerge when you approach conversations with an open, inquisitive mindset.

Your teenage years are a time of self-discovery, and curiosity is your compass. As you explore new hobbies, dive into fascinating books, and engage in stimulating discussions, each experience becomes a brush stroke in the masterpiece of your identity. Embrace the journey and let your curiosity lead the way.

Exploring New Interests and Hobbies

Hobbies are more than just pastimes; they're gateways to new passions, hidden talents, and a lifelong love of learning. In a world that can feel like an endless cycle of academic pressure and social expectations, hobbies provide a much-needed escape – a chance to lose yourself in something you genuinely enjoy.

Stress-Busting Hobbies

Being a teenager can be stressful. Between exams, extracurriculars, and the ever-shifting landscape of social dynamics, it's easy to feel overwhelmed. But here's the good news: nothing keeps stress at bay like engaging in hobbies that are near and dear to your heart.

You know the calm that washes over you as you lose yourself in the flow of a favorite activity – whether it's the rhythmic strokes of a paintbrush, the satisfying click of knitting needles, or the exhilarating rush of mastering a new skateboard trick. As you immerse yourself in these pursuits, your body releases a cascade of feel-good chemicals that melt away tension and promote a sense of well-being.

But the benefits of hobbies go beyond just momentary stress relief. When you carve out time for activities that truly light you up inside, you create space in your life for joy, self-expression, and personal fulfillment. Hobbies become a sanctuary where you can recharge your batteries and approach life's challenges with renewed energy and perspective.

Discover Hidden Talents

One of the most thrilling aspects of trying new hobbies is the opportunity to uncover talents you never knew you had. By stepping outside your comfort zone and embracing new experiences, you embark on a journey of self-discovery that can be deeply transformative.

Perhaps you'll find that you have a natural gift for capturing emotions through photography, or an uncanny ability to bring characters to life on the page. Maybe you'll discover a hidden aptitude for woodworking, or a knack for whipping up culinary creations that make your friends' taste buds sing.

As you explore different hobbies, you'll develop a rich tapestry of skills and experiences that make you a more well-rounded, adaptable individual. And who knows – you may even stumble upon a passion that could one day blossom into a fulfilling career path.

Find Your Tribe

Navigating the social landscape of teenage life can be daunting, but hobbies provide a natural way to connect with like-minded peers. When you join a club, team, or class centered around a shared interest, you instantly tap into a community of people who get you.

Picture the camaraderie that comes from working towards a common goal with your robotics team, or the deep discussions that arise during a book club meeting. These shared experiences create a bond that goes beyond the superficial, fostering friendships built on mutual understanding and respect.

And the best part? The connections you make through your hobbies often have a way of extending beyond the confines of the activity itself. You may find that the teammates who sweat alongside you on the field become your biggest cheerleaders in life, or that the friends you make in art class become your trusted confidantes.

So don't be afraid to put yourself out there and try something new. You never know who you might meet or what doors might open as a result.

Resources That Feed Curiosity

In a world that's constantly evolving, lifelong learning is the key to staying ahead of the curve. And the good news is that you don't need a classroom to keep expanding your mind. With a wealth of resources at your fingertips, you can embark on a journey of continuous discovery from anywhere, at any time.

Online Learning: A World of Possibilities

Welcome to the digital age, where the power to learn is quite literally at your fingertips. With platforms like Coursera, edX, and Udemy, you have access to an endless array of courses, tutorials, and educational content spanning every subject imaginable.

Want to learn how to code your own mobile app? There's a course for that. Curious about the intricacies of Ancient Egyptian history? You can dive deep into the topic with interactive lessons taught by world-renowned experts. The beauty of online learning is that you can tailor your education to your unique interests and goals, all at your own pace.

But online learning is about more than just convenience. Many platforms offer immersive, hands-on experiences that rival traditional classroom settings. Through virtual labs, real-world projects, and collaborative forums, you can develop practical skills and connect with a global community of learners who share your passions.

Books and Podcasts: Portable Inspiration

In a world of flashy digital distractions, there's something uniquely powerful about the timeless mediums of books and podcasts. With a good book or a thought-provoking podcast, you can transport yourself to new worlds, explore groundbreaking ideas, and gain wisdom from some of the most brilliant minds of our time.

Imagine immersing yourself in a memoir that chronicles a remarkable journey of resilience, or losing yourself in a science fiction novel that challenges your assumptions about the nature of reality. Through the written word, you can travel to the far reaches of human experience and imagination, all from the comfort of your favorite reading nook.

And when you're on the go, podcasts offer a portable dose of inspiration and enlightenment. Whether you're tuning into a history podcast that brings the past to life, or a science show that explores the cutting edge of discovery, you can transform your commute or workout into a mind-expanding adventure.

Community Learning: Strength in Numbers

While online resources and solitary pursuits have their place, there's something uniquely powerful about learning in a community setting. When you join a workshop, attend a seminar, or participate in a group project, you tap into the collective energy and wisdom of your peers.

Imagine the rush of collaborating with a team of like-minded individuals to bring a creative vision to life, or the thrill of engaging in a lively debate about a complex philosophical question. In these moments, you not only expand your knowledge and skills, but also learn from the diverse perspectives and experiences of those around you.

And the benefits of community learning extend far beyond the realm of academics. Through shared experiences and challenges, you develop crucial life skills like communication, collaboration, and empathy. You learn how to navigate different personalities, resolve conflicts, and work towards common goals – all skills that will serve you well in any future endeavor.

So, seek out opportunities to learn and grow alongside others. Join a study group, volunteer for a community project, or attend a local workshop. You never know what insights you might gain or what lifelong connections you might make.

The beauty of lifelong learning is that it's an ever-evolving journey. As you grow and change, so too will your interests and pursuits. Embrace the twists and turns, the challenges and the triumphs. Above all, never stop asking questions, seeking answers, and exploring the boundless possibilities of the world around you.

Because in the end, the most valuable education is the one that never stops – the one that keeps you curious, engaged, and forever reaching for new heights.

TRY IT: Curiosity Challenge

This chapter has emphasized the power of curiosity and the importance of embracing lifelong learning. Now, it's time to put those principles into practice.

Your challenge is to engage in three different exploratory activities that will broaden your horizons and nurture your natural inquisitiveness:

1) Explore a New Online Course: Visit a platform like Udemy and find a subject or skill that sparks your interest, but you haven't had the chance to explore. Select a course and commit to completing at least a few modules. Reflect on how it challenges your existing knowledge and pushes you to think in new ways.

2) Discover New Music: Step outside your usual music preferences and seek out artists, genres, or styles that you're unfamiliar with. Notice how the new sounds make you feel and what they reveal about the limits of your current musical knowledge.

3) Read a Book Outside Your Comfort Zone: Browse your local library or bookstore and select a title that takes you beyond your typical reading habits, whether it's a memoir, work of non-fiction, or a novel set in an unfamiliar culture or time period. Pay attention to how this new literary experience challenges your assumptions or broadens your understanding of the world.

After engaging in these three exploratory activities, take some time to reflect on your experiences in your journal. Consider what new passions or areas of interest you uncovered, how these explorations stretched your thinking, and how they might shape your future goals.

Chapter 8

The Art of Decision-Making

"The risk of a wrong decision is preferable to the terror of indecision."
— Maimonides

You're standing at a crossroads. In one direction lies the safe, familiar path you've walked a hundred times before. In the other, an uncharted trail winds its way into the unknown, full of uncertainty... *and potential.*

Which do you choose?

This moment of hesitation — of weighing your options and overthinking the potential outcomes — is one you'll face countless times throughout your life. Decisions, big and small, shape the very fabric of your world, whether you're deciding which extracurricular activity to join, which friendship to nurture, or how to spend a lazy Saturday afternoon.

The thing about these decisions is that they're rarely clear-cut. Sure, some choices are simple enough. Pizza or tacos. Netflix or YouTube. But the decisions that truly matter? Those are messy. They challenge you to think deeply, confront your fears, and even put your core values to the test.

Decision-making is a skill. One that can be learned, practiced, and honed over time. You don't need to have all the answers right away. What you do need is a reliable framework for making choices that not only reflect your deepest values, but also help you grow as a person.

In this chapter, we're going to explore that framework in-depth, arming you with the tools and strategies to navigate life's crossroads with confidence, wisdom, and an unwavering commitment to designing the future you desire.

The Weight of Every Choice

Choosing what to have for lunch isn't likely to alter the course of your life. However, many of the smaller choices we make on a daily basis can add up to something much bigger than we might initially realize.

The takeaway here is that it's not just the big, *"life-altering"* decisions that shape the trajectory of our lives. It's the small, everyday choices we make that quietly build the foundation for who we ultimately become.

Let's take this a step further…

The Butterfly Effect of Small Decisions

Have you ever heard of the concept of the *"butterfly effect"?* It's the idea that tiny, seemingly insignificant actions can set off a chain reaction, leading to massive, far-reaching outcomes. In the context of decision-making, this principle is everything.

Let's say, for example, that you decide to spend just 10 minutes a day practicing a new skill, like photography or coding. On its own, that might not seem like much. But over the course of a year, those daily 10-minute sessions add up to over 60 hours of dedicated practice. That's enough time to transform a casual interest into a genuine, marketable skill set.

On the flip side, small negative choices — like skipping one too many workouts or zoning out during class — can also snowball in ways that profoundly impact our lives. By recognizing the power inherent in these seemingly insignificant decisions, we can take proactive control of the narrative, understanding that each small choice is, in essence, a vote for the kind of person we're becoming.

Imagine a scenario where you decide to start meditating for just 5 minutes each morning. At first, it might feel like a tiny, almost negligible habit. But over time, that daily practice of mindfulness and self-reflection could have a profound impact, helping you manage stress more effectively, cultivate greater self-awareness, and make more thoughtful choices throughout your day. Those 5 minutes can quite literally reshape the trajectory of your life.

By being mindful of the butterfly effect at play in our decision-making, we empower ourselves to make choices that align with our values and long-term aspirations, rather than simply falling victim to the momentum of our habitual behaviors.

Why Decisions Feel So Overwhelming

If the idea of making decisions fills you with a sense of dread or paralysis, take comfort in the fact that you're not alone. There are several common reasons why decision-making can feel so overwhelming:

Fear of Regret: No one wants to make the wrong choice and be haunted by a lifetime of *"what-ifs."* The specter of regret can be paralyzing, even when the stakes feel relatively low. We tend to agonize over potential mistakes, convinced that any misstep will haunt us forever.

Too Many Options: Ever tried to pick a movie to watch from an endless streaming menu? It's exhausting, right? When presented with an abundance of possibilities, it's easy to get stuck in a loop of indecision, unable to determine the best path forward.

Pressure to Be Perfect: Society often makes it seem like every choice we make carries the weight of the world. But the reality is that life isn't a straight, perfect line. No single decision is going to define you forever. The pressure to make the *"right"* choice can be crippling, causing us to overthink and second-guess ourselves.

The good news is that you don't have to fear the decision-making process. Every choice you make, whether it ultimately works out or not, offers valuable lessons about yourself and your goals. The key is to approach each crossroads with an open, growth-oriented mindset.

The Foundation of Decision-Making

Before tackling any major life decision, it's essential to have a solid foundation in place. This means taking the time to know yourself honestly — your core values, your current priorities, and your long-term vision for the future.

Clarifying Your Core Values

Your values are like a personal compass, guiding you toward decisions that align with the kind of person you want to be. Take some time for deep reflection, and ask yourself:

- What do I care about most in life?

- What motivates me to keep going, even in the face of challenges?
- Whose qualities and achievements do I most admire, and why?

Your answers might reveal that you place a high value on creativity, kindness, adventure, or personal growth. Once you've identified your core values, decision-making becomes less about "*what*'s *right or wrong*" and more about "*what feels most true to who I am.*"

Values provide an anchor — a stable point of reference that can ground you when the path ahead feels uncertain. Imagine you're trying to decide between pursuing a lucrative but unfulfilling career or taking a risk on a creative passion project. If one of your core values is "*making a positive impact,*" the choice suddenly becomes clear — <u>even if it's the more challenging path</u>.

Understanding Your Priorities

Every decision we make involves some degree of trade-off. You simply can't do everything at once, so it's crucial to have a clear sense of what matters most to you in the present moment. Perhaps academics are your top priority this semester, or maybe you're focused on cultivating deeper friendships and relationships.

Try ranking your current priorities like this:

1. School and learning
2. Family and personal relationships
3. Exploring hobbies and interests

When you know what's most important, it becomes easier to say "*yes*" to things that support your goals — and "*no*" to things that don't quite align.

Imagine you're debating whether to join the school's student council or participate in a community service club. If your priority is building stronger friendships right now, the service club might be the better fit, as it would allow you to engage with your peers in a meaningful way.

Prioritizing doesn't mean permanently relegating certain aspects of your life to the back burner. It's about being intentional and discerning with how you allocate your time and energy in the present so that you can continue to grow and evolve in the future.

Techniques for Smart Decision-Making

Now that you've laid the groundwork by clarifying your values and priorities, let's explore some practical strategies for navigating life's crossroads.

Weigh the Pros and Cons

When your mind is spinning with all the possible options, grab a pen and paper and make a simple pro-con list. Seeing the trade-offs of each choice laid out in front of you can provide much-needed clarity.

For example, imagine you're trying to decide whether to join the school newspaper. Your pros and cons might look something like this:

Pros:

- Build valuable writing skills
- Meet new people and expand your social network
- Add an impressive extracurricular to your college applications

Cons:

- Less free time and personal flexibility
- Potential stress during busy exam periods

Once you see the complete picture, the best path forward often becomes much more evident. The decision might still be a bit uncomfortable to make — *which is completely normal* — but this technique allows you to thoughtfully examine each option, rather than relying on gut instinct or emotion alone.

Tap Into Trusted Advice

While the ultimate decision is yours to make, seeking input from people you trust can provide an incredibly valuable outside perspective. A teacher, for instance, might offer insights you hadn't considered, or a close friend might remind you of personal strengths you may have overlooked.

The key is to use this advice as a guide, but not to let others decide for you. Their role is to provide an outside viewpoint, not to tell you what to do. Trust your gut instinct to make the final call.

Tapping into a support network can be particularly helpful when you're feeling stuck or uncertain. Talking through your thought process with someone you respect can often reveal hidden biases or assumptions you weren't even aware of. Their fresh perspective may illuminate new angles you hadn't considered.

Short-Term vs. Long-Term Thinking

Sometimes, what feels good or convenient at the moment isn't actually what's best for your long-term well-being. Let's say you're trying to decide whether to skip studying for an upcoming math test in order to go out with friends. Sure, the evening of fun might be enjoyable, *but how will you feel when the test rolls around and you're woefully unprepared?*

To navigate these types of dilemmas, ask yourself:

- How will I feel about this choice tomorrow?
- Next week?
- A year from now?

Thinking through the long-term effects can help you make decisions that genuinely align with your priorities and values.

This long-term mindset is crucial, as it prevents us from getting caught up in the lure of instant gratification. It allows us to step back, look at the bigger picture, and choose paths that may be more challenging in the short term, but ultimately serve us better in the long run.

Learning From Every Choice

Not every decision you make is going to lead to success. It's a fact. It's just the way it is. Some will feel more like missteps or setbacks — but those moments are just as valuable as the "*wins*" in your life.

Reframing Mistakes as Lessons

When a choice doesn't pan out the way you'd hoped, it's natural to experience feelings of disappointment or self-doubt. But rather than spiraling, try to reframe the experience in a more constructive light.

Ask yourself:

- What did this teach me about myself?
- What will I do differently next time a similar situation arises?
- How can I apply this newfound knowledge to future decisions?

Remember, mistakes aren't failures — they're stepping stones on the path to greater self-knowledge and resilience. Each "*misstep*" brings you one step closer to understanding yourself and how to navigate life's challenges more effectively.

Reframing setbacks in this way empowers you to view them not as dead-ends, but as opportunities for growth. The lessons you glean from these experiences can inform and strengthen your decision-making prowess, making you more equipped to handle whatever comes next.

Celebrating Your Courage

It's important to remember that making decisions, especially difficult or uncertain ones, requires a significant amount of bravery. So whenever you summon the courage to choose a path, take a moment to acknowledge and celebrate that achievement. You stepped up and took charge of your life, and that's something worth honoring, *even if the outcome wasn't perfect.*

Too often, we're quick to beat ourselves up over decisions that didn't work out as planned. But recognizing the inherent courage it takes to make a choice, regardless of the result, is a powerful act of self-compassion. It reinforces the idea that you are willing to take risks, learn from your experiences, and continuously grow as a person.

Avoiding Decision-Making Traps

As you navigate the decision-making process, be mindful of a few common pitfalls to avoid:

Analysis Paralysis: Overthinking a situation can leave you stuck in a loop of indecision. Remember, no decision is set in stone. You can always adjust course if needed. The key is to take action, even if it's a small first step.

Letting Fear Win: It's normal to feel scared or uncertain when faced with a difficult choice. But don't let those feelings of fear hold you back. Trust that you have the resilience to handle whatever comes next.

Following the Crowd: Just because "*everyone else is doing it*" doesn't mean a particular path is right for you. Make choices that authentically reflect your own values and priorities, not those of your peers.

The Right Choice

The antidote to these decision-making traps is to stay grounded in self-awareness and trust your internal compass. When you find yourself getting stuck in analysis paralysis, for example, take a step back and ask what your core values are telling you. If fear is holding you back, summon the courage to move forward anyway, knowing that you have the strength to adapt to whatever lies ahead.

The Power of Taking Ownership

When you take ownership of your decisions — both the successes and the setbacks — you step into a profound sense of personal power. Each choice becomes an opportunity to learn, grow, and actively shape the life you want to live.

So, don't wait for perfect clarity or certainty. Trust yourself, take a deep breath, and move forward with confidence. The future is yours to design.

The Adventure of Choosing

Decision-making isn't about always getting it right or making the *"perfect"* choice. It's about having the courage to choose, the humility to learn from your experiences, and the determination to keep moving forward, even in the face of challenges.

The path ahead may wind and twist in unexpected ways, but that's all part of the adventure. Embrace the journey, my friend. You've got this.

Along the way, remember to celebrate your victories, no matter how small. Acknowledge the bravery it takes to make tough choices. And when setbacks arise, as they inevitably will, reframe them as opportunities to grow stronger, wiser, and more resilient.

Your life is not a straight line, *nor should it be!* It's a vibrant, ever-evolving tapestry, with each decision you make contributing a unique thread to the overall design. Trust the process, lean on your values and priorities, and enjoy the adventure of charting your own course.

The world is waiting for the remarkable person you are becoming. So go forth, make your mark, and never stop exploring the endless possibilities that lie before you.

TRY IT: Your Decision-Making Roadmap

Every decision shapes the path you're walking. Whether it's big or small, having a clear plan can help you navigate with confidence. Let's turn what you've learned into a practical tool that makes decision-making less stressful and more intentional. Follow these steps to create your personal Decision-Making Roadmap and take charge of your future.

1) Identify Your Values

Write down 3-5 things that matter most to you, like kindness, creativity, or growth. These are your compass points to guide every decision.

2) List Your Priorities

What's most important to you right now? Rank your top 3 priorities—school, friendships, hobbies, or anything else. Knowing your focus makes decisions simpler.

3) Pick Your Tools

Choose 1-2 strategies from the chapter that works best for you, like making a pros-and-cons list or talking to someone you trust. Decide when and how you'll use them.

4) Learn From Mistakes

Write down one question to ask yourself when things don't go as planned, like: "What can I do differently next time?" This keeps mistakes from holding you back.

Reflection:

Every decision you make is a step toward the future you're creating. Your roadmap is a reminder that you have the tools to navigate life's twists and turns with confidence.

Chapter 9
Developing Emotional Intelligence

"Self-awareness is the foundation upon which we build the house of our lives."
— Rasheed Ogunlaru

You've already learned the power of curiosity, the importance of embracing challenges, and the transformative nature of lifelong learning. But what if I told you there was one more essential ingredient for unlocking your full potential?

The final piece of the puzzle is something called **emotional intelligence.**

In simple terms, emotional intelligence is the ability to understand, manage, and communicate your emotions in healthy, productive ways. It's about getting in tune with your emotions and using that self-awareness to make wiser choices in your relationships and everyday life.

Imagine a scenario where you're having an off day. The stress from a tough class, the lingering family drama, and the ever-shifting social dynamics of high school have all come to a head. And then, in a moment of frustration, you snap at your best friend over something trivial. The hurt and confusion in their eyes leave you feeling guilty and unsure of how to make amends.

But what if, in that charged moment, you had the presence of mind to pause and reflect on your emotions?

You might have realized that the overwhelming anxiety and irritability bubbling within you were the true culprits, *not your friend*. With a little self-awareness, you could have expressed your feelings openly: *"I'm so sorry, I've just been really stressed out lately and it's making me short-tempered. I didn't mean to take it out on you."*

This ability to navigate your inner landscape is the hallmark of emotional intelligence — and it's the key to unlocking your growth mindset in every facet of your life. When you can understand your own emotions and empathize with those around you, you gain the resilience to tackle challenges head-on, the flexibility to adapt to change, and the social skills to build meaningful connections.

The 4 Pillars of Emotional Intelligence

I'm sure you've encountered people in your life who seem to be at the complete mercy of their emotions. Maybe it's the classmate who flies off the handle at the slightest provocation, or the family member who spirals into a meltdown over the most minor inconvenience. Their emotions dictate their reactions, and they're unable to regain control or respond constructively.

Then, there are those individuals who seem to stay cool, calm, and collected, even in the most stressful situations. They're able to pause, reflect on their feelings, and make thoughtful decisions about how to proceed. What's the secret behind their composure? It all comes down to the four key pillars of emotional intelligence.

Pillar 1: Self-Awareness

First and foremost, we have self-awareness — the foundation upon which all emotional intelligence is built. This is your capacity to recognize your own emotions, understand how they shape your thoughts and behaviors, and develop a keen sense of your strengths, weaknesses, and triggers.

When you cultivate self-awareness, you gain the power to **pause**, reflect, and ask yourself:

"Okay, why am I feeling this way? What's the root cause of my anxiety/frustration/sadness?"

This moment of introspection gives you the ability to manage your emotions, rather than simply letting them control you.

Self-awareness is the key to unlocking your emotional intelligence.

When you can clearly identify the root causes of your feelings, you're empowered to make conscious choices about how to handle them. This foundation will serve as the bedrock for all the other pillars of emotional intelligence.

Pillar 2: Self-Regulation

Next up, we have self-regulation — the ability to navigate your inner landscape with intention and discipline. This is all about resisting impulses, controlling your reactions, and making conscious choices about how to respond to life's challenges.

Think of it like hitting the brakes when you feel a sudden rush of anger or frustration. Instead of lashing out, self-regulation allows you to take a step back, take a deep breath, and choose a more constructive path forward. Maybe you need to excuse yourself for a quick walk or journal about your feelings before re-engaging.

We've all encountered people who seem to operate on a hair trigger, exploding at the slightest provocation. They might start yelling, slamming doors, or making hurtful comments without a second thought. This lack of self-regulation can very quickly damage relationships and make it difficult for them to navigate challenges effectively.

But with practice, you can develop the discipline to control your impulses and respond in ways that serve you, rather than sabotaging your progress. Self-regulation is about finding balance and maintaining composure, even in the face of intense emotions.

Pillar 3: Motivation

Ah, motivation — the internal drive that propels you to pursue your goals and dreams. It's not just about chasing external rewards and accolades, but finding joy and fulfillment in the journey itself. When you cultivate this intrinsic motivation, you build remarkable resilience, allowing you to bounce back from setbacks and stay the course, no matter what obstacles arise.

We've all known someone who seems to give up at the first sign of difficulty, while others persevere through even the toughest challenges. The difference often lies in their motivation. The person with stronger emotional intelligence is driven by an internal desire to learn, grow, and improve rather than just seeking external validation or accolades.

Imagine you're working towards mastering a new skill, like playing an instrument or perfecting your coding abilities. The emotionally intelligent person finds genuine satisfaction in the process of improvement, celebrating each small victory along the way. Their intrinsic drive and belief in their potential will carry them through, allowing them to achieve their goal with a profound sense of accomplishment ultimately.

Pillar 4: Social Skills

Last but not least, we have social skills — your ticket to better communication, collaboration, and empathy. In a world where social dynamics can change in a flash, strong interpersonal abilities are essential. By actively listening, making eye contact, and showing genuine interest in others, you'll build trust, understanding, and the capacity for meaningful connection.

I'm sure you've experienced the difference between talking with someone who has excellent social skills versus someone who doesn't. The former makes communication feel effortless and enjoyable, while the latter can create tension, misunderstandings, and an overall unpleasant dynamic.

Emotionally intelligent individuals understand the importance of being attuned to others' needs and perspectives. They actively engage in conversations, pick up on social cues, and adapt their communication style to the situation at hand. This ability to connect with and empathize with those around them is a skill that can transform all of your relationships.

Emotional Intelligence and the Growth Mindset

As you've learned, emotional intelligence is the key to unlocking your full potential and navigating life's ups and downs. But what many people don't realize is how closely this skill is tied to the growth mindset principles we've explored throughout this book.

The hallmarks of emotional intelligence — self-awareness, self-regulation, motivation, and social skills — are all fundamental to cultivating a mindset focused on continuous improvement and resilience. When you develop these abilities, you gain the tools to tackle challenges head-on, adapt to change, and forge meaningful connections.

Think about it — a growth mindset is all about embracing setbacks as opportunities for growth rather than seeing them as fixed limitations. Emotional intelligence gives you the self-awareness to recognize when you're stuck in a negative spiral, the self-regulation to pause and respond constructively, and the motivation to persist through difficulties.

Similarly, being able to understand and empathize with the perspectives of others aligns perfectly with the growth mindset's emphasis on learning from diverse experiences and viewpoints. The more attuned you are to the thoughts and feelings of those around you, the better equipped you are to collaborate, communicate, and find creative solutions to complex problems.

In many ways, emotional intelligence and the growth mindset are two sides of the same coin. They're complementary skill sets that, when developed in tandem, allow you to approach life's challenges with a powerful combination of self-knowledge, resilience, and interpersonal finesse.

So, as you continue to nurture your emotional intelligence, see it as an extension of the growth mindset principles you've been honing throughout this journey. The more you can understand, manage, and communicate your emotions, the more you'll be able to unlock your true potential and become the adaptable, empowered individual you're meant to be.

With this foundation in place, let's now dive deeper into the key components of emotional intelligence, starting with the cornerstone of this essential life skill: *empathy*.

Empathy: The Cornerstone of Meaningful Connections

At its core, empathy is about stepping outside of our limited perspectives and striving to see the world through someone else's eyes. It's about cultivating the compassion and openness to truly listen, acknowledge, and validate the experiences of those around us. Empathy allows us to forge more profound, more meaningful connections, navigate conflicts with greater understanding, and cultivate a heightened awareness of the diversity that enriches our social landscape.

Let's dive into the core elements that make empathy such a powerful force:

Active Listening

Active listening is a fundamental aspect of empathy, crucial for clarifying misunderstandings and strengthening interpersonal bonds. Imagine being in a conversation where the other person continuously interrupts or seems distracted — it can feel incredibly frustrating and disconnected.

Active listening, on the other hand, involves giving your full attention, making eye contact, and responding appropriately to what the other person is saying. These small gestures, like putting away your phone or using verbal affirmations, show that you value the speaker's words and create a safe space for open dialogue.

By actively engaging in this way, we can better understand the feelings and perspectives of others, preventing conflicts that often arise from miscommunication. When someone feels truly heard and understood, they're more likely to reciprocate that sense of trust and connectedness, leading to more meaningful exchanges.

Perspective-Taking

Another vital component of empathy is perspective-taking - the ability to see the world through someone else's eyes and acknowledge their unique experiences and feelings. This practice helps reduce judgment and promote compassion.

For instance, if a friend seems distant or upset, instead of immediately assuming they're angry with you, try imagining what they might be going through. Are they stressed about an exam? Dealing with issues at home? Recognizing that everyone has their own battles can foster a more open and understanding approach.

Moreover, perspective-taking helps us appreciate diversity. As we learn to recognize that people think and feel differently based on their backgrounds, cultures, and personal histories, we enrich our worldview and become more adaptable communicators. We start to understand that our perceptions and opinions are not the only valid ones, opening us up to a richer, more nuanced understanding of the human experience.

Expressing Empathy

Putting empathy into action through words and gestures is pivotal for building trust, especially during conflicts. Simple actions like offering a comforting hug, listening patiently, or saying *"I'm here for you"* can have a significant impact on how others feel supported.

The key is to express empathy from a place of genuine care and understanding. During heated arguments, for example, acknowledging the other person's feelings can diffuse tension and pave the way for constructive dialogue.

This is important stuff, so let me give you some detailed examples of what this might sound like:

"I can see how much this situation is affecting you. It's understandable to feel frustrated and hurt when you don't feel heard. I want you to know that your feelings are valid, and I'm here to listen and support you in any way I can."

"I'm so sorry you're going through this tough time. It breaks my heart to see you in pain. Please know that you're not alone – I'm here for you, ready to listen or just sit with you in silence if that's what you need."

"I can't imagine how overwhelming this must be for you right now. It's okay to feel lost and unsure. We'll figure this out together."

These empathetic expressions show that we're not just concerned with our own needs, but that we genuinely value the other person's perspective and emotional experience. This, in turn, helps create an environment where both parties feel heard and respected, making it much easier to find mutually satisfactory solutions.

Cultural Awareness

Empathy also requires cultural awareness, as every society has its norms and customs for communicating and expressing emotions. Being culturally sensitive means recognizing these differences and adjusting our behaviors accordingly.

For instance, maintaining eye contact is considered respectful in some cultures, while in others, it might be seen as confrontational. By understanding and respecting these nuances, we can interact more effectively with people from diverse backgrounds, enriching our social experiences and broadening our empathetic reach.

Cultural awareness also helps us appreciate the diversity of emotional expression. What may be considered an appropriate display of emotion in one culture could be seen as inappropriate or even disruptive in another. By recognizing and honoring these differences, we avoid making assumptions or judgments, and instead create an environment where everyone feels validated and understood.

Cultivating empathy is an ongoing journey of self-reflection and growth. By actively listening, considering different perspectives, expressing genuine care, and embracing cultural diversity, we can forge deeper, more meaningful connections with the people in our lives.

When we make a conscious effort to step into someone else's shoes, we unlock the ability to foster more compassionate, collaborative, and enriching interactions. Empathy has the power to bridge divides, resolve conflicts, and help us all feel a little less alone in this complex world. It's a skill worth cultivating, not just for our personal growth, but for the betterment of our communities and the world at large.

TRY IT: Empathy in Action

For this activity, you'll have the opportunity to put your empathy skills into action through a real-world interaction.

Identify a situation in your life where you can deliberately apply the principles of active listening, perspective-taking, and empathetic expression.

This could be anything from a conversation with a friend who's going through a difficult time, to a group project where you need to collaborate effectively with your peers. Whatever the context, your goal is to approach the interaction with heightened empathy and awareness.

1) Identify the Opportunity: Reflect on your daily life and relationships. Where do you see an opportunity to practice empathy? Perhaps it's a friend who has been more withdrawn lately, or a group assignment where tensions are running high. Choose a situation that feels meaningful and important to you.

2) Prepare Your Mindset: Before the interaction, take a few deep breaths and mentally prepare. Remind yourself to approach the situation with an open and curious mindset. Your goal is not to fix the other person's problems but to truly listen, understand, and validate their experience.

3) Engage with Empathy: During the interaction, pay close attention to the other person's verbal and nonverbal cues. Use techniques like reflective listening, validating their feelings, and offering empathetic statements.

4) Observe and Reflect: After the interaction, take time to reflect. How did the other person respond? What did you learn about their perspective? How might this have unfolded differently without your empathy skills?

5) Celebrate Your Growth: Recognizing your progress is essential. Acknowledge the empathy and emotional intelligence you demonstrated. Celebrate the meaningful step you've taken.

Empathy is a skill that takes practice, but the rewards are immeasurable. By engaging in this *"Empathy in Action"* activity, you're honing your abilities and making a positive impact on the people around you.

Chapter 10
Designing Your Future

> *"The best way to predict the future is to create it."*
> —Peter Drucker

Imagine standing at the edge of a vast, open landscape. It's your future, stretching out in every direction. But here's the twist: there are no paths, no roads, no signs. Instead, every step you take carves out a new trail, shaping where you go next. It's exhilarating. It's overwhelming, and most importantly — *it's yours to design.*

This isn't just a metaphor. *It's reality.* Your future isn't something that just happens to you. It's something you actively create through choices, actions, and the mindset you bring to every moment.

But how do you start?

How do you design a future that feels aligned with who you are?

That's what this chapter is about. We'll break the process into six actionable steps. Each one helps you move from dreaming about possibilities to building a life you're proud of.

As you dive into these steps, you might notice some familiar ideas from earlier chapters. That's no accident—it's intentional! These key concepts are trusted tools in your growth mindset toolkit, and revisiting them will strengthen your foundation. With this groundwork in place, it's time to look ahead and start shaping the future you've been working toward.

Let's begin.

Step 1: Discover What Drives You

Every meaningful journey begins with a sense of direction. But finding that direction requires understanding what truly matters to you — your values, passions, and unique vision for the life you want to live.

Why Values Are Your Compass

Think of values as your internal compass. They guide your decisions, helping you prioritize what's important and filter out distractions. When your actions align with your values, life is meaningful and fulfilling. When they don't, even success can feel hollow and pointless.

For example, if you value creativity but spend all your time following rigid routines, you might feel stifled. Conversely, if you value making a difference but focus on goals that feel self-serving, you might struggle to find motivation.

The trick lies in understanding your core values so that you can use them to help guide your path forward.

Discovering Your Core Values

To uncover your values, start by asking yourself these questions:

- What inspires me? Think about moments when you felt most alive or connected.
- What frustrates me? Sometimes, what you dislike in the world reveals what you care about changing.
- What do I admire in others? Consider the qualities you respect and want to emulate.

Let's say you admire honesty, creativity, and kindness. These become touchstones for your decisions. Whenever you're faced with a choice, ask: *Does this align with my values?*

Step 2: Define Your Vision

Once you've identified your core values, it's time to create a compelling vision for your future. This isn't about predicting every detail, but rather about gaining clarity on the kind of life you want to create.

Creating a Vision That Excites You

To begin crafting your vision, find a quiet space where you can reflect without interruption. Close your eyes and allow your imagination to run free, picturing your ideal future in as much detail as possible.

- Where are you living?
- What are you doing with your time?
- Who are the people in your life?

As you visualize your ideal future, don't hold back. This is your chance to dream big and imagine a life that genuinely excites you.

Maybe you see yourself:

- Launching a successful YouTube channel that showcases your passions and creativity
- Traveling the world, learning about different cultures, and making new friends
- Developing a groundbreaking app that makes a positive impact on people's lives
- Pursuing a fulfilling career in a field you love, like music, art, or science

Once you have a clear mental picture, write it down in vivid detail. Use sensory language to describe what you see, hear, and feel in your envisioned future.

As you reflect on your vision, ask yourself:

- How does this vision align with my core values?
- What parts of this vision feel most exciting, inspiring, or meaningful?

For example, let's say your vision includes becoming a successful YouTuber. If you value creativity, community, and self-expression, you might envision:

"I see myself creating engaging, inspiring content that resonates with a diverse global audience. My channel is a vibrant hub of creativity and connection, where I collaborate with other passionate creators and engage in meaningful discussions with my subscribers. Through my videos, I'm able to express my unique voice, share my talents, and make a positive impact on people's lives. My work is both challenging and fulfilling, allowing me to continuously grow, learn, and push the boundaries of what's possible."

Anchoring Your Vision in Reality

While dreaming big is essential, it's also important to identify concrete steps you can take to bridge the gap between where you are now and where you want to be.

Continuing with the example above, you might begin by:

- Researching popular channels in your niche and analyzing what makes them successful
- Developing your unique voice and on-camera presence through practice and feedback
- Learning key skills like video editing, scriptwriting, and SEO
- Networking with other creators and collaborating on projects
- Creating a consistent posting schedule and engaging with your audience regularly

By breaking your larger vision down into manageable steps, you make it feel more attainable. Each small action you take builds momentum, propelling you forward on the path to your ideal future.

Remember, your vision can evolve as you grow and learn. Stay connected to the core of what you want to create, and use it as a guiding light to navigate your journey.

Here is the expanded version with a word count of 919:

Step 3: Set the Right Goals

Dreams without action are just wishes. Goals are the bridge between where you are now and where you want to be. They turn your vision into concrete, achievable milestones that you can work towards every day.

Moving Beyond SMART Goals

In a previous chapter, we explored the SMART framework for goal setting — Specific, Measurable, Achievable, Relevant, and Time-bound. While this is a great starting point, designing a future that truly aligns with your values and aspirations requires going a bit deeper, or even being willing to bend and flex along the way.

Consider these additional layers when crafting your goals:

Flexible Goals: Life is unpredictable, and your priorities may shift over time. Build flexibility into your goals so you can adapt as needed without losing sight of your overall vision. This might mean setting a range instead of a fixed target ("I want to save $500-$1000 per month" instead of "I will save exactly $750 per *month")* or building in regular checkpoints to reassess and adjust your goals as needed.

Process-Oriented Goals: While it's essential to have a clear end-result in mind, focusing solely on the outcome can be daunting and demotivating. Instead, try setting process-oriented goals that prioritize the habits and actions that will get you there. For example, instead of saying, *"I want to write a novel,"* set a goal to write 500 words every day. By focusing on the process, you build momentum and make progress more manageable.

Meaningful Milestones: Big, audacious goals are exciting, but they can also feel overwhelming. Break them down into smaller, manageable milestones that you can celebrate along the way. Let's say your ultimate goal is to launch your own podcast. Start by setting incremental goals like:

1. Research equipment options and choose a microphone
2. Brainstorm a list of 20 potential episode topics
3. Write scripts for your first three episodes
4. Record and edit a short practice episode
5. Design your podcast cover art and create a website

By focusing on these bite-sized steps, you turn a daunting project into a series of achievable tasks. Each milestone you hit builds momentum and confidence, propelling you forward towards your larger goal.

Aligned with Values: As you set goals, make sure they align with your core values and the vision you created in the previous step. Ask yourself, *"Does this goal move me closer to the life I want to create? Is it aligned with what matters most to me?"* If a goal feels out of sync with your values, consider how you can reframe it or find an alternative path that feels more authentic.

Remember, goal-setting is not a one-time event, but an ongoing process. Regularly review and reassess your goals to make sure they're still relevant and aligned with your vision. Celebrate your progress along the way, and don't be afraid to adjust your course as needed. The path to your dreams is rarely a straight line, but with clear, flexible goals as your guide, you'll stay motivated and on track.

Step 4: Build Systems for Progress

Goals give you a destination, but systems are the vehicle that gets you there. In other words, goals are the *"what"* and systems are the *"how."* Without reliable systems in place, even the best intentions can stall out.

The Science of Habits

At the core of any effective system are habits — the small, consistent actions you take on a daily or weekly basis. Your brain is wired to automate repetitive tasks, turning them into habits that require less conscious effort over time. When you repeat an action often enough, it becomes automatic, freeing up mental energy for more significant, more complex decisions.

For example, if you build a habit of reviewing your goals every Sunday evening, staying focused and on track becomes second nature. You no longer have to expend willpower or motivation to keep your goals front and center; it simply becomes a part of your routine.

Designing Systems That Work

To create systems that support your goals, start by identifying the daily or weekly habits that will move you closer to your desired outcome. If you're working towards better physical health, your system might include meal prepping on Sundays, going for a run every morning before school, and attending a yoga class twice a week.

Next, create cues or triggers that remind you to perform these habits. One effective strategy is to pair a new habit with an existing routine. Want to build a journaling habit? Try doing it immediately after brushing your teeth each night. By linking your new habit to an established one, you make it easier to remember and follow through.

Finally, track your progress and celebrate your wins along the way. Use a simple checklist, habit tracker, or app to record your daily actions. Seeing your consistency build over time can be a powerful motivator to keep going, even when you don't feel like it. And when you reach a milestone or achieve a goal, take time to acknowledge and celebrate your hard work. Positive reinforcement helps cement new habits and keeps you motivated for the journey ahead.

Step 5: Visualize Your Success

We've talked about this previously, but its importance rings especially true for designing your ideal future. Visualization is a powerful tool for keeping your goals front and center and priming your brain for success. By vividly imagining yourself achieving your goals, you engage the same neural pathways that are activated when you actually perform an action. In other words, visualization is like a mental rehearsal that prepares you to handle challenges, recognize opportunities, and perform at your best.

The Power of Mental Rehearsal

Elite athletes have long used visualization to improve their performance. Before a big race, a sprinter might close their eyes and imagine every aspect of their performance, from the moment they settle into the starting blocks to the feeling of crossing the finish line victorious. This mental rehearsal helps build confidence, reduce anxiety, and program the mind and body for success.

You can apply this same principle to your own goals. Let's say you have a big class presentation coming up. In the days leading up to it, take a few minutes each day to close your eyes and vividly imagine yourself delivering the presentation with confidence and ease. Picture yourself speaking clearly, engaging your audience, and fielding questions with poise. The more detailed and immersive your visualization, the more powerful its impact will be.

Creating a Vision Board

Again, you're already aware of this particular tool, but its value in helping you design your future cannot be overstated. A vision board is a collage of images, quotes, and symbols that represent what you want to achieve. It can include pictures of your dream college, inspiring quotes about perseverance, or a photo of someone who embodies the qualities you want to develop.

The key is to make your vision board as specific and meaningful to you as possible. Choose images and words that evoke a strong emotional response and make you feel excited and motivated when you look at them. Place your vision board somewhere you'll see it every day, like your bedroom wall or your locker at school. By keeping your goals and dreams visually front and center, you prime your subconscious mind to look for opportunities and take actions that move you closer to your desired future.

Visualization and vision boards are powerful tools for keeping your motivation high and your focus sharp. By regularly taking time to imagine your success and surround yourself with reminders of your goals, you train your mind to stay positive, proactive, and resilient in the face of challenges. So dream big, imagine vividly, and watch as your vision begins to manifest in reality.

Wyatt's Journey: How He Designed His Future

Meet Wyatt, a sixteen-year-old with a fascination for the ocean. From a young age, he's been captivated by marine life, spending weekends glued to nature documentaries and doodling whales and dolphins in his notebooks. His favorite place in town? The local aquarium, where he'd spend hours marveling at the shimmering jellyfish and the mesmerizing movements of stingrays.

Wyatt's dream? To become a marine biologist. But for a long time, that dream felt like a distant, unreachable goal. That is, until he decided to follow a structured plan like the one outlined in this chapter. Here is how he applied the teachings of this chapter to design his future.

Discovering His Values

Wyatt started by identifying what mattered most to him. He reflected on his love for discovery, his passion for nature, and his deep care for protecting the environment. These values pointed him toward a career where he could explore and contribute to preserving marine ecosystems.

He jotted down his core values in his notebook: *curiosity, environmental stewardship, and learning.* These became his guiding principles as he began crafting a plan for his future.

Defining His Vision

With his values in mind, Wyatt envisioned his future. He pictured himself working on a research vessel, diving into the depths of the ocean to study coral reefs, and contributing to conservation efforts for endangered species. He wrote down a clear statement:

"I want to be a marine biologist who helps protect ocean ecosystems and educates others about the importance of marine life."

He also started thinking about the small, immediate steps he could take to begin his journey.

Setting a Goal

Wyatt set an actionable goal to kickstart his path:

"By the end of this year, I will volunteer at the local aquarium and take an online course in marine biology basics."

The aquarium had always been his favorite spot in town, so he reached out to their volunteer coordinator, explaining his passion for marine life and his desire to learn. To his excitement, they welcomed him onto their team to help with guest tours and assist in the care of the smaller exhibits.

Building a System

To stay on track, Wyatt built a system that fit into his busy high school schedule. He volunteered at the aquarium every Saturday morning, where he shared his enthusiasm with visitors by leading discussions about marine ecosystems. During the week, he set aside Tuesday and Thursday evenings to work on an online course about marine biology, watching lectures and completing quizzes on topics like oceanic ecosystems and animal behavior.

He used a planner to track his schedule and even created a checklist to measure his progress—finishing one module in his course for every two weeks of volunteering. Seeing those checkmarks accumulate kept him motivated.

Visualizing Success

Each night before bed, Wyatt spent a few quiet minutes picturing his future. He imagined himself scuba diving alongside colorful schools of fish, recording data on shark migrations, and presenting his findings at scientific conferences. He also visualized smaller victories, like feeling confident explaining ocean conservation to aquarium visitors or acing a quiz in his online course. These vivid mental rehearsals kept his excitement alive and helped him stay focused on his path.

Wyatt even created a vision board above his desk, filled with photos of coral reefs, inspiring quotes from marine biologists, and even a postcard from the aquarium's gift shop that read: *"Protect What You Love."*

Cultivating Resilience

Of course, Wyatt faced setbacks along the way. On his first day volunteering at the aquarium, he accidentally spilled a bucket of water while cleaning a tank, earning some teasing from the staff. He felt embarrassed and out of place. But instead of letting that moment discourage him, Wyatt reminded himself that every expert starts as a beginner.

He journaled about the experience, reflecting on what he could learn. *"I'll ask more questions next time,"* he wrote. *"And I'll double-check everything before moving a tank!"* Slowly but surely, he gained confidence, and the staff began to trust him with more responsibilities, like preparing food for the aquarium's sea turtles.

When his online course got tough—especially the module on ocean chemistry— Wyatt pushed through by breaking the material into smaller sections and dedicating extra time to study. He leaned on his systems and his vision to keep him motivated.

By the end of the year, Wyatt had completed his online course, gained hands-on experience at the aquarium, and even received a glowing recommendation letter from the volunteer coordinator. But more importantly, Wyatt felt a new sense of confidence in his ability to pursue his dream.

Wyatt's hard work paid off. Not only did he make progress toward his long-term dream, but he also discovered how much he loved sharing his passion for marine life with others — a skill he knew would serve him well in his future career.

What about you?

What's your big dream?

Follow the steps in this chapter to design your ideal future and start making small and consistent steps toward your goal. I assure you that you'll be shocked by how quickly you can make measurable progress toward your ideal future.

TRY IT: Your Future-Planning Blueprint

Follow these steps to create your personalized blueprint:

Step 1: Identify Your Core Values

Write down 3–5 values that matter most to you. Think about what inspires you, what frustrates you, and the qualities you admire in others.

Example: *Creativity, helping others, curiosity.*

Step 2: Envision Your Ideal Future

Take five minutes to imagine your dream life. Where are you? What are you doing? Who's with you? Write a short paragraph describing this vision in as much detail as possible.

Example: *"I'm running a wildlife sanctuary, caring for animals, and educating people about conservation."*

Step 3: Set One Actionable Goal

Choose one small, specific step that aligns with your vision. Make sure it's achievable in the next 1–3 months.

Example: *"Volunteer at a local animal shelter on weekends."*

Step 4: Build a System

Create a simple routine to support your goal. Include when and how often you'll take action.

Example: *"Spend Saturday mornings volunteering and Wednesday afternoons researching animal care."*

Step 5: Visualize Success

Close your eyes and imagine yourself achieving your goal. What does it feel like? What steps got you there? Write a sentence or two describing this moment.

Example: *"I see myself at the shelter, confidently helping care for the animals and learning new skills."*

Step 6: Plan for Setbacks

List one or two challenges you might face and how you'll overcome them.

Example: *"If I feel nervous about volunteering, I'll remind myself that everyone starts somewhere and ask lots of questions to learn."*

Reflection

After completing these steps, take a moment to reflect:

- What excites you most about your plan?
- What's one thing you can do today to move closer to your goal?

Keep this blueprint somewhere visible, like your desk or journal, and revisit it often. Every small action adds up, bringing you closer to the future you're designing!

Chapter 11

Maintaining Momentum

"Don't Watch the Clock; Do What It Does. Keep Going."
— Sam Levenson

You and your best friend decide to hike up the local mountain. You're pumped. The sun is shining, the air is crisp, and the views? Incredible. But about halfway up, your legs start burning. Your once-perfect rhythm slows, and suddenly the summit feels ridiculously far away. Meanwhile, your friend is bounding ahead like a mountain goat, grinning ear to ear.

"*Come on!*" they yell. "*We're so close!*"

For a moment, you wonder, *"Why am I even doing this?"* The climb feels endless, and your motivation tanks. That's when your friend doubles back, pats you on the shoulder, and says, "*It's not just about the peak — it's about the climb. Look around!*"

And they're right. You pause, take in the view, and something shifts. The mountain hasn't gotten smaller, but your perspective has changed. You can do this.

Life's challenges are like that hike. Some days, you're fired up and unstoppable. Other days, you're dragging, wondering if the effort is even worth it.

Momentum — the energy that keeps you going — isn't something you find; *it's something you create*. It's a mix of strategy, self-awareness, and resilience that allows you to keep moving forward, even when the path is challenging.

This chapter is about how to maintain that momentum. You'll learn how to reflect on your goals, track your progress, and celebrate along the way. You'll also discover how to adapt when life throws you curveballs and how to keep your motivation alive during tough times. By the end, you'll have a clear toolkit to stay on track and enjoy the climb.

Are You Climbing the Right Mountain?

Here's a hard truth: Not every goal you set will stay relevant forever, *and that*'s *okay!* The key is learning when to push forward and when to pivot.

Take a moment to reflect on your current goals.

Are they still lighting a fire in you?

Or are they starting to feel like obligations?

For instance, maybe you set a goal to ace your math class because you thought it would help you pursue engineering. But somewhere along the way, you realize your real passion lies in art. Does sticking with engineering still make sense?

Adjusting your goals isn't giving up; it's leveling up. It's saying, *"I've grown, and my priorities have grown with me."* Maybe the new goal is to apply to art school or start an independent design business. Whatever it is, don't be afraid to shift course if it means aligning your efforts with what truly inspires you.

Practical Tip: Schedule a regular "*goal check-in*" with yourself. Once a month, take 15 minutes to ask:

- Does this goal still excite me?
- Does it align with my values and long-term vision?
- What progress have I made, and what's holding me back?
- How can I adjust or refine this goal to better fit who I am now?

This habit keeps your goals fresh and relevant, ensuring you're climbing the right mountain. It also gives you the flexibility to adapt as your circumstances and passions evolve.

Turn Mountains Into Steps

Big dreams can feel overwhelming, like staring up at a massive peak with no trail in sight. The secret? Break it down into smaller, manageable steps.

Imagine you want to write a novel. Thinking about 300 pages can be paralyzing. But what if your first step was just outlining the plot? And the next was drafting one chapter? Suddenly, it feels doable.

Real-World Example: Remember Wyatt's dreams of becoming a marine biologist? His long-term goal feels massive: years of schooling, internships, and fieldwork. So, he breaks it down:

1. Volunteer at the local aquarium.
2. Take advanced biology in high school.
3. Research colleges with strong marine biology programs.
4. Apply for summer research internships.
5. Declare a marine biology major in college.

Every small step builds momentum and makes the more significant goal feel achievable. Plus, as Wyatt completes each milestone, he gains valuable experience and insights that inform the next phase of his journey.

Practical Tip: Write down your big goal and break it into 3–5 smaller milestones. Focus on completing one at a time. Each success will fuel your motivation to tackle the next.

Celebrate the Wins — Big and Small

Imagine playing a video game without checkpoints or bonus rounds. Boring, right? Goals are the same. Celebrating milestones keeps the journey exciting and reminds you of how far you've come.

When you hit a small win — like finishing a big homework assignment or running your first mile without stopping — take a moment to celebrate. High-five yourself, blast your favorite song, or treat yourself to something fun. These little victories are just as important as the big ones.

Why It Matters: Celebrations release dopamine, the feel-good chemical in your brain. This reinforces positive behavior, making you more likely to keep going. Recognizing your progress also gives you a sense of momentum and purpose, preventing you from getting discouraged.

Practical Tip: Create a reward system for your goals.

Small wins = small rewards (e.g., a favorite snack, an hour of free time).

Big wins = big rewards (e.g., a movie night, new gear for your hobby).

Set aside a dedicated *"celebration fund"* in your budget so you always have something to look forward to. These small acts of self-appreciation can make a big difference in sustaining your motivation.

Build a Scoreboard — Track Your Progress

Ever noticed how satisfying it is to check something off a to-do list? That's the power of tracking.

A scoreboard gives you a visual reminder of your progress. It could be as simple as a notebook, a habit-tracking app, or a whiteboard in your room. Seeing your progress keeps you motivated and accountable.

If your goal is to practice guitar every day, mark an "X" on your calendar for each day you practice. Watching those X's pile up creates a sense of achievement and builds momentum.

Practical Tip: Experiment with different tracking tools until you find one that works for you. Apps like Habitica or Notion are great for digital tracking, while journals or sticky notes are perfect for analog fans. The key is to find a system that feels intuitive and easy to maintain.

You can also get creative with how you display your progress. Some people like to color in a grid or add stickers to a wall calendar. Find a method that keeps you engaged and excited to mark your achievements.

Embrace Change

Life is unpredictable. New interests emerge, old passions fade, and external factors throw curveballs. Learning to adapt your goals is a crucial skill.

Take Jack, for example. He started high school with dreams of being a professional skateboarder. But after an injury and a newfound love for graphic design, his focus shifted. Instead of clinging to his original goal, Jack pivoted. He started designing skateboards and launched a small online shop, combining his love for skating and creativity.

Adjusting doesn't mean failure; it means growth. Sometimes, the path you envision at the start isn't the one that ultimately fulfills you. The key is remaining open to exploration and following the trail that lights you up.

Practical Tip: When you feel stuck or uninspired, ask yourself:

- Is this goal still aligned with who I am and what I value?

- What changes can I make to reignite my passion for this pursuit?
- Are there adjacent interests or skills I could explore that might be a better fit?

Avoid getting boxed in by your initial plan. Stay curious, experiment, and be willing to adjust course if it means getting closer to your true calling.

Stay Motivated During Tough Times

Even the most driven people hit slumps. The key to pushing through is having strategies to stay motivated.

Coping Strategies: When stress hits, try mindfulness techniques like deep breathing or journaling. For example, before a big test, take three deep breaths to calm your nerves and clear your mind. You can also try meditation, yoga, or simply going for a walk to reset.

Lean on Your Network: Surround yourself with people who lift you up. Whether it's a supportive friend, a teacher, or a family member, having someone to cheer you on makes all the difference. Share your struggles and let them encourage you.

Visualization: Picture yourself achieving your goal. Close your eyes and imagine crossing the finish line, hearing the applause, and feeling the rush of success. This mental rehearsal can keep you focused when the going gets tough.

Affirmations: Use positive self-talk to counter doubts. Say things like, *"I've got this,"* or *"Every step brings me closer to success."* Repeating these affirmations builds confidence and resilience.

Reframe Setbacks: When you hit a roadblock, avoid seeing it as a failure. Instead, view it as a chance to learn and grow. Ask yourself, *"What can I take away from this experience that will make me stronger?"*

Having a toolkit of coping strategies allows you to weather the storms and keep moving forward, even when motivation starts to wane.

Build Habits That Last

Success isn't just about bursts of motivation; it's about consistent habits that support long-term growth.

Start Small: Pick one habit that aligns with your goal and stick to it. For example, if you want to run a 5K, start by jogging for 5 minutes a day.

Track Consistency: Use a habit tracker to build streaks. Watching your progress over time keeps you committed.

Stay Flexible: If a habit stops working, tweak it. Life changes, and your routines should too. Experiment until you find what works best for you.

Expanding Your Mindset

As you work through the steps of designing your future, it's essential to keep an open, expansive mindset. Far too often, we unconsciously limit ourselves, constraining our dreams to what we think is *"realistic"* or *"attainable."* But the truth is, your future holds a world of limitless possibilities that extend far beyond your current circumstances.

When you take the time to deeply reflect on your values, passions, and greatest aspirations, you may find that your initial vision feels a bit... *small*.

Maybe you start by imagining yourself in a stable, respectable career, living a comfortable life. But as you dig deeper, you realize that what truly excites you is the prospect of starting your own business, or traveling the world as a digital nomad, or spearheading a social impact initiative that could change lives.

Don't be afraid to dream bigger. In fact, embracing a genuinely expansive vision is essential to designing a future that feels energizing, meaningful, and in alignment with your most profound sense of purpose. By consciously pushing the boundaries of what you think is possible, you open yourself up to opportunities and pathways you may have never considered before.

Of course, it's important to balance that expansiveness with practicality. You don't want to get so carried away by lofty visions that you lose sight of the concrete steps required to turn them into reality. But by cultivating an open, curious mindset, you can continue to refine and elevate your goals in ways that feel both exciting and achievable.

Fueling Your Journey with Curiosity

As you work through the process of designing your future, it's crucial to maintain a spirit of curious exploration. Rather than approaching this journey with a rigid, prescriptive mindset, stay open to discovery, adaptation, and ongoing evolution.

Curiosity is the driving force behind innovation, resilience, and personal growth. It's what compels you to ask questions, experiment with new approaches, and continuously seek out fresh perspectives. And in the context of designing your future, it's an essential quality to cultivate.

After all, the world is constantly changing, and the path from your current circumstances to your desired destination will inevitably be filled with surprises, obstacles, and unexpected opportunities. The more open you are to asking "why?" and "how?" — the better equipped you'll be to navigate those twists and turns.

Curiosity allows you to reframe challenges as intriguing puzzles to solve, rather than roadblocks to overcome. It sparks your creativity, fueling innovative solutions. And it keeps you attuned to signals and insights that could dramatically alter the trajectory of your plans.

By approaching this process with curiosity, you give yourself the freedom to adapt, refine, and improve upon your original plans. You don't get stuck in a single, rigid trajectory, but rather remain open to the insights and epiphanies that will undoubtedly arise along the way.

So, as you dive into the process of designing your future, make curiosity your constant companion. Celebrate the thrill of discovery. Embrace the lessons hidden within setbacks. And always, always keep your mind open to the possibility that your dreams may grow and transform in ways you never could have predicted.

After all, the future isn't static — it's a living, breathing entity, shaped by your choices, your actions, and the openness with which you approach each new chapter. By nurturing your curiosity, you ensure that the journey of designing your destiny remains an exciting, fulfilling, and constantly unfolding adventure.

Chapter 12
Conclusion

Your Future Starts Now

By aligning your goals with your values, building systems that support your progress, and cultivating resilience, you have everything you need to design a life that feels meaningful and fulfilling.

Remember, this isn't a one-time process. Your vision will evolve, your goals will shift, and new opportunities will arise. The key is to stay curious, adaptable, and committed to growth.

So, take the first step today. Write down your values, set a goal, or start visualizing your success. The future is yours to design — one choice, one action, one moment at a time.

Momentum isn't about rushing to the finish line; it's about finding joy in the journey and staying committed to your path. By reflecting on your goals, celebrating your wins, and embracing change, you'll build the resilience to tackle any mountain — one step at a time.

Now, climb your mountain!

Ben Clardy

www.ingramcontent.com/pod-product-compliance
Lightning Source LLC
Chambersburg PA
CBHW070907120626
46546CB00001B/174